Chained to the Desk

A GUIDEBOOK FOR WORKAHOLICS, THEIR PARTNERS AND CHILDREN, AND THE CLINICIANS WHO TREAT THEM

THIRD EDITION

Bryan E. Robinson, PhD

New York University Press
New York and London

NEW YORK UNIVERSITY PRESS
New York and London
www.nyupress.org

References to Internet websites (URLs) were accurate at the time of writing.
Neither the author nor New York University Press is responsible for URLs
that may have expired or changed since the manuscript was prepared.

Library of Congress Cataloging-in-Publication Data

Robinson, Bryan E., author.
 Chained to the desk : a guidebook for workaholics, their partners and children, and the
clinicians who treat them / Bryan E. Robinson. — Third edition.
  p. ; cm.
 Includes bibliographical references and index.
 ISBN 978-0-8147-2463-7 (cloth : alk. paper) — ISBN 978-0-8147-8923-0 (pbk. : alk. paper)
 I. Title.
 [DNLM: 1. Behavior, Addictive. 2. Family Relations. 3. Work—psychology. WM 176]
 RC569.5.W67
 155.2′32—dc23
                                    2013037226

New York University Press books are printed on acid-free paper,
and their binding materials are chosen for strength and durability.
We strive to use environmentally responsible suppliers and materials
to the greatest extent possible in publishing our books.

Manufactured in the United States of America

10 9 8 7 6 5 4 3 2 1

Also available as an ebook

There is a candle in your heart, ready to be
Kindled.
There is a void in your soul, ready to be
Filled.
You feel it, don't you?

—Rumi

Contents

Acknowledgments

It's hard to believe that this book is now in its third edition. I have many people to thank for its continued success. My deepest appreciation goes to the anonymous individuals who took the time to write about their courageous struggle with work addiction and how it damaged their lives, as well as their inspiring stories of recovery. Special thanks to Dr. Nancy Chase, Annie O'Grady, Art Campbell, Stephanie Wilder, Daffie Matthews, George Raftelis, Annemarie Russell, Gloria Steinem, Roger Catlin, and Tom Dybro.

I want to extend my appreciation to the staff of New York University Press for their enduring support and tireless promotion of my work. And to my professional colleagues and friends who have been so supportive of me over the years. I want to especially thank Dr. Patricia Love, Dr. Kristin Neff, Dr. Gayle Porter, and Tony Schwartz for taking the time to read the manuscript and write an endorsement.

Last but certainly not least, my heartfelt thanks go to the hundreds of readers who have called and e-mailed me, searching for help in their battle with workaholism. It has always been my wish that Chained to the Desk would give hope and courage to workaholics waging an inner battle against themselves, as well as to their loved ones who also suffer from this best-dressed problem of the twenty-first century. If you're searching for answers, I hope this book helps you find the peace and serenity that you're seeking.

Introduction

Glorification of an Illness

This is a man for whom work always came first. Now he can't even remember it.

— Chris Wallace, *Fox News Sunday* anchor, on the final days of his hard-driving *60 Minutes* father, Mike Wallace, who died in 2012

Recording artists have always known something about the work world that the American workforce still doesn't get. Cyndi Lauper sang it: "When the working day is done, girls just wanna have fun." Michael Jackson crooned it in *Off the Wall*: "So tonight gotta leave that nine-to-five upon the shelf and just enjoy yourself." And Dolly Parton warned us about working nine to five: "It'll drive you crazy if you let it."

And Dolly's right. It will, *if you let it*. But you don't have to worry about nine to five workdays anymore. In the twenty-first century, we have 24/7 workdays and soaring job pressures in our technologically driven work culture. "It's enough to drive you crazy if you let it." The key is not to let it, but that's easier said than done.

❖ Do you feel like you're tethered to your smart phone?

❖ Are you working far more than forty or fifty hours a week?

❖ Are you eating fast food or vending machine snacks at your desk or skipping lunch altogether?

❖ Do you stay in constant contact with work even on weekends, holidays, and vacations, or forfeit your vacations to keep on working?

❖ Do you get nervous or jittery when you're away from work?

1

If you answered "yes" to some of these questions, you could be a workaholic, a problem that has continued to swell since the first and second editions of this book. Increasingly, American workers find themselves on a tightrope, trying to hold that line between calm and frantic activity, looking for a way to balance crammed schedules and keep clever work gadgets from infiltrating their personal time.

I Only Work on Days That End with "Y"

Chained to the Desk is a metaphor for the agonizing work obsessions that haunt you even when you're away from your desk. If you're a workaholic, chances are you openly admit your obsession with work while concealing the darker side of the addiction. Perhaps you testify to your passion for work, your nonstop schedule—all of which present you in a favorable light. But you fail to mention your episodes of depression, anxiety, chronic fatigue, and stress-related illnesses—consequences of working obsessively for days on end.

To say that the general public and media do not take workaholism seriously is an understatement. When it's not praised, workaholism is dismissed as a joke. One light-hearted portrayal in a newspaper cartoon shows a huge, empty meeting room with a sign posted at the front that reads, "Workaholics Anonymous." The cartoon's caption says, "Everybody had to work overtime." Advertisers bathe workaholism in the same glamorous light that they poured over cigarettes and liquor in the ads of the 1930s. A Lexus ad in the *Wall Street Journal* boasted, "Workaholic? Oh, you flatter us: The relentless pursuit of perfection." A radio commercial for a truck praised the versatility of the "Workaholic 4 by 4." If you tell people you're a workaholic, they usually chuckle. The label is tossed around with abandon in social gatherings, not as a problem but a badge of honor. Corporate climbers wear the workaholic name with pride, proclaiming their loyalty on behalf of the company, announcing that they binged for eighteen hours or three days on a project as something of which to be proud. But rarely do you hear adults boast about a three-day drunk or proclaim that they binged on an entire apple pie.

The Buzz on Workaholism

Workaholism is the best-dressed of all the addictions. It is enabled by our society's dangerous immersion in overwork, which explains why we can't see the water we swim in, and why many therapists look blank when the spouses of workaholics complain of loneliness and marital dissatisfaction. There are hundreds of studies on alcoholism, substance abuse, compulsive gambling, and eating disorders, but only a handful on workaholism, a profound omission.

The term *workaholic* was coined by Wayne Oates in the first book on the subject, *Confessions of a Workaholic*, in which Oates described workaholics as behaving compulsively about work in the same ways that alcoholics do about alcohol.[1] More than forty years later, no consensus exists among clinicians on how to define or categorize workaholism.

I use the terms *workaholism* and *work addiction* interchangeably throughout this book. I define *workaholism* as *an obsessive-compulsive disorder that manifests itself through self-imposed demands, an inability to regulate work habits, and over-indulgence in work to the exclusion of most other life activities.* The frantic work habits of workaholics activate their stress response, and their neurological systems are on constant red alert. Although workaholism is a form of escape from unresolved emotional issues, the relief it provides has an addictive quality. The addictive nature of workaholism comes from the fact that workaholics are temporarily delivered from deeper red alert conditions through the distraction of working. But because the deeper issues are not addressed, constant working is necessary to keep the smoldering coals from becoming wildfires.

Trending Now: Some Things NEVER Change

This is the third edition of *Chained to the Desk*. The first edition appeared in 1998, the second in 2007. During this fifteen-year span, a lot has happened to advance the understanding of workaholism. The problem is being recognized and addressed in more and more countries worldwide. Workaholics Anonymous has over a thousand members and holds meetings around the world—in Paris, Sydney, London, Reykjavik, and Bangkok.[2] On average, I receive several queries a month from researchers and graduate students studying the problem in such countries as Hungary, Poland, Spain, Slovenia, Turkey, the Netherlands, Japan, Canada, Australia, and the United Kingdom.

A 2011 dissertation by a graduate student at Central Queensland University, in Australia, was titled "Problematic Use of Smartphones in the Workplace: An Introductory Study."[3] The research reported in the dissertation used the Work Addiction Risk Test (WART), a test that I created to measure workaholism (which you will get to take later in the book). Findings showed a strong link between workaholism and the negative impact of smart-phone use such as addictive highs, withdrawal symptoms, interpersonal conflict, and problems at work.

Other studies around the world report that the seeds of workaholism are being planted early. In a 2011 global study conducted by the International

Center for Media and the Public Agenda, researchers asked 1,000 young adults from the United States to Hong Kong to give up all electronic media for twenty-four hours.[4] Deprived of their MP3 players, cellphones, and laptops, their stress levels went through the roof. They experienced elevated heart rates and increased feelings of anxiety, panic, irritability, restlessness, and depression —all symptoms of addiction and withdrawal. Some even said they felt as if they had lost their identities. Such withdrawal reactions are typical of workaholics who are deprived of work opportunities.

Extreme work habits have become commonplace in a world characterized by the frenzied pace of life, fear of being left behind, and desperation to achieve. For example, a disturbing report showed Chinese college students hooked up to IV drips. Under life-and-death pressure to gain acceptance to the college of their dreams, they were cramming for the 2012 National College Entrance exams. They had been losing precious time running to and from health clinics, so amino acid IV drips were installed to fight fatigue, giving students more time to study.

Working Faster, Furious, and Frenzied

In 1998, the same year that the first edition of this book was released, the Families and Work Institute reported that the average American worker clocked 44 hours of work per week, an increase of 3.5 hours since 1977 and far more than workers in France (39 hours per week) and Germany (40 hours).[5] And according to the Center for American Progress, American families worked an average of 11 hours more per week in 2006 than they did in 1979.[6]

Shortly after the publication of the first edition of Chained to the Desk, we entered a new century. A lot happened in terms of work and workaholism by the time the second edition was released in 2007. In the 1990s "blackberries" were something you consumed, not something that consumed you. If you had a "Bluetooth," you went to the dentist instead of to work. By 2007 the 1990s workday phrase "nine to five" had become obsolete, replaced by the "24/7" of the new millennium. These trends were an indication of how work had slithered its way into every hour of our day—the "smart phoning" of our lives. But how smart are we, really?

During the seven years between the first and second editions of this book, we worked longer and longer hours. According to US News and World Report, the workweek jumped from forty-four hours in 1998 to forty-seven in 2000.[7] And the Organization for Economic Cooperation and Development reported that Americans put in 20 percent more hours in 2012 than in 1970, with sixty-hour workweeks becoming the norm.[8] Along with that time increase, work stress skyrocketed. Studies show that after financial worries, job pressures are the second major cause of stress among Americans. According to the American Psychological Association, 62 percent of Americans said their jobs caused them stress in 2007, but the figure had jumped to 70 percent in the association's 2011 follow-up study.[9]

The No-Vacation Nation

Even more disturbing has been the slow evaporation of vacation days. Years ago I never went on vacation without my laptop, cellphone, and mountains of work (See "My Story," the opening case study in chapter 1). Although my old habits have changed, they are typical of today's employees, many of whom haul tons of work with them on vacation. But an increasing number of workers no longer take vacations at all.

The Economic Policy Institute of Washington, D.C., discovered that the average American worker took only two and a half weeks of vacation and holidays in 1990—less than the average worker in any other developed country, including Germany, where workers take six weeks a year. In 2004 Management Recruiters International reported that nearly half of US executives said they wouldn't use all of their earned vacation because they were too busy at work.[10] In 2010 a CareerBuilder survey found that 37 percent of working Americans did not take all their vacation days, an increase from 35 percent in 2009. And of those who did take all their time off, 30 percent worked while on vacation.[11]

In 2012 the average American worker left 9.2 vacation days on the table—up from 6.2 days in 2011—and most people said they did so because they were stressed out by the extra work they had to do around any vacation: "We have to get ahead of our workload in order to leave, and then we have to catch up to our workload upon our return."[12]

Fear is another reason. Increasingly, patients in my clinical practice say they are afraid to take vacation days for fear they will not be perceived as team players. Some even say they are afraid to leave the office for lunch, because if positions were cut they would be the first to go. This worry has increased nationwide. In 1977, 45 percent of people felt secure in their jobs, according to the Families and Work Institute. That number dropped to only 36 percent in 2006.[13]

To make matters worse, once the recession began in 2008, the concept of workaholism became an even harder sell, especially in a declining economy

where people were desperate for work so they could stave off mortgage fore-
closures and reduce their escalating debt. Many American workers were eager
to accept heavy workloads and job stress if that meant they could make ends
meet and feel more secure in their jobs.

Psst, Denial Is Not a River in Egypt

Despite these disturbing trends, the concept of workaholism has been rele-
gated to the pop psychology bookshelves. A book on workaholics by Marilyn
Machlowitz in the 1980s applauded the workaholic lifestyle, presenting it as
a virtue rather than a vice and suggesting that workaholics are actually happy
because they are doing what they love.[14] And supporters of work addiction
reform have been the targets of ridicule and butts of jokes, as the following
commentary from *Fortune* magazine illustrates: "Along with heroin, gambling,
sex, and sniffing model airplane glue, work is now taken seriously as something
people often get addicted to, in which case they need to get cured. . . . The references to work addiction are instantly psychiatric. The phrase is enveloped in
psychobabble about inner insecurities, lives destroyed, and—could it be otherwise?—support groups needed."[15]

Another shocking example of denial is the professor in the Netherlands who
coined the term *engaged workaholics*. The professor argues: "If you love what
you do, where's the harm in doing too much?" I wonder if that's something anyone would tell an alcoholic, shopaholic, drug addict, or compulsive gambler.[16]

These kinds of comments reflect ignorance about a condition that wreaks
misery and havoc on millions of people in this country. Obviously, a lot of education is still needed even for mental health professionals, which brings me to
an even more disturbing state of affairs. Although *workaholism* has become a
household word, it has not been accepted into the official psychiatric and psychological nomenclature. The American Psychiatric Association considers it a
symptom of obsessive-compulsive personality disorder. Jeffrey Kahn, a consultant for the association's committee on psychiatry in the workplace insists
that "other professionals who think workaholism is an addiction or a diagnosis
in and of itself are 'missing the boat.'"[17] It's also shocking that in 2006 a representative of the Priory, Great Britain's high-profile clinic for addiction, charged
that "workaholism is just something journalists like to write about."[18]

As of this writing, The American Psychiatric Association is preparing the
new diagnostic guidelines for substance use and addictive disorders that it will
publish in the fifth edition of the *Diagnostic and Statistical Manual of Mental
Disorders* (DSM-5) in May 2013.[19] The DSM is the standard classification of
mental disorders used by mental health professionals in the United States.

The American Psychiatric Association is recommending that this diagnostic category include both substance use disorders and nonsubstance addiction such as gambling. The association's recognition of behavioral addictions as true addictions is a groundbreaking action. But unfortunately workaholism—or work addiction or overworking—is not included as a nonsubstance addiction in the DSM-5. This oversight has occurred despite the fact that the association is recommending further study of Internet use disorder as an addiction and is recognizing other addictive disorders that are related to the use of caffeine, inhalants, and tobacco.

Many clinicians—vast numbers of whom are workaholics themselves—still do not recognize workaholism as a problem. They see nothing wrong with eighteen-hour, pressure-cooker days. They deny that workaholism is a factor in their patients' problems or in troubled relationships in the couples who see them for psychotherapy. Although workaholism surrounds us daily, they look on it much as we do caffeine or prescription drugs—as harmless, even beneficial. But not only has the problem of workaholism not gone away, it has worsened. Hence, the third edition of *Chained to the Desk*.

Why Will This Book Be Helpful?

This book provides an inside look at work addiction that debunks the myths, refutes false claims, and sets the record straight, using the clinical, empirical, and case studies that are currently available. Since the first and second editions of this book, new studies have emerged that provide deeper insights into the condition and into the effects it has on the workaholic's family.

From California to the Carolinas, men and women have recounted their agonizing bouts with work addiction and the devastation left in its wake. It's no accident that personal stories in San Diego resemble the accounts of those in Atlanta. It's no coincidence either that patient after patient in Charlotte who grew up with workaholics describe haunting feelings that are strikingly similar to those of children of workaholics in Peoria, St. Louis, and Houston.

It's not a fluke that partners of workaholics in New York describe experiences that are almost identical in every detail to those of partners in other parts of the country. These personal accounts are not scientific in the quantitative sense, but they carry their own validity. They document the psychological experiences of individuals affected by work addiction—and the details in so many accounts provide such an uncanny match that the emerging profiles cannot be attributed to chance alone. In this respect we have a qualitative science of work addiction derived from the parallel themes and feelings that have been observed by clinicians in the field.

This is the first book to show the devastating effects of overworking on the workforce as a whole and on those who live and work with workaholics—their partners, offspring, and business associates. It contains new and innovative research not reported anywhere else on the outcomes of adults who carry the legacies of their workaholic parents and the problems this creates in their own adult relationships. Each chapter opens with a case study, followed by information assembled from hundreds of case reports and a small body of clinical and empirical research.

I have drawn on my own personal experiences, the research I've conducted at the University of North Carolina at Charlotte, my vast clinical practice with workaholics and their families, and correspondence from around the world. This information is presented in a readable way for workaholics and their families in the general public who might be struggling with these issues.

Combining scientific knowledge and clinical practice with personal accounts, this book is unique because it's also the first informative source for clinicians to help them respond to the work addiction epidemic sweeping this country. Written for psychologists, social workers, marriage and family therapists, counselors, health educators, the clergy, medical practitioners, teachers, healthcare administrators, heads of corporations, and employee assistance personnel, *Chained to the Desk* reveals the origin and scope of work addiction, its pervasiveness within the family system, and how professionals can diagnose, intervene, and provide treatment for workaholics and their families.

A Makeover for the Third Edition

You may notice that the third edition of this book has been given a makeover. For starters, it has a new organization: Part I ("Work Addiction: The New American Idol") describes the problem of workaholism. Part II ("Recovery from Work Addiction") focuses on the solution and includes four new chapters: chapter 9, "Your Workaholic Brain"; chapter 10, "Mindful Working"; chapter 11, "Your Work Resilient Zone: Finding Your Positive, Compassionate Self"; and chapter 12, "Work-Life Balance and Workaholics Anonymous."

Each chapter opens with updated case studies and concludes with revised strategies and tips for clinicians to treat workaholics, their loved ones, and their employers and colleagues in the workplace. Within the chapters, I have included sections called "Recharging Your Batteries," which contain practical recovery steps for workaholics and their families. A new appendix contains psychometric information about the Work Addiction Risk Test (WART) and further information on reading material, support organizations, and websites relating to workaholism.

Here's what else is new:

❖ Cutting-edge research on work stress and efficiency
❖ Information on stress, the workaholic brain, and neuroplasticity
❖ News about the effects of electronic devices
❖ Myths about the virtues of multitasking and overtime
❖ Groundbreaking mindfulness techniques and resilience
❖ The latest research on finding your work resilient zone and work-life balance
❖ A more reader-friendly writing style

Idle Moments without Imperatives

If you're like most people who grow up in the United States, you've probably heard the adage, "An idle mind is the devil's workshop." For many people, doing is more valued in our culture than being, and the more you do, the greater your worth.

Chained to the Desk is for you and anyone struggling with the insidious and misunderstood addiction to work. It aims to provide both counseling and consolation when you cannot find them elsewhere. It shows you how to work hard, find your work resilient zone, be kind and compassionate to yourself, keep a positive attitude, and maintain balance with the three Rs: relaxation, recreation, and relationships.

May this book help you, the reader, find a place in your life where career success and personal and intimate fulfillment reside side by side—where you will know more about special times without imperatives, with idle moments when there's nothing to rush to, fix, or accomplish. And where you can give yourself the gift of being present in each moment.

Bryan Robinson
November 2013

Part I

Work Addiction

The New American Idol

Who, Me? A Workaholic— Seriously?

They intoxicate themselves with work so they won't see how they really are.

—Aldous Huxley

Bryan (My Story)

There was a time when I needed my work—and hid it from others—the way my alcoholic father needed and hid his bourbon. And just as I once tried to control my father's drinking by pouring out his booze and refilling the bottle with vinegar, the people who loved me sulked, pleaded, and tore their hair out trying to keep me from working all the time. Every summer, for instance, just before we left on vacation, my life partner, Jamey, would search my bags and confiscate any work I planned to smuggle into our rented beach house on the South Carolina shore. But however thoroughly he searched, he would always miss the tightly folded papers covered with work notes that I had stuffed into the pockets of my jeans.

Later, when Jamey and our close friends invited me to stroll on the beach, I'd say I was tired and wanted to nap. While they were off swimming and playing in the surf—which I considered a big waste of time—I secretly worked in the empty house, bent over a lap desk fashioned from a board. At the sound of their returning footsteps, I'd stuff my papers back into my jeans, hide the board, and stretch out on the bed, pretending to be asleep.

I saw nothing strange about my behavior; it's only in hindsight that I say that I was a workaholic. By this, I mean something quite different from saying that I worked hard. I mean that I used work to defend myself against unwelcome emotional states—to modulate anxiety, sadness, and frustration the way a pothead uses dope and an alcoholic uses booze.

Since childhood, work had been my sanctuary—my source of stability, self-worth, and meaning, and my protection against the uncertainties of human relationships. In elementary school, the subject I hated the most was recess. When a teacher forgot to assign homework over Christmas vacation, I was the one who raised his hand to remind her. In high school I wrote, directed, and produced the church Christmas play, also designing and building the sets and acting the lead role of Joseph. Doing everything for the play gave me a sense of control and mastery that was missing from my chaotic family life, where furniture-breaking fights between my mother and my father were a regular occurrence.

As an adult, the thought of a vacation or weekend without work was terrifying to me, and I structured my life accordingly. I carried a full college teaching load and volunteered for committee assignments, while also writing books, conducting research, and establishing a full clinical practice. Ignoring Jamey's frequent pleas that we "just do something together," I would work in my windowless office in our basement through evenings, weekends, Thanksgivings, and Christmases. I even worked through most of the day of my father's funeral: while my mother and sisters broke bread with our old neighbors, I was in my university office twenty-five miles away, working on a project so insignificant that I no longer remember what it was.

When I stopped thinking of myself as an extraordinarily talented and dedicated professional with a great deal to offer the world and realized how empty my life had become, I hit bottom. Until then I'd been proud of my workaholism and well rewarded for it. Jamey might complain that I was never home—and that when I was, I didn't listen—but my university colleagues called me responsible and conscientious. Jamey might call me controlling, inflexible, and incapable of living in the moment. But the promotions, accolades, and fat paychecks that came my way built an ever-stronger case against his accusations, and I used them to further vilify him: *Why couldn't he pull his own weight? Why couldn't he be more supportive? Why didn't he appreciate my hard work and the creature comforts it provided? Why was he constantly bothering me with problems that distracted me from earning a decent living?*

After nearly fourteen years together, Jamey—who had been trying without success to talk to me about my absence from our relationship and his growing problems with alcohol—told me that he had found someone who *would* listen to him, and he moved out. My first book had been published, and I had two more books and several funded research projects in the works. I was also recovering from surgery for stress-related gastrointestinal problems. My life was crumbling under my feet, and there was nothing I could do about it. I lost weight. I couldn't eat. I didn't care if I lived or died.

I was a chain-smoking, caffeine-drinking work junkie, dogged by self-doubt. I had no close friends. I didn't smile. I felt that my colleagues didn't really appreciate my hard work and were breathing down my neck. My memory got so bad that members of my family wondered if I was developing an early case of Alzheimer's. I snapped at colleagues, and they snapped back. I once angrily confronted a college librarian, demanding the name of the irresponsible faculty member who had kept, for three months, a book I wanted. She gave me the name: my own. Work had been the one thing that I had always done well, and now even that was failing me. Yet I couldn't stop working.

In the summer of that year Jamey and I reconciled, and in the fall he checked himself into a treatment center for alcoholism. When I eagerly took part in the family treatment component to "help Jamey with his problem," a facilitator confronted me with my own work obsession. I joined Workaholics Anonymous, entered therapy, and began my climb out of the pit into a saner life. And Jamey and I started to understand the crack in the foundation of our relationship. Today we celebrate decades together in sobriety.

Now, instead of spending my Saturdays in my basement office, I look forward to weekends of yard work, hiking, or matinees at the movies. When we go to the South Carolina shore, I don't pretend to nap anymore. I'm swimming in the surf or walking on the beach with friends. I enjoy and savor my life and my time with Jamey as much as I had once savored my endless work. But old habits die hard. One day while I was working on a writing project, Jamey yelled from upstairs. At first, I felt the workaholic's instinctive annoyance— *Don't you know how important my projects are?* But this feeling was immediately replaced with love and gratitude as I realized he was calling me to a big breakfast of French toast, warm maple syrup, and butter.

Who, Me? A Workaholic?

In a society based on overwork, my behavior had plenty of camouflage. Flextime, twenty-four-hour Walmarts, and electronic devices have vaporized the boundaries that once kept work from engulfing the sacred hours of the Sabbath and the family dinnertime. iPhones, iPads, and laptops have blurred the spatial boundaries between workplace and home: you can e-mail a memo at midnight from the kitchen table, bend over a laptop on an island in paradise, or call the office via cellphone from the ski lift. But work performed in exotic environments is still work, however much you tell yourself it's play. And when any place can be a workplace and any hour is work time, you can work yourself to death, just as some people drink themselves to death in a culture in which any hour is cocktail hour. Little in our present culture teaches workaholics when or how to say no.

Along with my colleagues at the University of North Carolina at Charlotte, I studied workaholics and their families for twenty years. Although no formal records are kept on the numbers of workaholics, we estimate from our extensive studies that one-quarter of the population can be classified as workaholic. But the concept of workaholism is a hard sell. You might be thinking that some of these trends and statistics apply to you. You work hard and put in long hours because you have a mortgage, two children approaching college, and two cars loans. If you don't work hard, how would you stay afloat financially?

Actually, you might not be a workaholic at all. You might be a hard worker. There's a big difference between hard work and workaholism. Hard work put us on the moon. Chances are that from time to time you put more hours and effort into working than into being with loved ones or relaxing. Starting a new business can be an all-consuming affair at first. If you're trying to find a cure for a disease, it can make you single-minded. Or if you're a new employee, you might want to make a good impression as you start your job. These examples are exceptions that most of us encounter at some point in our lives, but workaholics routinely operate in this fashion, using their jobs as escape. So it's possible for you to work long hours, carry a mortgage, send your kids to college, pay for the two cars, and not be a workaholic. Working long hours alone does not make you a workaholic.

Perhaps you're a single parent or someone who has to work overtime to make ends meet, and you're thinking, "From morning to night, it's go, go, go. I'm barely scraping by as it is, and now you're saying I have another problem?" This is not necessarily the case. A workaholic is not the single mom who works two jobs to pay mounting bills. Neither is it the tax accountant who works extra-long hours on weekdays and weekends as April 15 approaches. True workaholics are driven by deeper, internal needs, rather than by external ones —not that it's tax season or that baby needs a new pair of shoes but that the process of working satisfies an inner psychological hunger. But if friends or loved ones have accused you of neglect because of your work habits—or if you have used or abused work to escape from intimacy or social relationships —you might want to take a closer look at your life.

The Workaholic Joy Ride: This Century's Cocaine

Overwork is this century's cocaine, its problem without a name. Workweeks of sixty, eighty, even a hundred hours are commonplace in major law firms and corporations; tribes of modern-day male and female Willy Lomans, manacled to cellphones, trundle through the nation's airports at all hours with their rolling luggage; cafes are filled with serious young people bent over laptops; young workers at dot-coms are available for work 24/7. Could this be you?

Some folks wear their workaholic label like a prize, but if you're like most workaholics, the picture is far more subtle. You don't party or stay out late. You don't waste your time or throw money down the drain. You're level-headed and rational. You've been called dedicated, responsible, and conscientious. You work long and hard, and you're always at your desk or available electronically.

At first the accolades and applause, slaps on the back, fat paychecks, and gold plaques make you feel it's all worth the effort. But after a while, the addiction starts to feel like an unwelcome burden. You have a lot on your plate. You've got to do it perfectly. Can you measure up? Will you be able to perform? Or will you let others down? You've got to prove that you can do it. If you fall short, you dig your heels in deeper. You can't let up because everyone's depending on you.

Burrowing itself deeper into your soul, work addiction is like a prisoner's chain that moves with you wherever you go. When you're not at your desk, your compulsive thoughts are still there. They beat you to the office before you begin the day. They stalk you in your sleep, at a party, or while you're hiking with a friend. They loom over your shoulder when you're trying to have an intimate conversation with your partner. You can't stop thinking about, talking about, or engaging in work activities. Like an alcoholic, you have rigid thinking—sometimes called "stinkin' thinking"—patterns that feed your addiction. When you're preoccupied with work, you don't notice signals, such as physical aches and pains or a reduced ability to function, that warn of serious health problems.

Your projects take priority over every aspect of your life. You get soused by overloading yourself with more work tasks than you can possibly complete. You toil around the clock—hurrying, rushing, and multitasking to meet unrealistic deadlines. You might even throw all-nighters, sometimes sleeping off a work binge in your clothes. The uncontrollable work urge engulfs you in a work fog called a brownout, numbing you to anxiety, worry, and stress, as well as to other people. Work highs, reminiscent of an alcoholic euphoria, run a cycle of adrenaline-charged binge working, followed by a downward swing. Euphoria eventually gives way to work hangovers characterized by withdrawal, depression, irritability, anxiety, even thoughts of suicide.

The Workaholic High

Many people insist that workaholism is not a legitimate addiction because it doesn't have a physiological basis, as chemical and food addictions do. But the truth is that work addiction is both an activity (overdoing) and a substance (adrenaline) addiction in the same way that cocaine and alcoholism are chemical addictions. Long-standing research shows that workaholics have greater anxiety, anger, depression, and stress than nonworkaholics and that they perceive themselves as having more job stress, perfectionism, more generalized anxiety, more health complaints, and greater unwillingness to delegate job responsbilities than nonworkaholics. In addition, workaholics are at higher risk for burnout.[1]

THE ADRENALINE RUSH

Studies have linked work addiction to the release of adrenaline in the body. Adrenaline—a hormone produced by the body in times of stress—has an effect similar to that of amphetamines, or "speed." The release of adrenaline, like other drugs, creates physiological changes that lead to highs—in the case of workaholism, "work highs"—that become addictive and may even be fatal.

Workaholics often describe the rush or surge of energy pumping through their veins and the accompanying euphoria as "an adrenaline high." Addicted to adrenaline, workaholics require larger doses to maintain the high that they create by putting themselves and those around them under stress. Some researchers believe workaholics unconsciously put themselves into stressful situations to get the body to pump its fix.

After a long week, a university professor left his office, butterflies in his stomach at the thought of facing an unplanned weekend. On his way out, he was handed a memo announcing grant-proposal deadlines. Suddenly, calm descended on him, and the adrenaline began to flow as he folded the three-inch-thick computer printout under his arm. Like an alcoholic with a bottle under one arm, who was assured of plenty to drink, the professor was calmed by the guarantee of having more to do; this knowledge filled the hours and gave him purpose. It was an anesthetic, a tranquilizer. But after the proposal was written, the feelings of emptiness, unrest, and depression returned.

Adrenaline addiction, in effect, creates addictions to crises that lead the body to produce the hormone and give workaholics their drug. On the job, workaholics routinely create and douse crises that require the body's adrenaline flow. Pushing subordinates or themselves to finish designated assignments within unrealistic deadlines is one way crises are achieved. Another is biting off too much at one time or attempting to accomplish many tasks at once. But while the workaholic gets high, coworkers and subordinates experience stress and burnout and many of the same emotions as children in alcoholic homes do —notably, confusion and frustration caused by unpredictability. The adrenaline flow also boomerangs for the workaholic in the form of physical problems. Too much adrenaline blocks the body's ability to clear dangerous cholesterol from the bloodstream. Elevated cholesterol levels clog arteries, damage their inner lining, and can cause heart attacks.

HITTING BOTTOM

Progressive in nature, your addictive work behaviors are unconscious attempts to resolve unmet psychological needs that have roots in your upbringing. Your work addiction can lead to an unmanageable everyday life, family disintegration, serious health problems, and even death. The Japanese have a name for the ten thousand workers a year in that country who drop dead from putting in sixty-to-seventy-hour workweeks: *karoshi*—death from overwork. We have no comparable term in the English language. Otherwise healthy Japanese workers keel over at their desks after a long stretch of overtime or after consummating a high-pressured deal, usually from a stroke or heart attack. *Karoshi* among corporate workers in their forties and fifties has become so common that the Japanese workplace has been dubbed "a killing field."[2] And some economists in India have referred to work addiction as "a poison by slow motion."[3]

In the United States, members of Alcoholics Anonymous often speak of the moment they "hit bottom." The glamour peels off like old varnish, alcohol stops working for them, and they can no longer think of themselves as simply bons vivants or men about town. Workaholics, too, hit bottom: a spouse may threaten divorce; a long-ignored back problem or stress-related illness like psoriasis may become painfully disabling; or valued employees may quit, tired of trying to meet impossible deadlines. Some workaholics hit bottom before they can admit they have a problem and get the help they need. Some become so depressed they cannot get out of bed. They find themselves alone, unable to feel, and cut off from everyone they care about. Marriages crumble, and health problems hit crisis proportions. Breaking through the denial shakes workaholics into facing the truth and getting the help they need.

Many of the workaholics I see in private practice are dragged there kicking and screaming by their partners; others finally burn out, or get tired of being perceived as the impossible boss at work and the tyrannical parent at home. "It finally reached a point that I hit a wall!" exclaimed Ed, smacking his right fist into his left palm, "and I couldn't escape it anymore. I was either going to deal with it or I was going to die."

Despite longer hours and more determination, your life is falling apart. Your company doesn't appreciate your hard work. Your boss is breathing down your neck. No matter how hard you try, nothing seems to satisfy him. You're impatient and restless at work, your tolerance for slow-moving coworkers lessening. You resent the fact that you get to work earlier and stay longer than anyone else in the office. You feel contempt for colleagues who don't work on weekends or who "goof off" on holidays.

You have a comfortable income, and your family appears to have all the material comforts. Not only does work addiction look good on you, the workaholic, but your family also appears to be thriving from the outside. Behind closed doors, though, you're breaking down inwardly, and your loved ones are suffering in quiet desperation. Your family doesn't appreciate your hard work and the creature comforts it provides. You can't depend on them to handle things at home in your absence, and they're constantly bothering you with problems that distract you from earning a decent living. They say that you're always working and that when you're not, your mind is off in the clouds. They drag you into their disputes, and your kids are out of control. Sometimes it feels like they are ganging up on you. You're starting to feel like an outsider in your own home. Your old friends don't call anymore, and you never seem to have fun.

Work is the one thing you do well, and now even it has soured. If you don't have your job, there's nothing left of you. Still, you keep plugging away, hoping it will get better. Your life has become cold, dark, and lonely—without meaning. You're dogged by self-doubt and failure. You wish you could talk to someone who would understand and help you remove the invisible chains.

If you've reached this point, you might feel as though there's no place to turn. Even the clinicians you seek out may be oblivious to your problem or ignorant of how to treat it. And when this happens, you feel even more disconnected from others, lonelier, and more hopeless. It is as if work has stolen your soul.

Could You Just Be a Hard Worker?

In a society where many people work long hours, it's important to make a distinction between hard workers and workaholics. If you're a workaholic, you're likely to be a separatist, preferring to work alone and focusing on the details of work.

In contrast, if you're a hard worker, you can see the bigger picture and work cooperatively with others toward common goals. As a workaholic, you're more apt to look for work to do. But if you're a hard worker, you enjoy your work, often work long hours, and focus on getting the job done efficiently. And you think about and enjoy the job you're engaged in at the present moment. In contrast, a workaholic mind-set drives you to think about working a disproportionate amount of time. Even during social activities or leisure times your mind wanders and you obsess about work.

Hard workers see work as a necessary and sometimes fulfilling obligation, compared to workaholics who see it as a haven in a dangerous, emotionally unpredictable world. A hard worker knows when to close the briefcase, mentally switch gears, and be fully present at the celebration of his or her wedding anniversary or a child's Little League game. But if you're a workaholic, you allow work to engulf all other quarters of life: sales reports might litter your dining table; your desk could be covered with dinner plates; you frequently fail to attend to your self-care, spiritual life, and household chores and break your commitments to friends, partners, and children to meet work deadlines.

If you're a workaholic, you seek an emotional and neurophysiological payoff from overwork and get an adrenaline rush from meeting apparently impossible deadlines; hard workers do not. If you're a hard worker, you're able to turn off your work appetite, while workaholics are insatiable. Workaholism keeps you preoccupied with work no matter where you are—walking hand-in-hand with someone you love at the seashore, playing catch with a child, or hanging out with a friend. If you're a hard worker, you're in the office looking forward to being on the ski slopes, compared to the workaholic on the ski slopes who is thinking about being back in the office.

If you're a true workaholic, your relationship with work is the central connection of your life, as compelling as the connection that addicts experience with booze or cocaine. You could be the lawyer who brings his briefcase on family picnics, while his wife carries the picnic basket; the therapist who schedules appointments six days a week, from 8:00 in the morning to 8:00 at night; or the real estate saleswoman who cannot have a heart-to-heart talk with her husband without simultaneously watching television, eating dinner, and going over property-assessment reports. In each case, work has become a defense against human relationships, and balance has been lost.

Workaholism is not a black-and-white matter. Just as *alcoholic* refers not only to the bum in the gutter but to the relatively well-functioning professor who gets quietly soused every night, *workaholism* describes a wide spectrum of behaviors. For some people, workaholism takes outwardly bizarre forms, such as working around the clock for three or four days straight and periodically catching a few hours' sleep in sweat clothes. For others, workaholism is

Cultivating Abstinence on the Work High Wire

Recovery from any addiction requires abstinence from the drug of choice. If you're chemically dependent, that means total sobriety because alcohol and drugs are not necessary for the body to sustain itself. But if you're a workaholic, you still have to work, just as compulsive overeaters have to eat. Abstinence for you, if you're a workaholic, means that you refrain from COMPULSIVE OVERWORKING and cultivate workaholic abstinence through work moderation and healthy work habits. The key is balance, not sacrifice. You don't have to choose misery in one arena or another to put balance into your life. It's possible to work hard, have all the material advantages that result from your hard work, and still have a full and satisfying personal life outside the office.

Healthy work habits, in contrast to workaholism, help you lead a more balanced life—one with time for social and leisure activities and personal and family pursuits. The payoff is a fresher, more clear-minded approach to your job that makes you more efficient at what you do. Chapter 2 guides you through a work moderation plan that helps you find the proper integration of work and personal time to support you in all areas of your life.

subtler: work is the place where life really takes place, the secret repository of drama and emotion. Family and friends are little more than a vague, if pleasant, backdrop.

By now you might be saying, "Fine, I'm a workaholic. It makes me miserable, but I prefer it to having to confront intimacy issues, living without my second home, taking my kids out of private school, and giving up all the other advantages work brings me." So you've settled on being miserable at work rather than being miserable at home. The belief that you can have happiness only at home or only at work, but not both, is all-or-nothing thinking (see chapter 4). Whether you're a workaholic or simply caught up in the workaholic pace of juggling work and family, this book can help you see that you don't have to give up your lifestyle to change your work habits.

Millions of Americans, although not workaholics in the literal sense, find themselves caught in a workaholic lifestyle that gives them some of the same physical and psychological symptoms that workaholics have: emotional burdens, exhaustion, and suffering from stress and relationship problems caused by the disproportionate amount of time and emotional energy put into work. They are consumed by never-ending, obsessive thoughts about work and work-related functions. Many are unable to be emotionally present with loved ones or engage in meaningful intimate, spiritual, and social relationships. And their partners feel lonely, isolated, and guilty in these empty relationships, questioning their own sanity as friends and employers applaud the workaholics for their accomplishments. If this sounds familiar, keep reading to see if you could be chained to the desk.

Are You Chained to the Desk?

There are different degrees of workaholism. Some people fall in the low to mild ranges, and others fall in the higher ranges. The greater the degree of your workaholism, the more serious your physical and emotional side effects will be. Let's take a look at your work patterns.

Could you be chained to the desk? Or are you just a hard worker? To find out in a flash, you can take the Work Addiction Risk Test (WART) on my website, www.bryanrobinsononline.com, click "show results," and see your score in seconds. Or you can rate yourself right here using the rating scale of 1 (never true), 2 (sometimes true), 3 (often true) or 4 (always true). Put the number that best describes your work habits in the blank beside each statement. After you have responded to all twenty-five statements, add the numbers in the blanks for your total score. The higher your score (the highest possible is 100), the more likely you are to be a workaholic; the lower your score (the lowest possible is 25), the less likely you are to be a workaholic.[4]

WART scores are divided into three ranges. After you've taken the WART, here's how to interpret your score:

❖ Red light: If you scored in the upper third (67–100), you're chained to the desk. You are highly workaholic with poor work-life balance, and you might be at risk for burnout. In addition, research suggests that your loved ones might be experiencing emotional repercussions as well.

❖ Yellow light: If you scored in the middle range (57–66), you tend to become busy and work to the exclusion of other life events. Your work habits are mildly workaholic. But with modifications, you can find work-life balance and prevent job burnout.

❖ Green light: If you scored in the lowest range (25–56), you're a hard worker instead of a workaholic, and your risk for burnout is low. You have good work-life balance, and your work style isn't a problem for you or others.

The Work Addiction Risk Test (WART)

_____ 1. I prefer to do most things instead of ask for help.

_____ 2. I get impatient when I have to wait for someone or when something takes too long.

_____ 3. I seem to be in a hurry, racing against the clock.

_____ 4. I get irritated when I'm interrupted while in the middle of something.

_____ 5. I stay busy with many irons in the fire.

_____ 6. I engage in two or three activities at once, such as eating lunch, checking my email, and talking on my cell phone.

_____ 7. I overcommit myself by biting off more than I can chew.

_____ 8. I feel guilty when I'm not working on a project.

_____ 9. It's important that I see the concrete results of my work.

_____ 10. I'm more interested in the final outcome of my work than in the process.

_____ 11. Things don't move fast enough or get done fast enough at work to suit me.

_____ 12. I lose my temper when things don't go my way or work out to suit me.

_____ 13. I ask the same question over again without realizing it, after I've already been given the answer.

_____ 14. I work in my head thinking about future projects while tuning out the here and now.

_____ 15. I continue working after my coworkers have called it quits.

_____ 16. I get angry when people don't meet my standards of perfection on the job.

_____ 17. I get upset when I'm not in control at work.

_____ 18. I tend to put myself under pressure from self-imposed work deadlines.

_____ 19. It's hard for me to relax when I'm not working.

_____ 20. I spend more time working than socializing with friends or enjoying hobbies or leisure activities.

_____ 21. I dive into projects to get a head start before plans are finalized.

_____ 22. I get upset with myself for making even the smallest mistake.

_____ 23. I put more thought, time, and energy into work than into relationships with loved ones and friends.

_____ 24. I forget, ignore, or minimize celebrations such as birthdays, reunions, anniversaries, or holidays.

_____ 25. I make important job decisions before getting all the facts and thinking them through.

Tips for Clinicians

The workaholic's problem is doubly difficult when clinics and clinicians don't tune their radars to detect workaholism. Here are some tips to help you, the clinician, treat workaholism instead of suggesting that workaholics just cut back on work hours, subtly pressuring the partner to adapt to the workaholic's work obsession, or missing the problem altogether.

ESTABLISHING ABSTINENCE

An alcoholic who decides to get sober and joins Alcoholics Anonymous is expected to follow simple, black-and-white rules. He or she may be told, "Just don't drink, no matter what" and "Go to ninety meetings in ninety days." But workaholics can't quit working any more than compulsive eaters can quit eating. Transformation involves becoming attuned to shades of gray and making gradual, gentle changes. The goal is not to eliminate work and its joys but to make it part of a balanced life, rather than the eight-hundred-pound gorilla that sits wherever it wants. First, of course, workaholics have to recognize that there's a problem and be reassured that you, the therapist, do not plan to force them to quit work or even necessarily to reduce their work hours.

Just like in my own recovery, in the clinical work I now do with workaholic clients, therapy usually involves an ordinary, commonsense blend of emotional and interpersonal work, cognitive techniques, family-of-origin work, self-nurturing exercises, pencil-and-paper exercises, and behavioral tactics to help people reorganize time and space so that they're not working or thinking about work 24/7. The only thing unique about therapy with workaholics is focusing the microscope so that overwork comes into view as a problem to begin with.

I often tell workaholic clients that the goal is not to cut back on work hours, which they find immensely relieving. The goal, rather, is to create watertight compartments between work and other areas of life and prepare for easy transitions between them. Some solutions are simple, modest, and practical. Mildred, an overweight, forty-three-year-old psychotherapist had no sense of containment for either her work or her diet. She scheduled clients six days a week, any time between 8:00 a.m. and 8:00 p.m. She literally didn't know when her plate was full because, rather than using a plate, she would open the refrigerator and drink or eat directly from a milk container or take-out carton. At my suggestion, she discarded a day planner that listed the hours from 7:00 a.m. to 11:00 p.m. and replaced it with one that stopped at 5:00 p.m. I also suggested that when she ate, she pour the milk into a glass and dish a serving of food onto a plate.

Before she made these changes, Mildred had felt as though she had to be available to all people all the time. But keeping a more limited day planner and serving herself food on a plate reminded her, physically and practically, that she had choices, could set limits, and could decide for herself when she would see a client or have a glass of milk. This empowerment and self-care helped her slowly revise boundaries that had been blurred since childhood, when she had acted as her depressed mother's emotional caretaker. Over time, she was able to question old beliefs that had confused legitimate self-care with selfishness.

PUTTING "TIME CUSHIONS" INTO WORK SCHEDULES

As a clinician, you can help workaholic clients make transitions between work and other activities and learn not to schedule themselves so tightly that there's no time for bathroom breaks or travel between appointments. By showing them how to schedule "time cushions" around appointments, you can help them drastically reduce tension. One man invariably fought with his fiancée when he returned home because she would be eager to talk intimately while he was still tense and preoccupied with work. Once he started to schedule "time cushions," his days became less harried. He also started using his drive home not to chew over the events of the day but to decompress, play enjoyable music, and practice relaxing exercises as he mentally thought ahead to seeing his fiancée. By the time she met him at the door, he was actually glad to see her and capable of making the transition from hectic schedule to relaxed, intimate conversations.

SETTING BOUNDARIES AROUND WORK HOURS

In your sessions, be sure to address problems in boundary setting and help clients say no when choices are available to them or when they're already over-committed. The boundaries that workaholics set depend on their unique lifestyles. Some clients can limit their work to eight hours a day, with no weekend or holiday work, and can recognize that additional hours are not honorable but a "fix." Others don't have that flexibility. Still others do, but have trouble saying no.

You can challenge clients to set weekly boundaries creatively and to evaluate from week to week their success at maintaining healthy boundaries. But be prepared to challenge their many justifications for their inability to maintain the boundaries they set. The next week then becomes another opportunity for them to practice this skill.

Many of the techniques I now use with clients are ones that I used myself. I ditched a day planner that went from 7:00 a.m. to midnight and got one that limited my work to the hours between 8:00 a.m. and 5:00 p.m. I also set specific hours for working at home, worked only in my study, and gave myself fifteen-minute time cushions between appointments to give myself time to stretch or get where I needed to go. I renewed old friendships and developed new ones. And I confronted the fact that I had been hiding from the world since third grade, using work to keep me from close relationships even though I hungered for them. Closeness had felt scary and unpredictable, and I'd worked to keep even Jamey at arm's length. I felt out of control with someone who in an instant could break my heart like a brittle twig.

Change was not easy for me, and there was no specific moment when the light switch came on. Instead, it was more like the subtle changing of the seasons. I started to see Jamey with fresh eyes, watching him care for his orchids and realizing the wisdom contained in the pleasure he got from simply working in the yard. One weekend I accepted his invitation and tried working with him, just to do something together. Much to my surprise, I discovered how much I, too, relished the smell of cut grass, the feel of warm earth, and chats with neighbors.

SEEING THE WATER YOU'RE SWIMMING IN

As a practitioner, I know I'm not alone. Many of you face similar challenges in your own lives. It's one of the hazards of work that is not merely a job but a calling. It's easy for callings to overwhelm other areas of our lives, to become not only our livelihoods but our sole source of spiritual meaning and an oddly safe arena for intense emotional connection without too much personal risk.

Chances are that you too are particularly vulnerable to the blurred boundaries that can promote workaholism. We have the dangerous freedom to set our own hours; to juggle training, supervision, workshops, and clinical work; to labor on research projects in our home offices until midnight; to leave our cellphones and laptops on—and we have trouble saying no to clients who insist on evening or weekend appointments.

When we live this way ourselves, swimming in the soup of a work-obsessed culture, it's hardly surprising that we miss the clues our clients and their partners give us about the misshaping power of overwork on their families' lives. By way of analogy, before the 1980s many therapists who were not aware of the ramifications of alcoholism worked earnestly with couples without directly addressing substance-abuse issues and wondered why they seemed to be treading water.

As mental health professionals, we have also failed to notice that workaholism is the unacknowledged common element in many of our treatment failures. We hear that a man isn't devoting time to his relationship with his wife, and we may be unaware that his compelling and unacknowledged relationship to work may be at the bottom of the couple's distress.

This is a larger issue than it may seem at first. In the case of alcoholism, therapists eventually got more sophisticated and began to see it for what it was, to refer clients to Alcoholics Anonymous or rehab as a condition for continuing therapy, and to understand that until the centrality of the relationship to the substance was addressed, little else was likely to change. It's time we got more sophisticated about overwork as well. We need to see it as yet another way that vulnerable human beings seek, for understandable reasons, a sanctuary from the uncertainties and vulnerabilities of really living their present lives, with all their textures and disappointments.

When we as clinicians restore balance to our own lives, we will be far more likely to recognize, and effectively treat, this century's problem without a name when it bedevils the clients and families who come into our therapy offices for help.

2

How to Spot
Work Addiction

*I didn't need to use drugs because my
bloodstream was manufacturing my
own crystal meth.*

—Workaholics Anonymous Member

Roger

As a sixty-five-year-old physician, I was forced into retirement by multiple
health and legal issues, and I surrendered my medical license in the fall of 2009.
When I look back, it's clear that the seeds of my work addiction sprouted in
childhood. I mowed lawns in junior high, became a construction laborer as
soon as I could drive, waited tables in college, and worked two jobs, seven days
a week, every summer. I had little if any free time.

In medical school, I worked day and night three days straight in the hospital
by choice. As an intern at the San Diego Naval Hospital, I was selected the
"Hot Dog of the Year." As a resident and fellow, I developed numerous clinical and teaching programs that were not required of me, but they earned me
attention, distinction, and honors.

I was always busy and loved it that way. I considered work my hobby, not
a job. After the internship, I worked eighty-hour workweeks, giving most of
myself to my career, having little left over for my wife and children. I purchased
a home with eight acres and a barn where I had plenty to do. Like my father
did when I was a child, I took my family on beach vacations but was always
ready to get back to work. I took a fax machine and computer on vacation
and had my staff FedEx charts that I processed and sent back. I rationalized
that I didn't want to return to work with a pile on my desk. But truth be told,

working gave me a high, making me feel important in ways that nothing else could. Work transcended everything.

While working a full anesthesia practice, I developed a pain clinic that consumed a great amount of my time and soul, plus thousands of hours of work and great effort. I reasoned that the time and effort drain was acceptable because I provided a nice home, with a place for my wife's horses, and all our children went to the best private schools. I worked my ass off and loved it! Work had become a compulsion. I received awards from the medical society for what I contributed to the medical community and to patients. It was great, and I was having fun. Or so I thought.

As the workload continued to escalate, I couldn't keep up. Then I discovered hydrocodone. The painkiller helped me focus, work longer hours, and churn out a greater quantity and higher quality of work. When back pain started interfering with my productivity, the painkiller became a necessity to keep up with the workload. It was easy to get, often sent to the office as samples.

Altogether, I had five back surgeries, two neck spine fusions, one knee and both hip replacements, two shoulder surgeries, and hand surgery. I was proud that it never took me more than a week to return to work, that my staff was amazed, and that no one tried to stop me. Then one day a representative from the state's impaired physician group visited me, inquiring about a complaint he had received. I assured him I didn't have a problem. Afterward I sought help from an addictionologist on my own. He said I should stop using hydrocodone. But I was blind to my out-of-control work compulsions and didn't know how to change.

I continued working until 2:00 or 3:00 a.m. and got up at 5:00 or 6:00 a.m. to return to the office. I became so tired that I developed fatigue-induced paranoia. I would fall asleep for a few seconds while driving, almost totaling the car more than once. At home, before reaching the bed one time, I damaged our house by a water spill when I fell asleep in the shower.

I continued to perform over seventy injections and other surgical procedures each week and see patients in the office. I couldn't get ahead of the work, yet I couldn't say no to taking on more. I used eight different medications to keep me going, each on a schedule. And I went to great lengths, making sure I had enough in reserve, so I'd have the energy they provided for me to work. My rut became deeper, but I saw no way out. I couldn't ask for help for fear of being ruined financially and having my personal life destroyed. Constantly anxious, my blood pressure spiked to a dangerous level of 170/110, and I had constant headaches.

Eventually, I was reported to the state board of medicine and was sent to a drug addiction program for evaluation. I told them about my inability to stop working compulsively, yet I was diagnosed as a drug addict. With a wrong diagnosis, I was prescribed the wrong treatment. I had taken charts and a Dictaphone with me so I could continue working in rehab. When they found out, they were upset but still didn't see my problem.

Upon returning home, I tried working without painkillers but couldn't. With my old pill source still in place, I returned to work while going to mandatory AA meetings, ultimately passing ninety-one random urine drug screens over a five-year period. The rut and downward spiral continued for another five years, as did my drug use to support my work addiction.

Hooked on work, I pulled further away from my family and was dying inside. Then came the dreaded call that told me to shut down my practice. I was actually relieved to receive the call. I enrolled in a high-powered drug rehab program for professionals for three months where I explained that my real problem was work addiction. Again I was ignored and told "the treatment is all the same."

Once home, I finally found a therapist who listened and made the diagnosis of work addiction with or without drug addiction. I felt like jumping for joy! It had taken only seven years for an accurate diagnosis. Treatment from several other experts on workaholism and many tests all supported the diagnosis of work addiction without chemical addiction.

I can trace my struggles with work addiction to my childhood, when my father worked all the time. He had been a breadwinner for his family since the ninth grade, when his father died. I saw little of him, except when I was in trouble. Although I'd said I'd never do what my father had done, I'd become just like him. I missed my children's youth and sacrificed my marriage to work. I'm sure some of my health problems were caused by my work addiction and the total lack of the ability to treat myself. I'm living out my father's life, and even though I recognize the need to change somehow, I'm still resistant.

My hopes are to avoid dying feeling totally useless and a burden to my family and society, and in pain. I'm still in good physical health and have the will and drive to regain my medical license and rebuild my family. Fortunately, my wife and children continue to be understanding and supportive. But the price I've paid for work addiction has been as great as that of any person with a chemical addiction. I'm living proof of that.

The Tell-Tale Signs of Work Addiction

If you're like Roger—addicted to work but unable to see the water you're swimming in—this chapter describes the warning signals so you can recognize the work addiction that's staring you in the face.

My research team at the University of North Carolina at Charlotte wanted to pinpoint some of the signs of work addiction. We compared a sample of 109 workaholics with nonworkaholics. Across the board, workaholics had statistically higher burnout rates, were more disconnected from their inner selves, and had less self-insight than nonworkaholics. Workaholics were more controlling and more impaired in their communication. In contrast, nonworkaholics showed more clarity, compassion, calmness, and confidence.[1] And it's no wonder, because workaholics focus—for the most part—outside themselves on the tsunami of work that they take on. Let's look at more of the signs.

The Ten Red Flags

Over the years, I have collected hundreds of case studies from self-described workaholics in my clinical practice. The following ten warning signs were synthesized from these case studies.[2] All ten signs are not present in every case, and they may appear in various configurations in different individuals. But they are useful guidelines to help you recognize workaholism.

1. *Rushing and hyperbusyness.* "As I'm walking out the door, I glance at my watch and realize I have ten more minutes before my next appointment. I just have to cram in one more thing. So I rush back to my desk, put in a call . . . and before I know it, fifteen minutes have passed. Of course, I'm late to the appointment."

Nothing moves fast enough for Jim. The more items he can cross off his list, the better he feels. When a job is left hanging, he feels anxious and afraid. To curb his anxiety, he has to have two or three activities going at once. So when he has the phone in one hand, he's pounding away on his computer with the other and mentally planning a third project.

If you're a workaholic, you feel compelled to have many things happening at once and to engage in two or three activities simultaneously because it gives you the sense that you're accomplishing more. To perform only one activity at a time feels underproductive. Typically, you schedule back-to-back appointments and don't give yourself enough time to complete tasks, the pressures of which provide an adrenaline rush. Or you create minicrises, such as when a balky computer system or paper-clip shortage flips you out.

2. *Need to control.* "I have to write, produce, and star in my life. I really don't have time to develop this new account, but I know if I hand it over to someone else, it won't be handled right. I'll have to work nights to write and design this new ad campaign, but it's worth it. In the long run, we'll keep the client. I'd rather do it myself than waste time with a bunch of bad ideas from everyone else."

Sally's successful advertising agency is built on her own strength. As a work-addicted employer, she has trouble delegating authority. Her need to control her life is prompted by insecurity; she's uncomfortable in unpredictable situations. Solo working gives her security. Projects come with a beginning, middle, and end. When she's in control of all three stages, she feels like her entire life is in control.

When you're chained to the desk, you fear that delegating tasks or asking for help will be perceived as signs of weakness or incompetence. And once something is out of your hands, you feel a loss of control. So you can't and won't ask for help. You tend to overplan and overorganize through work so that your environment feels predictable, consistent, and controllable—all of which inhibit spontaneity and flexibility.

3. *Perfectionism.* "I think I'm superhuman. I can't be content to accomplish something without laying the groundwork for something else. Fearing that I'll somehow fall behind or get out of control, I constantly have to be striving to accomplish some kind of goal or some block of work."

Lyn judges herself and others by inhuman standards. In her view, there's no room for mistakes. Anyone falling short of her idea of perfection is lazy. Even at home, Lyn is a critical judge: "This house isn't clean enough. Who left crumbs in the den? You forgot to wipe your feet. If I've told you once, I've told you a million times, 'Close that basement door when you come upstairs!'"

Chances are that if you're a perfectionist workaholic, you're difficult to work for and even more difficult to live with. You narrow your life to only those things at which you can excel. You judge yourself and others unmercifully. Your common sayings include "If you want it done right, do it yourself" and "If I do it, I know it's been done the way I want it done." Because of these superhuman standards, failure and anger at others for not meeting high standards are your constant companions.

4. *Difficulty with intimacy and crumbling relationships.* "At rehearsals, I would imagine my smiling dad in the front row. He looked so proud of me. His imagined presence really motivated me to learn my part. But when it came time for the actual performance, he had an out-of-town business meeting. He promised to dash back from the airport to catch my second act. All through the first act, I was distracted by opening doors and shuffling feet. I'd look into the audience, searching for his face. But as always, his meeting ran over, and he missed my school play."

If you're anything like Sandy's father, this wouldn't be the first play you missed. You would have a pattern of forgetting, ignoring, or minimizing the importance of family rituals and celebrations. A family member might have to remind you about birthdays, reunions, holidays, and anniversaries. And even if you make it to an event, you might have trouble concentrating because your mind is back at the office. Wedded to work, you have little time left over for others.

5. *Work binges.* "I self-impose deadlines all the time. The price I have to pay for procrastinating just isn't worth it. I go nuts. I panic. I can't sleep. I have such anxiety until a project is completed. So finally I just buckle down and do it. I get in this altered state where I chain-smoke, don't eat, screen all of my phone calls, and avoid sleep. When I'm done, it's like crawling out of a work cave. I look and feel pretty disgusting. But with that finished project in my hand, nothing else seems to matter."

Chances are you've occasionally worked overtime to meet a deadline. But when you're a workaholic, you strangle yourself with unrealistic deadlines and work binges to complete projects. You would rather work nonstop for days than spread tasks out over a reasonable time period. In extreme cases, you might mimic the alcoholic who stashes booze wherever he goes. Instead of hiding your booze, you shove a laptop into suitcases or under car seats. Even at leisure events, after promising not to work, you slip out your iPhone or shuffle papers inside pant or skirt pockets. It's as if you need a work "fix" everywhere you go.

6. *Restlessness and inability to relax.* "I always have this annoying voice in my head. It tells me I don't have the right to relax or unwind. This voice says, 'Look, fun is a waste of time. What do you have to show for it? Go do something productive, you jerk.'"

This symptom can show up when you feel guilty and useless whenever you are doing something that doesn't produce results. If you're exercising, cleaning, or doing a job-related activity, you feel okay. But if you're hanging out with friends, you might feel restless and irritable. Leisure activities are viewed as a frivolous waste of time, and you become so restless that you turn hobbies and recreation into productivity or money-making ventures.

7. *Work trances and "DWW."* Work trances or brownouts are comparable to the alcoholic's blackouts. During a work trance, you have memory lapses during long conversations because you're preoccupied with work. You tune out the here and now. Driving while working mentally (DWW) can cause you to drive through stop signs or past designated points on your route. Busily focusing on tomorrow's presentation, you might have trouble paying attention to the road. Chances are if you work and drive, you have a faulty driving record. Melanie described one work trance this way:

It was my boyfriend's birthday, and I'd spent most of the day with him. We were supposed to have dinner together. He was even going to cook. But just before dinnertime, I became so anxious I had to get out of his apartment. I hadn't done one work-related thing all day. I told him I needed to run home to change clothes. But once in my car, I found myself driving toward my office. I told myself I would merely type a few paragraphs and go over tomorrow's appointments. I don't remember the three hours that passed. It was 9:00 p.m. when I rushed to my car and floored it back toward his apartment. I was stopped by a police officer for speeding. I tried to explain my situation to him, but to no avail. When I finally made it back, my boyfriend had already eaten his birthday dinner alone. I felt so terrible. Yet even worse, I didn't know why I did it.

8. *Impatience and irritability.* Since time is your most precious commodity as a workaholic, you hate to wait. You'll try almost anything to get to the front of the line at the grocery store, restaurant, or movie. You're easy to spot at the doctor's or dentist's office—the one hypnotically gazing into a smart phone or with an open laptop, pad of paper, and a fast-scribbling pen.

In the long run, your impatience can result in impulsivity and premature decisions. You might start projects before gathering all the facts. You make avoidable mistakes because you bypass research and exploration.

9. *Self-inadequacy.* "Work was my security, promising to fill the hours and give me purpose, meaning, and self-esteem. But as soon as a project was done, the emptiness, unrest, and depression returned. The only time I felt good about myself was when I was producing 'things' so that I could constantly prove that I was okay."

Natalie gets a temporary high when she completes a project. In between achievements, she feels empty and lost. This feeling of inadequacy bothers her until she is immersed in her next project. Work is the one thing that used to bring her love and attention from her parents when she was younger. She still believes she has to prove herself in order to be accepted by others.

As a workaholic, you seek self-worth through performance and achievement. Your sense of inadequacy and poor self-esteem cause you to emphasize production with concrete results that give you a temporary high and feeling of value.

10. *Self-neglect.* Self-care is at the bottom of your list if you're a workaholic. Your job trumps taking care of yourself. You pay little attention to your physical condition, which is probably on a downhill slide. And nutrition, rest, and exercise are no-shows in your life. When coping mechanisms such as

TABLE 2.1

Warning Signs of Work Addiction

Physical signs	Behavioral signs
Headaches	Temper outbursts
Fatigue	Restlessness
Allergies	Insomnia
Indigestion	Difficulty relaxing
Stomachaches	Hyperactivity
Ulcers	Irritability and impatience
Chest pain	Forgetfulness
Shortness of breath	Difficulty concentrating
Nervous tics	Boredom
Dizziness	Mood swings

chain-smoking, caffeine abuse, and compulsive eating are added to the picture, your health deteriorates further.

Even when real symptoms such as headaches, ulcers, or high blood pressure crop up, you say you don't have time to go to the doctor. Although you know there's a problem, you convince yourself to ignore it. Table 2.1 presents the physical and behavioral warning signs that accompany work addiction.

The Many Faces of Work Addiction

All workaholics work too much, but not all workaholics act alike. Some are too careless, others too ploddingly scrupulous; some can't get started, others plunge in on a dozen projects and finish little. The end result of these differing work styles may look the same from the point of view of a therapist or an unhappy spouse—an unbalanced life dominated by long hours at the office —but each style expresses a different set of emotional and cognitive vulnerabilities, and each needs different therapeutic treatment.

As you consider the signs and traits, keep in mind that not all workaholics fit the general pattern. Work addiction has many faces:

❖ The CEO who sneaks a cellphone and laptop into the hospital where she has just undergone major surgery

❖ The minister zipping down the highway at seventy miles an hour, scribbling notes for his sermon, swearing and promising to remember his iPhone next time so he won't have to slow down

❖ The psychotherapist who cannot say no to the patients who need her and ends up overscheduling herself, burning out in the process

❖ The architect who confides that she mentally worked on a client's house during sexual intercourse with her husband

❖ The supermom who has a career, manages the house, is a driver for the kids' carpool, gets dinner on the table, and perhaps even takes a class at night

Workaholics are not always the Donald Trumps of the corporate world. Sometimes they look more like Martha Stewart. In fact, the number of women workaholics is climbing as women enter more traditionally male-dominated fields. Workaholics are not always in corporate or office jobs, nor are they always in high-paying positions. Plumbers, electricians, waitresses, and maintenance workers are included in the ranks of workaholics.

The broad umbrella term *workaholism* is only a starting point. There are four major categories of workaholism: the *relentless*, the *bulimic*, the *attention-deficit*, and the *savoring* workaholic. Maybe you can see yourself, a loved one, or a colleague in one of the following categories of workaholism.

Typology of Workaholics

	Work Initiation	
High Work Completion	Bulimic Workaholics (low work initiation / high work completion)	Relentless Workaholics (high work initiation / high work completion)
Low	Savoring Workaholics (low work initiation / low work completion)	Attention-Deficit Workaholics (high work initiation / low work completion)

Work Initiation
Low ————————————————→ High

THE RELENTLESS WORKAHOLIC

The stereotypical workaholics are what I call *relentless workaholics*—those who work compulsively and constantly day and night, holidays and weekends. How do you know if you're a relentless workaholic? There's no letup and few periods of down time in your life, and leisure and recreation are rare. Gary describes what happens:

> When I'm fatigued and have had only three hours of sleep after staying up all night at the computer, something in my body and my mechanism keeps me moving, even when there's no energy left. It isn't easy for me to give up, no matter what the clock says. I take a break to eat and try to work out once in a while. But I usually don't stop until eleven or twelve o'clock at night, and many times not until two in the morning. Because I want to bear down on myself, I tend to put too much on my list, stay up past the time I should have, and do projects that really could be done the next day. I want to make sure that I put forth some blood, sweat, and tears so that I'll remember I've done the work and I didn't come by it in an easy way. I have headaches almost every afternoon to the point that I'm keeping the makers of Extra Strength Tylenol in business. I'm tired all the time, but I don't allow myself to get the kind of rest I need. I haven't made time for it because there's too much work to be done.

You know you're a relentless workaholic if, instead of dragging your feet on deadlines, you complete work tasks weeks ahead of schedule. When you approach a project with a six-month deadline as if it were due tomorrow, it gives you an adrenaline charge. You let nothing and no one stand in your way of getting the job done. Having the project finished early leaves you time to focus on other work items. Work is more important to you than relationships, and you disregard other people's feelings because you're focused on task completion. Marge was so praised for her tireless dedication by her hospital bosses that it stimulated her to do more, despite her husband's objections. Her work addiction got so bad that she actually stepped over dog excrement for days on her way out the door because she didn't have time to pick it up. After her marriage ended, Marge lamented her belated revelation:

> Only after I was separated from my husband did I realize I wasn't supposed to do all of this as part of my job. I'm aware that I've been addicted to my own adrenaline for a long, long time. My mind never stopped at night, because I was running on adrenaline. When I couldn't sleep, I'd put a yellow pad by my bed. Every time I had a thought, I'd turn on the light and write the thought down, thinking it would help me sleep. My husband wanted to know why I couldn't

turn it off. But the adrenaline made me feel like I didn't need sleep, except for two or three hours a night. But I wasn't tired. I was having a ball and on a roll!

Once a task is completed, if you're a relentless workaholic, you move to the next item on the agenda and have many activities going at once. You are a hard-driving perfectionist; your work is thorough, and your standards practically unreachable. You are a dyed-in-the-wool workaholic—you take work seriously, performing to nothing short of the highest standards.[3] Overcommitted, you abhor incompetence in others and tend to be productive and highly regarded by others.

THE BULIMIC WORKAHOLIC

The second category is the *bulimic workaholic*, who has out-of-control work patterns that alternate between binges and purges. How do you know if you're a bulimic workaholic? Faced with a time crunch, you create adrenaline as you engage in frantic productivity that is followed by inertia. You overcommit, wait until the last possible minute, then throw yourself into a panic and work frantically to complete the task. Jenny worked for two or three days straight and slept off her work high for two days. She collapsed, sleeping in her clothes, just like an alcoholic sleeping off a drinking binge:

> When I used to binge, I would take on a project and stay up until three or four in the morning to get it finished, just compulsively thinking that morning's not going to come and that if something happened to me, I have to have it done today. That binge would go into fourteen and sixteen hours, and then I'd have two or three hours of sleep and then go on a roll and do this for two more days. Then I would be exhausted and sleep it off. It's almost like I've heard alcoholics talk about sleeping off a drunk. I would sleep off that binge of work. Sometimes I would sleep in my clothes, and I hated it! I just hated it!

In contrast to relentless workaholics, whose productivity is clearly visible, you know you're a bulimic workaholic if you go through long periods where you don't work. In fact, no one would know you're a workaholic if they caught you in one of your down times. When it comes to deadlines, you procrastinate and then put yourself under the gun to finish. Procrastination and frantic working are two different sides of the same coin of work bulimia. Fear that you won't do the task perfectly underlies your procrastination. You might become so preoccupied with perfection that you cannot start a project. Yet while you engage in behaviors that distract you from the task, you obsess over getting the job accomplished. Outwardly, your work bulimia makes it appear that you're avoiding work, but in your mind you're working obsessively hard.

Although physically present during family gatherings or Workaholics Anonymous meetings, others see you as preoccupied, working in your head. During your procrastination phase, when you feel paralyzed and unable to work steadily and within healthy boundaries, you are what is referred to as a *work anorexic*—someone for whom avoidance of work is as much a compulsion of work addiction as overworking is because of your obsession with it.[4]

THE ATTENTION-DEFICIT WORKAHOLIC

Lee represents the third type of workaholic, the *attention-deficit workaholic*. How do you know if you're engaged in this workaholic style? You're adrenaline-seeking, easily bored and distracted, constantly seeking stimulation. Lee leaves the house most mornings in a huff because either his wife or kids did something to upset him. On the way to work he weaves in and out of traffic, shaking his fist and cursing at other commuters.

By the time he gets to the office, Lee has settled down and is ready to work. You know you're an attention-deficit workaholic when your appetite for excitement, crisis, and intense stimulation is a strategy that you unwittingly use to focus. You're often the revved-up workaholic who clicks her nails on table tops, twiddles his thumbs, or fidgets, pacing about erratically. You like risky jobs, recreation, and living on the edge at work and play.

Living on the brink of chaos gives you a constant adrenaline charge. Lee seeks diversion from boredom through stimulation in a relatively safe fashion, such as creating tight deadlines, keeping many projects going at one time, taking on big challenges at work, and being chronically unable to relax without intense stimulation. The adrenaline charge could also cause you to live on the edge and engage in high-risk jobs or activities such as playing the stock market, parachute jumping, or working triage in a hospital emergency room.

You have difficulty staying focused on tasks. You get bored with the details of your work and jump ahead to the next item on the agenda to get another charge. You might even create crises over the smallest things to get the adrenaline rush, possibly throwing a fit because there is no paper in the fax machine. Research shows that it's not uncommon for workaholics to generate the crisis and then get attention and praise for resolving it.[5]

Some but not all attention-deficit workaholics are struggling with undiagnosed attention-deficit disorder (ADD). Adrenaline acts as self-medication that functions as an antidote for the ADD and provides the needed focus that allows you to buckle down to work. Unlike bulimic workaholics, who are paralyzed by perfectionism when they should be starting a project, you start many projects but can't complete them. Unlike relentless workaholics who compulsively follow through, you leave projects unfinished and half-baked to move on to the next excitement. Easily bored with the details of the follow-through stage, you get high from creating ideas and brainstorming the big picture, then launching projects without finishing them.

One expert described this type of workaholic as *the innovators*: "They cannot keep their attention focused long enough to finish what they have created. Moreover, they report boredom with follow-through. Upon deeper investigation, I discovered that these workers were hooked on the adrenaline rush of the new idea, and felt let down by the painstaking development work. They jumped to the new projects to get their high. Of course, with inadequate product development, these great innovations were just sitting on the shelves and not making profit for the company."[6]

The compulsion to jump impulsively into work projects before plans have been thought through or solidified makes it hard for you to complete projects in a timely manner. Instead of giving serious consideration to alternate behaviors or possible consequences or waiting and planning, your need for immediacy often locks you into a course of action. You proceed with projects without paying thorough attention to details or receiving valuable input from others. The results can be disastrous if your addiction outruns careful thought and reflection. Nowhere is the adage "haste makes waste" more appropriate. When your lack of forethought causes you to make impulsive decisions without all the facts, you might wonder why you're constantly backtracking to clean up your own messes.

THE SAVORING WORKAHOLIC

The fourth type, the *savoring workaholic*, is a contrast to attention-deficit workaholics because he or she is slow, deliberate, and methodical. How do you know if you're a savoring workaholic? You are a consummate perfectionist, terrified deep down that the finished project is never good enough. It's difficult for you to tell when something is incomplete or when it's finished. You savor your work just as alcoholics savor a shot of bourbon.

When Norm balances his accounts, he'll take eight hours to do some tabulating that most people could do in one hour. According to his wife, Norm has the same sort of intoxication with work that people who eat too much do with food. "He's always working but never seems to accomplish much," Norm's wife said, "Sometimes I look at what he's done, and it doesn't look like he's produced anything. For all I know, he's adding up the same column of numbers day after day."

You know you're a savoring workaholic if you inadvertently prolong and create additional work when you're almost finished with a task. You are notorious for creating to-do lists that often take longer to generate than completing the task would. Norm says he takes great pride and pleasure in producing to-do lists and marking off each item as it is completed: "Creating lists dictated my work life. I always found a way to fill in any extra spaces or lines on my yellow pad with obscure chores so I'd always be busy." He says each line that's marked off is a great sense of satisfaction for him: "It's a visible trophy to my sense of accomplishment."

When savoring workaholism runs your life, your detailed, self-absorbed work style makes it hard to function on a team. Norm drives colleagues and loved ones crazy with his nitpicking and inability to let things go because tasks rarely seem finished to him. Colleagues complain that you drag your feet because you have to dot every *i* and cross every *t*. When others are ready to move on, you hold them back by overanalyzing, taking ideas apart, thinking them through from every angle, getting bogged down in detail, and sending things back to committee fifteen different times. Because projects seem incomplete to you, even when others deem them finalized, you have difficulty with both the closure of old tasks and the initiation of new ones in your work.

Work Moderation

Abstinence for those who are chemically dependent means total sobriety. But if you have to work, you can find work moderation by abstaining from compulsive overworking and freedom from negative thinking. For some workaholics, an effective work-moderation plan includes specific activities and time commitments. For others, it's a broad framework that provides maximum flexibility and balance in the four areas of life: work, play, relationships, and self. Giving time and thought to your work in proportion to other activities in your life becomes the primary goal. There's a general consensus that the best predictor of a positive approach to work is a full life outside work. A full personal life that acts as a psychological buffer can dissipate your work's negative effects and augment the positive ones.

Steps to Developing a Work Moderation Plan

As a beginning to a work moderation—or self-care—plan, imagine your life as four spokes in a wheel: self, relationships, play, and work.

1. *Self*: attending to the personal needs of rest and physical exercise, relaxation, self-esteem, spiritual practices, nutrition, and stress-reduction exercises

such as deep breathing or meditation (I include a detailed discussion of the benefits of meditation in chapter 10).

2. *Relationships*: spending time and nurturing relationships with significant loved ones and friends whom you consider your family. Your family can be a spouse; it can include both a spouse and children; it can include unmarried same-sex or opposite-sex partners with or without children; or it can comprise other adults such as your parents or siblings. Your family, whether related or unrelated to you, and your friends comprise your major support system.

3. *Play*: spending time in fun activities and social pastimes such as hobbies, recreation, and leisure.

4. *Work*: being effective and productive on the job, enjoying what you do for a living, working harmoniously with coworkers, and working moderately while giving equal time to other areas of your life.

You can use the form in the next section to develop a self-care plan.

Tips for Clinicians

The symptoms of work addiction are often overlooked. If you're like most clinicians, you'll want to know the symptoms and be able to recognize them. Once you identify the pattern, you can take the first step in treating work addiction by helping clients develop a self-care plan. Together with your client, you can identify his or her type of workaholism, along with accompanying problems, and match counseling goals with the specific type of work addiction. It's important for you to evaluate your own work addiction tendencies and think about a self-care plan of your own if applicable.

USING THE WART

I developed the Work Addiction Risk Test (WART), shown in chapter 1, as a tool to screen for the symptoms of work addiction. The WART has been tested for its clinical preciseness. Statistical studies show that it has high reliability and validity. Scores on the instrument tend to be consistent over time, and it measures what it is supposed to measure.[7]

You can use the WART to identify problem areas and set goals. Together with clients, I encourage you to use the WART to pinpoint areas of concern that need modifying. Then you can apply some or all of the tips presented throughout this book. Rereading the test and identifying statements that clients rated 3 or 4 will tell you a lot about how they're living their lives. Then they can think of ways to reduce the risk involved in each situation. In other words, how can they change their lives so that they can honestly rate the statements 1

Computing Your Self-Care Quotient

1. Start by computing your NOW percentage:
   How are you living your life? Indicate the percentage of time you NOW
   devote to each of the four areas below. (The percentages must add up to 100.)

SELF	_____
RELATIONSHIPS	_____
PLAY	_____
WORK	_____
TOTAL	100%

2. Next compute your GOAL percentage:
   What would be your goal for a more balanced life? Indicate the percentage of
   time you would devote to each of the four areas below if your life were more
   balanced. (The percentages must add up to 100.)

SELF	_____
RELATIONSHIPS	_____
PLAY	_____
WORK	_____
TOTAL	100%

3. Then compute your self-care quotient:
   Enter the four NOW and GOAL percentages in the spaces below. Then subtract the NOW from the GOAL percentages to get your self-care quotient.
   A positive score means the area needs more time. A negative score means the
   area needs less time.

	SELF	RELATIONSHIPS	PLAY	WORK
GOAL	_____	_____	_____	_____
NOW	_____	_____	_____	_____
BALANCE	_____	_____	_____	_____

4. Your Work Moderation Plan
   After reviewing your four balances, name three or four actions you can take in
   each area to bring more balance to your life. Putting the actions into practice
   becomes the basis of your self-care plan. After you try your plan for a week,
   revise it by deciding what you want to keep, add, or delete.

   Self:

   Relationships:

   Play:

   Work:

or 2? You can help clients set goals for each situation that they'd like to change, moving them in the direction of reversing their compulsive work patterns.

The psychologists Wayne and Mary Sotile modified the WART for those they call *high-powered couples* and discovered that it provides a vehicle for stimulating helpful conversation among couples.[8] Consider encouraging couples to read the WART together and decide how much each item pertains to them. After tallying their two scores—a "mine" and a "yours" score—they can note how they define their own and each other's "work." They can note where they agree and disagree in how they rated themselves and each other. They can note changes in perceptions of each other and answer such questions as "Have you changed in ways that your partner is not recognizing?" or "What small changes in your own and in your partner's work style or work orientation might make a difference in the quality of your day-to-day life together?"

MATCHING COUNSELING GOALS TO WORKAHOLIC TYPE

Some work addicts consistently fit in only one category of workaholic; others mix and match, blending categories or alternating among them. For example, a perfectionist may sometimes procrastinate on a major project like a bulimic workaholic and at other times be unwilling to let go of finished work like a savoring workaholic. And an attention-deficit workaholic may sometimes procrastinate and at other times impulsively start projects, only to lose interest and abandon them. Whatever the type of overwork, a careful assessment can help you unravel the assumptions and fears that lie beneath it and point the way to an effective therapeutic approach.

Workaholics in different categories experience different kinds of job and family problems. I recommend collaborating with your workaholic clients to set therapeutic goals that match your client's type of work addiction. Relentless workaholics need help with impulse control, forethought, and attention to detail. They need to slow down the pulse and rhythm of their daily lives —to deliberately eat more slowly, talk more slowly, walk more slowly, and drive more slowly. Developing a work pace commensurate with that of their colleagues and learning to delegate tasks can give them the breathing room they need to stay in the present.

Goals for work bulimics might include devising a more consistent, steady work style and setting boundaries around the times they work. If workaholics in this category learn to accept imperfection, they can move from a stance of "I either do it perfectly or not at all" to "It's okay if my rough draft contains misspelled words, bad grammar, and incomplete and imperfect ideas." Then bulimic workaholics can get started earlier and spread their work out over more realistic time spans. Some workaholics need more help with procrastination and lethargy, along with concurrent mental obsessions and working. Others need a self-care plan that helps them change their frantic, nonstop approach to work, a plan that might include time out.

In my private practice I have noticed that many adrenaline-seeking workaholics also have a dual diagnosis of attention-deficit disorder (ADD). In your clinical work, make sure you're aware of that possibility and of your client's need for medication when the dual diagnosis exists. Attention-deficit workaholics perform best in positions where they can initiate ideas and delegate the implementation of them to others. Instead of multitasking, they benefit from making a list of daily (or weekly) goals and sticking with one task on the list until it's completed before starting another one.

The physicians Edward Hallowell and John Ratey, authors of *Driven to Distraction*, describe what they call the high-stimulation ADD individual who abhors boredom. Similar to attention-deficit workaholics, the client with high-stim ADD seeks diversion from boredom and is unable to relax without intense stimulation. This appetite for excitement and crisis is a strategy that these clients unwittingly use to self-medicate themselves with adrenaline, which helps them focus on their work.

Hallowell and Ratey write: "It may be that the thrill of danger helps focus the individual in a way similar to that of stimulant medication, inducing changes at the neurotransmitter level. Stimulant medications, the standard for ADD, enhance the release of epinephrine (adrenaline) in the brain. High-risk behavior does the same thing. Hence such behavior may constitute a form of self-medication. In addiction, a high-risk situation may supply the extra motivation that we know can help with focusing. When one is highly motivated, once again there is a change at the neurotransmitter level that enhances focusing."[9]

Sometimes it's difficult to treat attention-deficit workaholic clients without proper medication, thereby reducing their appetite for crises and high stimulation so that therapy can have the maximum benefit. Once it's clear that medication is not necessary, you can employ other traditional therapeutic techniques to reduce stress. You can inform clients that it's acceptable to indulge themselves once in a while by setting aside a block of time to soak in a long, warm bath; relax by a fire or on a cool screened porch; or listen to soft music by candlelight.

Encourage them to block out all work-related thoughts that try to enter their mind. Teach them thought-stopping techniques to make this easier. Advise them that they may feel bored or restless the first time they try it and urge them not to become discouraged. The only way to get over adrenaline withdrawal is to go through it. When restlessness occurs, encourage clients to exercise vigorously, use deep-breathing techniques, or meditate but in any case try to keep a low-key mood at all costs until the anxiety abates (see the appendix for resources on meditation and relaxation techniques).

Those who practice savoring workaholism can benefit from widening their work lens, functioning as team members, and trusting their work group's assessment of when it's time to move on. They often find themselves becoming productive when they learn to let go, distinguish between perfectionism and high standards, and work more efficiently without getting bogged down with minutiae and losing sight of their goals.

HELPING CLIENTS WITH WORK MODERATION

You can use the form in the "Recharging Your Batteries: Computing Your Self-Care Quotient" section to help clients develop a self-care plan of abstinence, tailored to their personal needs, lifestyles, and preferences. The plan includes ways to include in their lives more social and leisure activities, hobbies, and family, as well as personal and spiritual time. A work-moderation component includes setting regular work hours devoid of binges and purges, planning ahead for deadlines, and spreading projects out over a realistic time span. Putting the plan on paper for one week helps clients see how they are spending time and which parts of their lives get overlooked. Such a plan helps them lower their perfectionistic standards and set more reachable goals, delegate, and outsource work in the office and at home.

3

When Work Addiction Hits Home

Work is the refuge of people who have nothing better to do.

—Oscar Wilde

Jena

For years I lived with loneliness, disappointments, broken promises, anger and chaos, created by my husband's addiction to work. Nobody can ever understand my pain when they see the million-dollar house I live in or my beach house, the cars, boat, clothes, travel. I have luxury that some people don't even dare to dream about, and most importantly I have my dedicated husband who works so hard for the family.

I've been living like a single mother for my three sons, watching my husband's work addiction run out of control. Hudson is competitive, seeking perfection in everything he does, killing himself working weekends until 3:00 or 4:00 in the morning, taking no lunch breaks, conducting business while wolfing down meals, even while in the bathroom. He works while driving and has had several accidents as a result. When Hudson is not working, his mind is constantly on work. On the beach in Europe, Hawaii, or Florida, he's thinking about work, oblivious to what's going on around him. We go to dinner with friends and he misses lengthy conversations that took place during the evening. He cannot relax and feels he's wasting time if he's not engaged with work.

Our life revolves around his impossible work schedule. I'm pursuing him, and he's constantly distancing himself. I enabled him without realizing it, at the time thinking I was being supportive, but then things got out of control when he couldn't draw the line.

He told me his job needed him more than I did. He ignored my birthdays and holidays because he didn't have time and we could always "have them later." Of course, "later" never came. Meanwhile, family and friends concluded that something had to be wrong with me, something he was trying to avoid, something driving him to work so much. It seemed an unlikely explanation for the behavior of a man who often worked at his computer seventy-two hours straight without food or sleep. But I accepted it and believed that there was something I needed to do differently.

After twenty-five years of marriage, it grew more difficult to hold out hope that our life would ever change, that Hudson's walls of denial would break down, that he'd ever begin any kind of recovery process. Then I began to struggle with severe bouts of depression. As I became more miserable and lonely, I sought counseling. Hudson wasn't part of our daily lives, and I became weary of filling him in on our details and schedules. Tired of being a single parent, I spent many hours drumming into him the importance of his role as husband and father. He was an outsider, a stranger to the kids and me, as if he didn't know his own family. Plus, it was hard to watch the kids deal with the fact that they couldn't change their dad, a tremendous heartbreak for them. Still, I was obsessed with trying to figure out how to get him to cut back his time at work, be part of the family.

Counseling helped me see that I had to let go of my obsession, release my focus on Hudson's workaholism. I began to look at my own behavior. It was difficult to admit that I couldn't fix my husband, more difficult to admit that much in me needed fixing. And that's what I focused on. As long as I obsessed about him, nothing was going to change. It was a frightening time because it meant letting go of all the habits and ways of dealing with what was familiar to me. It meant stepping into the unknown, but that's when I started to see genuine progress in my own recovery from workaholism.

As Hudson's work addiction progressed, my loneliness increased, not just from Hudson's absence but from the pain inflicted by a lack of understanding from friends and professionals. No more wry smiles and patronizing pats on the back for me when work addiction is mentioned. It's a devastating addiction and it hurts.

Out of the Shadows

Now that you know the signs of work addiction and how to recognize it, let's look more closely at how it affects other family members, giving them a whole set of mental health problems of their own. My research suggests that workaholism has devastating systemic effects on other family members that can be as severe as—or even more severe than—the familial effects of alcoholism.[1] But there is one major difference between the spouses and children of alcoholics and those who live with workaholics: Clinicians give the partners and children of alcoholics understanding, professional help, and referrals to self-help programs like Al-Anon. When the partners and children of workaholics complain, they get blank looks. Therapists—some of whom are workaholics themselves—often suggest that the partner simply accept and adapt to the workaholic's schedule or tell the spouse not to be a "pop psychologist."

Asked what a spouse can do to change a workaholic, one management consultant gave some less than helpful advice in a popular magazine interview: "Family members should make every effort to be exposed to the workaholic's work world. They should meet for lunch if possible. Even a small child can be taken to the office, shop or lab on a weekend. To make time together enjoyable, they must simplify household chores—pay bills and shop by phone, for example, and buy a microwave oven. Most important, they should anticipate spending a lot of time on their own. As one stockbroker told me, 'I may be a lousy father, but when Merrill Lynch needs me, I'm here.'"[2]

The message here is to center your life around the workaholic and his or her work schedule, join in the addiction whenever possible, and settle for being alone a lot. In other words, bite the bullet and enable the problem to continue. (See the discussion of practitioner denial in the section on "Tips for Clinicians" at the end of this chapter.)

Although our culture so often admires this sort of "dedication" to work, it's not surprising that wives and husbands often bring their workaholic partners into my office, insisting that the partners invest in the marriage. As you saw in Jena's case, spouses of workaholics say they feel like widowed partners and solo parents. With little support from the workplace, the mental health system, or their families, many are self-doubting and depressed.

"There are times when I feel that I would actually be relieved if my husband were dead," said Dora, married to a driven attorney. "He doesn't hit me, he doesn't drink, and he doesn't use drugs. There are a lot of things he *doesn't do*—the most important being that he doesn't do anything with me or our three kids." When Dora asked him to spend more time with the family, he called her an ingrate and said he was only working day and night for her, the kids, and their future.

Treating Workaholism as a Family Disease

In exposing work addiction's nature as a disease, I employ a family systems addictions model. The principal view from this perspective is that addictions are transmitted through the breakdown of the family system, rendering it dysfunctional. If you're a workaholic, this breakdown is shown in the behavior from your family of origin and in your intimate relationships as an adult, including those with your children. Addictive behaviors are intergenerational and are passed on to future generations through family dynamics, which often change from one generation to the next. Through the way the family operates —its rules, beliefs, and behavior patterns—addictive behaviors such as alcoholism, work addiction, and codependent relationships can become an intergenerational cycle. Work addiction is viewed as a learned addictive response to a dysfunctional family of origin. It requires a nonmedical model of treatment such as family-of-origin work and marriage and family therapy.

Work addiction is a family disease, one that affects you and other members of your family in a devastating way. Thinking of the family unit as a system can help you understand the disease concept. Suppose I wanted to know how the cardiovascular system works. I might go to a medical lab, locate a heart and the attached blood vessels, and then carefully dissect and study them. I would learn something about the basic structure of the cardiovascular system, such as that the heart has four chambers and a number of valves. But I would still not know how these chambers and valves work, because the heart would not be functioning. Only by studying the cardiovascular system while it is functioning in a living person could I see how the chambers and valves pump blood through the body. And I cannot know what happens to the heart when a person is running, for example, without seeing the cardiovascular system in relationship to the whole body system. This holistic approach teaches me that while the person is running, the muscles of the body require more oxygen than they do at rest and the heart beats faster to supply that oxygen. In other words, the total body system is affected by the running and must change to adjust to it.

The same is true of the workaholic family. It's difficult to fully understand what happens to you as a family member without understanding the interworkings of your total family system. When you look at your family as a whole, you'll see that each member is part of a functioning system, with each person interdependent on the others. As your family works together to run smoothly, change in one part of the family system results in changes in the other parts. Your family system will always try to keep itself balanced, organizing around problems and thus often causing them to continue. Your workaholic family automatically alters how it functions to accommodate the workaholic's extreme work patterns. Out-of-control working throws your whole family off kilter, causing the other members to shift the way they function in order to keep themselves in stasis and maintain a closed system.

You and your family members are negatively affected by work addiction and often develop mental health problems as a result. The workaholic's career dictates your family's rules, which get enforced despite their negative effect on the emotional well-being of individual members. There's often a tacit family contract that allows workaholics to work, while their partners align with the children against them and the workaholic forfeits a hierarchical family position in order to pursue a career.[3] To better understand the workaholic family structure, let's look at the Smith family.

Family Ties: The Smith Household

Because of failing health, Jack Smith, a forty-three-year-old workaholic, saw his physician, who said that the best antidote for Jack's addiction was taking long weekends and vacations. Jack complied with the doctor's orders, but he lugged his legal files across Europe and halfway around the world. His wife, Dorothy, said that both Jack and she knew those files would never be opened, because she would not allow it. For years she had complained to Jack's doctor about his constant working and how lonely she was on trips, visiting museums alone while Jack holed up in the hotel working. Even when they took long weekends to their Adirondack mountain retreat, Jack carried a portable phone in his fishing boat. According to Dorothy, Jack maintained direct and constant contact with the other attorneys in his law firm in New York City. A constant source of conflict in their marriage, Jack's workaholism had driven a wedge between the couple and between him and his now-grown children.

When the three children were small and came along on picnics, Dorothy carried the blanket and picnic basket while Jack carried his briefcase. Jack's preoccupation with work angered Dorothy, who felt like a single mother rearing the children on her own. And the children are angry at their father because he kept them at arm's length. Although the children have become successful adults, they admitted to Dorothy that they never believed they could do anything good enough to please their father.

Dorothy regretted that Jack was "missing in action" during most of their marriage, while she was "left holding the bag." When it came to child rearing, managing the house, or attending social gatherings, Jack would often break promises to meet her at various places. The family's tone and activities revolved around Jack's moods and whims. Family members postponed their plans, hoping by chance to be able to grab some time with Jack.

The children learned they could have these special times with their dad by photocopying legal papers for him or going to his law office on Saturdays and playing in an adjacent room while Jack worked on important cases. Even when they went fishing, the children resented their father's brownouts when his mind was back at the office. Dorothy even went to school to become a paralegal and took a job in Jack's office, working alongside her husband "just to nab some time with him." On those rare occasions when Jack tried to take an active role in his family life, he said he felt rebuffed by his wife, who felt he was intruding on her turf.

During the course of marriage therapy, the wise therapist introduced the concept of workaholism to Dorothy, which helped her see her husband in a different light: "Workaholic, huh? That sounds as if my husband's a sick man. That gives me a whole new way of looking at him—with more compassion and understanding."

Underlying Patterns of the Workaholic Family

The structural patterns of the Smith family are such that Dorothy and the children become extensions of Jack's ego, inevitably leading to family conflict.[4] Tending toward self-centeredness and self-absorption, workaholics typically need an overabundance of attention and want family members to cater to their work habits.[5] With the timing and synchronization of a Ginger Rogers–Fred Astaire dance routine, each family member gets drawn into the act by waltzing around the workaholic's schedule, moods, and actions, which determine the family's schedule, moods, and actions.

CIRCULARITY

If you're a family member of a workaholic, you may have noticed that, over the course of time, you've unwittingly developed certain habits in response to the work addiction. As workaholics work longer and harder, chances are that as a spouse, not unlike the spouses of alcoholics, you react by trying to get your workaholic to curb the compulsive behaviors and spend more time in the relationship. And chances are that your workaholic mate hears your reactions as demands, criticisms, or nagging and reacts by digging his or her heels in deeper, thus retreating further from the family. Feeling lonely, unloved, iso-lated, and emotionally and physically abandoned, you might align with others against the workaholic and retaliate with verbal resentment and emotional dis-tance. Eventually your workaholic mate is left outside your family unit because of his or her self-distancing and your retaliations and coalitions.

As a family member, it's natural for you to complain or become cynical about living with abusive work habits. A common refrain is that even when workaholics are physically present, they are emotionally unavailable and dis-connected from the family. As with Jena and Dorothy, spouses often single-handedly raise the children, complaining about having had the major portion of parenting responsibilities dumped on them. As a result of this one-sided arrangement, if you're like most workaholic spouses, you react with anger and resentment. Your workaholic partner, in turn, cites your verbal complaints to justify his or her physical and emotional aloofness. Thus, circularity often results: the workaholic claims that "I wouldn't work so much if you didn't nag all the time," whereupon the partner retorts, "I wouldn't bug you so much if you didn't work all the time."

Dorothy's presenting problem in therapy was Jack's remoteness and his exits from the relationship through work; Jack's presenting problem was Dorothy's constant criticism, and his resulting feeling that he couldn't please her. He felt that even his successful career was not enough to satisfy her. He rationalized his intentional exits from the marriage by demanding, "Why would I want to spend time with someone who's on my back about something all the time?" Dorothy had started to withdraw because she felt she was getting nothing from Jack emotionally. Jack defended himself with denial, claiming his hard work was for Dorothy and the kids, and he couldn't understand how she could criticize him on one hand and reap the benefits of his efforts on the other hand, much like Jena's husband did. As two experts observed, "for the suffering family, the final blow usually comes when the workaholic passes the blame by saying, 'I'm doing all this for you!'"[6]

POWER STRUGGLES AND ENABLING

Could your family's behavior patterns enable the very work addiction that you protest? If you're like Jena and most partners of workaholics, you might be playing the role of resentful enabler, trying to limit your partner's overwork while unwittingly supporting it. Just as many wives and husbands of alcoholics cover bounced checks or serve a hot dinner whenever the drinker returns from the bar, many partners of workaholics cover the workaholic's home chores, give alibis to children and party hosts, build family activities around the workaholic's impossible work schedule, and put dinner on the table at midnight for the umpteenth time after the workaholic promised to be home by 7:00. Barbara, the wife of the founder of Workaholics Anonymous, said, "Our lives revolve around the workaholics we married—around making excuses to friends why our spouses aren't at parties, making excuses to our children why daddy can't make birthday parties and baseball games."[7]

Partners of workaholics often plead, threaten to leave, insist on weekends together, and otherwise try to control the addictive behavior. Much as the partner of an alcoholic searches for hidden gin bottles—the way Jamey had once searched my luggage for work—these unhappy spouses live with loneliness, try to control the uncontrollable, and build up enormous amounts of resentment, experiencing the workaholic's emotional unavailability and unreliability as a personal rejection and failure.

I realize this sounds counterintuitive. But by assuming child-rearing duties, household responsibilities, and social commitments, you the family member provide the workaholic with the necessary freedom to work endlessly. Shielding workaholics from domestic worries and working alongside them, as members of the Smith family did, have the effect of enabling the compulsive working.

Even if you're a frustrated family member, demanding that your workaholic partner moderate his or her busy pursuits, you could unwittingly be enabling the work addiction. It's possible that you become just as obsessed with trying to get your workaholic to cut back on work hours as he or she is obsessed with working. The more you press her or him to take a break, a day off, or a vacation; to slow down; or come home early, the more threatened your partner feels and the more tenaciously she or he resists and retreats into work.

Typically, workaholics interpret these pressures as an effort to undermine their control. Cheryl said: "The more my husband complained about my working too much, the harder I worked." If you're a husband who dictates how his workaholic wife should set boundaries or reprimands her when she relapses, the more shamed and out of control she feels. From her point of view, the only solution is to escape further into a satisfying activity—her job—in an attempt to gain control and relief. Challenges to the compulsive working often result in defensive reactions. As you saw with Jack, he rationalized his long work hours as providing a better life and future for the family.

VILIFICATION OF FAMILY MEMBERS

If you're the family member of a workaholic, chances are that your hands are tied in many ways, giving you few options for dealing with the problem. Workaholism's looking-good camouflage, supported by our society, enables work addiction. As you saw with Jena, spouses often are branded as ingrates and blamed for wanting more despite the fact that their workaholic partners have given them abundant material comforts. With little or no support, Jena ended up in counseling for depression.

In another workaholic marriage, Madge ended up at the Duke University Medical Center to be treated for allergies, headaches, stomachaches, and other stress-related symptoms that workaholics have. The paradox was that Madge was the spouse of a workaholic: "I had to remove myself from my husband, or I was going to die. I had taken on his work addiction, and it was killing me. His multimillion-dollar business is everything to him. He's always working, always on a 'high.' People ask me why I complain. We have two beautiful kids, he has a great job, he makes lots of money, and I don't have to work. I have the dream life; why am I never smiling?"

If you're a family member, your fear of appearing unappreciative can have the effect of censoring you, preventing you from speaking out or seeking help, which further cements your family's denial. This denial can also cause you and other family members to wonder if you *are* the problem. If your friends and colleagues heap praise and financial rewards on your workaholic spouse, you might think that something is wrong with you, that you're terminally flawed or don't measure up in some way. And when you relax, you might feel unproductive and inferior.

PARENTIFICATION

When the generation lines that insulate children from the parental adult world get violated or blurred, children can become what family therapists call parentified.[8] If you were a *parentified child,* by definition you became a parent to your own parent, setting aside your own emotional needs for attention, comfort, and guidance to accommodate and care for the emotional needs and pursuits of a parent or another family member. Workaholics who were parentified as kids often pass their own parentification to their offspring, who are sometimes chosen to be emotional surrogates for the missing workaholic parent.

A typical example is the child who is elevated into an adult position within the family system to accommodate a parent's emotional need for intimacy by becoming the adult of the house during the workaholic's physical or emotional absence. Or the nonworkaholic spouse may be consumed by the single-parent role during the workaholic's absence, with the children (usually the oldest) becoming parentified—required to become overly responsible at a young age before they have reached emotional maturity themselves. They may assume household chores or caretaking responsibilities for young siblings to bring homeostasis to the family system. The void left when you have to sacrifice your childhood shows up years later as an oft-described "empty hole inside." (See chapter 5 for a further discussion of parentification.)

TRIANGULATION

Triangles across generations can occur when spouses become competitive with each other or the parental bond becomes more valued than the marital bond, as when a mother aligns with her daughter by sharing her despair over the workaholic father's emotional absence. The father is excluded, and the mother-child bond is strengthened at the expense of the marital bond.

This boundary violation can exacerbate the child's resentment of the absent workaholic father and increase tension between them. As emotions surface between father and offspring, the mother may intercede on the child's behalf, further eroding the marital and paternal bonds while solidifying the maternal bond. As alliances form, workaholics feel like bystanders in their own homes. They complain about feeling insecure and not fitting in with their families. Hudson believed that Jena and their three sons were conspiring against him. He blamed them for his unhappiness outside the office. In fact, he had helped create the barriers by extricating himself from their conversations and activities, because his mind was on work. He felt like an outsider, but he couldn't see how his own actions had contributed to the situation.

The Japanese would call Hudson a "seven-eleven husband," their term for marginal fathers who work from dawn to dusk and live on the fringes of their families: "For overworked and exhausted husbands, the home becomes just a place where familiar sleeping facilities are provided without much emotional nourishment. Such husbands tend to feel like fringe dwellers whose main responsibility is to bring money home, but not to be directly and significantly involved in family activities and raising their children. The seven-eleven husband is often so tired even on the weekends that family outings and chores around the house sometimes become additional sources of stress and fatigue. He tends to have a rather marginal family membership, and receives only limited substantive validation for his familial self from the family. When the family forms an internal alliance excluding the marginal father, he is likely to feel displaced and unwanted at home, which in turn reinforces his wish to be back in a familiar working environment."[9]

After alliances are solidified, spouses often resent having their turfs violated when workaholics try to become more actively involved in their families. Older children often rebuff the workaholic's attempts to reestablish close contact because they feel the reentry is too little, too late.

The Workaholic Family under the Microscope

My colleagues at the University of North Carolina at Charlotte and I tested anecdotal reports by conducting two empirical studies that showed family members are harmed by work addiction.

We launched the first study because we wanted to know if there was a relationship between work addiction and family-of-origin or current-family functioning.[10] After all, family systems and psychodynamic theories suggest that adult behaviors have their roots in the family of origin. A body of research had

Your Unspoken Workaholic Family Contract

Look over the section titled "Underlying Patterns of the Workaholic Family." Then ask yourself the following questions to get a picture of your family's unspoken contract with the workaholic:

1. Is CIRCULARITY present because of workaholism in your family?
2. Has anyone in your family ENABLED the workaholic?
3. Has a family member ever been VILIFIED when he or she has complained about work addiction?
4. Does PARENTIFICATION exist among children in your family?
5. Is TRIANGULATION present because of workaholism in your family?

If you answered yes to any of these questions, write a description below of the patterns you detect. Then describe what can be done to correct the patterns:

already linked a healthy family of origin to healthy functioning in adulthood, positive marital experiences, and overall family relationships.

We administered a battery of tests to 107 members of Workaholics Anonymous from Canada and five regions of the United States. Of our sample, 14 percent came from the Northeast, 24 percent from the Southeast, 4 percent from the Northwest, 39 percent from the Midwest, 18 percent from the Southwest, and 1 percent from Canada. The average age of the participants was forty-four, and 65 percent were women.

Respondents were classified into two groups on the basis of their responses to the following question: "Have you ever joined a group or talked with a professional counselor about your work habits?" Seventy people answered yes and were defined as the clinical group of workaholics; thirty-six said no and were defined as the nonclinical workaholic group.

Despite the clinical observation that workaholic adults come from dysfunctional families, we found no relationship between work addiction (based on WART scores) and family-of-origin dysfunction in the overall sample. But when the sample was divided into clinical and nonclinical groups, the findings changed. Clinical workaholics who had sought help for their condition, compared to those who had not sought help, were more likely to rate their families of origin as dysfunctional and lower in intimacy.

Our findings also positively linked work addiction to the family's current functioning, showing that workaholism wreaks havoc on the family as a whole. The more serious the work addiction, the worse the family was at communicating, solving problems, expressing feelings, valuing others' concerns, and functioning as a unit.

Using scores on the WART, we divided the sample into three groups: those at low, medium, or high risk for work addiction. The high-risk group rated their families as having greater problems in communication and in the exchange of information than the other groups did. In addition, those at high risk were more likely to rate their family members as having unclear roles and less established behavior patterns for handling family functions, compared to respondents in the low- and medium-risk groups. High-risk respondents also said their families were less likely to express feelings appropriately about various events occurring in the family. High-risk adults said their family members were less likely to be interested in and value each other's activities and concerns. And they perceived their families as unhealthy and more likely to have problems functioning in general, compared to respondents at low or medium risk.

Maintaining social and intimate relationships was also a problem for workaholics in the sample because of their work. The social relationships of men were affected to a significantly greater extent by their work than were those of women. Intimacy was a problem for the clinical workaholics, both in their families of upbringing and in the families that they established as adults. Perhaps workaholics in the clinical group, with more intimacy problems from their families of origin compared to those in the nonclinical group, had more problems with intimate relationships in adulthood, which may explain their motivation to seek help.

The second investigation conducted by my research team examined the influence of work addiction on adults who grew up in workaholic homes—the first study to be done on adult children of workaholics.[11] That study, as well as the earlier one, strongly supported clinical evidence suggesting that work addiction is associated with ineffective communication and that it contributes to brittle family relationships, marital conflict, and overall dysfunction within the family system.[12]

Tips for Clinicians

You can take a variety of clinical approaches when workaholic clients and their loved ones are entrenched in denial. You have seen that family members often are reluctant to come forward for fear of being vilified as ungrateful for the material rewards generated by the workaholic lifestyle. Typical workaholic families dance around this "elephant in the room" without acknowledging its presence, which builds tension and resentment. When you help couples identify and express their feelings about the problem, you can reduce tension and reactivity and set the stage for further work.

THE PRACTITIONER'S DENIAL

Uninformed clinicians often prescribe work as a solution to emotional problems, rather than identify it as a cause. Over the years, I've been appalled at the inability of the professional community to recognize, understand, and treat workaholics. I have been shocked and dismayed at the pervasiveness of workaholism among practitioners and their attendant denial about their own out-of-control work habits. I have also seen misdiagnosis after misdiagnosis because of this lack of awareness among clinicians.

Russell is a case in point. He had a six-week sabbatical from his job in Silicon Valley and decided to see a clinician for his workaholism. After six sessions, he stopped going because the therapist told him there was nothing wrong with him, that it was normal for people to work excessive hours in Silicon Valley. Back at work after his sabbatical, Russell said he felt lost again—he had returned to his old habits of overworking, thinking about work all the time, reaching for the next recognition like a drug addict searching for the next fix.

Dierdre also struggled with the therapeutic community's blindness about work addiction: "It's bad enough when family and friends don't get it, but it's truly horrifying when the therapist you hire doesn't get it. Nine different clinicians assured me they could help my husband and me, and each failed to notice the monster that eventually crushed our twenty-four-year marriage. The therapist even told me that words like 'addiction' were not helpful to the therapy. But as far as I'm concerned, to not name the monster is to keep it hidden and its power intact. I wish professionals had a full vocabulary and clear understanding to effectively help families struggling with this unidentified monster."

Thirty-seven-year-old Blake agreed to individual counseling for his work addiction. When Marilyn, his wife, was invited for a session, the therapist dispelled all notions of workaholism and told her to stop being "Dr. Marilyn" and stop reading "pop psychology." After only two visits, the therapist told Blake that he was not "marriage material" due to his childhood.

Emma from New Jersey called me in anguish to say that after her husband's successful recovery from alcoholism, he was doing a replay, only this time with workaholism. "It's déjà vu," Emma said. "Same story, different drug, but now it's work addiction that takes up 90 percent of his time. He eats, thinks, and breathes work. My marriage is going down the tubes again, and the therapists are saying, 'So what? He likes his job.'"

INITIAL SCREENING AND FAMILY CONTRACTS

As part of the initial screening, I recommend that you identify the structure of the workaholic family. Is there a tacit family contract, for example, that permits compulsive overworking? Are there unspoken expectations of children that place them in parentified roles that could cause long-term emotional problems? If you can bring these hidden factors into the light, you'll have more success in helping families restructure their behaviors.

Together with family members, you can diagram the structure of the family system to help clients see clearly where alliances, triangles, enabling, or exclusions exist. You will see cases where the marital bond has weakened (perhaps replaced by parent-child alliances or the elevation of children above the generational boundary into adult surrogate roles). Then you can work with couples to strengthen their relationships, consciously work at reinforcing the generational boundary, and perhaps even prevent further parentification of the children. After revealing the tacit family contract, you can assist families in rewriting a more deliberate and functional family contract that clearly defines family roles for each member and provides methods for encouraging open communication, valuing each other's concerns, and openly expressing feelings.

INTRODUCING THE CONCEPT OF WORK ADDICTION AS A FAMILY DISEASE

When you present the disease concept of work addiction to families, it usually brings them great relief and in many cases arouses compassion, as in the case of Dorothy. It can also help families reframe the problem, to go from seeing it as personal rejection to seeing it as a more complex condition that workaholics bring to the marriage. The disease concept also helps family members understand how they are affected in subtle ways that they're not aware of. With the disease concept, you can introduce a Twelve-Step approach and many of the principles of Alcoholics Anonymous and Al-Anon that have been extrapolated to work addiction (see chapter 12 for more information on the Twelve Steps). Some family members, like Jena, benefit from help in learning to detach from the addictive process and to focus on themselves and their children when offspring are involved.

As I have noted, work addiction is a "pretty addiction" that also looks good on the workaholic's offspring. It's important in your clinical work to educate yourself about the insidious damage that work addiction inflicts on workaholics' children and to tailor your approach to examine unrealistic expectations the family might have of children. Once you ascertain the family structure, you can look beneath the surface of this pretty addiction and discern potential anxiety and depression among children. Breaking the cycle of work addiction also is important. Protecting children from out-of-reach aspirations, unreasonable expectations, and parental perfectionism can prevent the development of Type A behaviors and the intergenerational transmission of work addiction.

CONFRONTING THE ENABLING

In your sessions, I suggest you raise the awareness of spouses and children about ways they are repeatedly pulled into the addictive work cycle. Then you can explain how to avoid enabling the addiction when loved ones are desperate to spend time with the workaholic family member. You can help families explore whether they have put their own lives on hold for their workaholic family member. You can help them understand that, as with any addiction, building their lives around the addict's behaviors only sets them up for further hurt and disappointment. Then help them explore ways they can include workaholics in family plans but without stopping the family's life. I discuss this issue in more detail in the section called "Recharging Your Batteries: The New Normal," in chapter 6.

TWELVE STEPS AND REFERRAL TO SUPPORT GROUPS

In conjunction with individual therapy, you can refer families to support groups composed of other people struggling with various addictive behaviors. In group therapy, members help one another see past denials and distractions that have prevented them from taking responsibility for their actions and putting balance in their lives.

Most large cities have support groups such as Workaholics Anonymous (WA) that provide literature and weekly meetings for workaholics. You can inform clients of Twelve-Step programs such as Workaholics Anonymous or Al-Anon to complement their individual therapy plans.

The Twelve Steps have worked for millions of people with a variety of addictions, including to alcohol and other drugs, food, gambling, and shopping. Continuing in the Twelve-Step tradition, Workaholics Anonymous provides a setting that is accepting, anonymous, and safe where workaholics share their strength, courage, and hope. They follow the Twelve Steps and work with other recovering workaholics and sponsors with solid records of personal growth who mentor newcomers. Under the guidance of their sponsors, members are encouraged to develop their own self-care plan of work moderation. Abstinence from compulsive working on a physical level is encouraged, as is developing a positive attitude that comes from surrender to a Higher Power.

The work plan is a guide to daily work that provides healthy limits and moves Workaholics Anonymous members toward a more balanced way of life. Chapter 12 provides more information about Workaholics Anonymous and describes how to find locations and contact members across the United States and Canada. Elizabeth described how she benefited from Workaholics Anonymous:

> Workaholics Anonymous gives me the opportunity to go and sit down with other people like me, with anonymity. I don't have to worry if I don't want the world to know about me, that what I say will go out of that room. It gives me an opportunity to share with others and to hear myself for an hour. It gives me a chance to calm down. It's very soothing to be with other people just like you who understand and know what you feel. At the same time, listening to them and what they've done to change their behavior helps you realize what you can do, because they share their experience, strength, and hope. They don't give advice.

SUPPORT FOR FAMILY MEMBERS

Family members often need help expressing their feelings of emotional abandonment, guilt, inadequacy, anger, resentment, and hurt to their overworked loved ones. Partners especially need help in developing constructive outlets for their feelings, such as keeping a journal, joining a support group, or getting individual therapy. They often benefit from understanding that they didn't cause and can't cure or control their partner's work addiction, and that their partner's problem is a cover for low self-esteem, past hurt and fears, and intimacy problems that remain unresolved.

An organization called WorkAnon was founded in suburban New York at the same time that Workaholics Anonymous started. WorkAnon serves spouses, other family members, and friends of workaholics in the same way Al-Anon serves as a family adjunct to Alcoholics Anonymous. Barbara, the founder of WorkAnon and wife of one of the WA founders, got a call one night from a distraught woman who had planned a special dinner for her twenty-fifth wedding anniversary, for which her husband never showed. The woman put his gift on the dining-room table and went to Barbara's house, and the two of them started WorkAnon. Some people come to WorkAnon with the idea that it will help them cure their spouse, relative, or friend of work addiction. But, like Al-Anon, WorkAnon is there to help nonworkaholics deal with their personal feelings about work addiction, not to cure their work-addicted partners or friends. Workaholics have to decide for themselves that they need help and take the responsibility for getting it.

Spouses and children who cannot find a WorkAnon or Workaholics Anonymous group in their area can attend Al-Anon. Although meant for families of alcoholics, Al-Anon addresses issues similar to those faced by people living with work addiction. The principles and group interaction can provide workaholics' partners with the support they need to face and deal with the work addiction.

In your work with workaholic families, consider establishing structured support groups for partners of workaholics similar to Al-Anon or WorkAnon. These special groups can help spouses cope with their own bruised self-esteem and feelings of guilt, stress, and isolation. It can be a haven for many families who feel alone and hopeless and who fear that their going public will lead to accusations and insults aimed at their lack of gratitude. Groups of this nature can provide support to help spouses feel connected to others who understand and achieve greater clarity about constructive actions they can take to change their lives.

4

Inside Your
Workaholic Mind

*Our greatest weapon against stress
is our ability to choose one thought
over another.*
　　　　　　　—William James

Kathy

When I'm honest, I realize there have been workaholic patterns in my life as long as I can remember. On the positive side, I had worked my way to a top senior management position in an international role by my mid-thirties. I was one of the few working females in a male-dominated industry. I had gotten there by sacrificing everything else. I worked Saturdays (if not Sundays, too). Although I enjoyed it, I made it a habit of only socializing with work colleagues.

I did my MBA part-time, which focused on a work project. I was fully consumed by work. I would get to the office by 7:00 a.m. and not leave before 10:00 or 11:00 p.m, for many years. I rarely dated, and if I did, it didn't last long as I was consumed by work. I was easily bored and annoyed. What few friends I had were all long distance, and I liked it that way. They didn't get in the way of work.

At one point, I prided myself on having an operation on a Friday and being back at work on Monday, despite the doctor's recommendation of two weeks' rest. I thought that was dedication. On some level, I loved it, but on another level, it was isolating and painful. Hard to admit, but I felt more comfortable talking about work than anything else. Work was my escape. But from what? I couldn't really answer that until I realized I'd gone too far.

If I could describe it, I was caught in quicksand at work, and the harder I

67

tried, the more I slipped and failed at my job. I was trapped. It took me a long time to even realize that I was failing. I was caught in a company with some significant growing pains but with my optimism, single-mindedness and work ethic, I was determined to fix it single-handedly, in spite of the odds. I was working in a foreign land with no way out physically, emotionally, or financially. I felt the daily deck stacked against me—the bullying, lying, unrealistic demands, and plans changing daily. I put my head down, digging deeper into my resolve to keep going.

For the first year, I was considered a star performer. I was the "hero," but little did I realize I was soon to be a "zero." I simply didn't see the signs (or truth be told, I did but chose to ignore them). Over many months, my role was being undermined by subtle unpleasant experiences:

Headcount and budgets were cut. When asked to deliver the same results, I complied.

My boss would set priorities, then add to them or change them, still expecting all of them to be delivered. I kicked myself but also would bend to pressure to say yes. And I said yes.

My boss demanded within one day's notice that I travel five hours to meet him. But on the flip side, he would also cancel meetings at a moment's notice —to all of which I would agree.

Executive meetings were directed to conversations from my peers that I needed to get along with my boss. As humiliating as it was, I would take feedback with a yes attitude.

Over the years, I'd built a reputation of being pragmatic and in some ways bending over backward for both my superiors and subordinates. I would make up for it by working extra effort or time. But this time it had gone too far. One too many yeses. Often I would kick myself for complying when I really meant to say no.

Having a strong sense of intuition, I had a gut feeling and put the puzzle pieces together of what was coming next. But in reality I could not process it, nor did I know what to do. With all the emotional pressures, I was miserable, exhausted, and trapped in a foreign country. One day, I was summoned to the Human Resources office and told I would be exiting. I was bitterly disappointed, having been so agreeable and worked so hard. I had never "failed." I had gone from "hero" to "zero" within twenty-four months. I was angry and mentally and physically exhausted.

The emotional roller coaster of the past two years had taken its toll. I was in pain with heartache, struggling to think clearly, complete tasks, or even get out of bed. I had lost patience with just about everyone and felt isolated. I had never tried so hard and gotten so little in return. I had taken this job in a remote foreign small town with no friends, no social life, and, for that matter, no contact with anyone outside of work. Far from family, I was out of touch. I secretly thought that being dead wouldn't be so bad. At least I could get some rest.

While it's easy to look at this particular company as an isolated case, I was in my mid-forties, thinking I had invested two painful years of my life with no benefits. I simply didn't have the wherewithal to endure that punishment again. I could've easily deflected it as a company in turbulent times and moved on. But now I had to examine the cause from my perspective and what I would do differently the next time. I happened to stumble upon an early edition of *Chained to the Desk*. As I was reading the first chapter, I began to cry. So much in the story was similar to my story and to what I was suffering.

In the past, I remember an employee telling me I was a workaholic, but I only looked at it as a good thing. I didn't see the cause or cure of it. Now I was ready to explore the cause. And I mused, "Could there be a cure?"

An Idle Mind Is the Devil's Workshop

Now that you are familiar with the signs of work addiction and the havoc it wreaks on families, let's look beneath the surface at the workaholic mind. This chapter explores in more detail the psychological workings of workaholics that are manifested in compulsive behaviors of accomplishing and achieving.

In the psychological realm, "an idle mind is the devil's workshop" is the reasoning of many workaholics like Kathy, who thinks she's nonexistent unless she's working.

When you're a workaholic, work defines your identity, gives your life meaning, and helps you gain approval and acceptance, just as Kathy described. It becomes the only way you know to prove your value and numb the hurt and pain that stem from unfulfilled needs. You believe you must earn the right to be, something that nonworkaholics believe is their birthright. Shame is often at the bottom of work addiction—a kind of self-loathing that has earned you the name of human *doer* instead of human *being*, a caricature that reflects your need to justify your existence. Chances are that, like Kathy, you believe you must overcompensate and do more than the average person to be legitimate: "For some reason I can't just be average. I have to do more or be more than the ordinary person. I've always felt that way—that I have to go over, beyond, and above what other people do. It makes me feel like I'm okay."

Even when friends and family think you're present and accounted for, in your mind you're working constantly—while driving a car, eating dinner, spending time with loved ones, and even while having sex and, sometimes, during Workaholics Anonymous meetings. You believe you can earn respect along with your place among others if you just work hard enough. The constant hurrying, the need to control, and the perfectionism mask your deep feelings of not being good enough. Work addiction has been dubbed the "addiction of choice of the unworthy."[1] Motivated by low self-worth, you define yourself by what you can accomplish. You gauge your value by what you can produce. And the more you do, the better you feel, as Dan describes: "I associate whether I have worth and value with what I achieve, and if I'm not achieving, I have no worth or value. It's like who I am depends on whether I'm able to achieve, not that I'm a good person, not that I have a lot of good qualities and characteristics. But if I achieve, I have worth and value. That's real distorted, but that's where I'm at."

Your workaholic mind feeds on tangible success, quantifying observable outcomes. Outward manifestations of your importance include how much money you make, how many sales accounts you land, how many pieces of real estate you sell, how many projects you can complete around the house, and how quickly you can get superb food on the table. Typical of most workaholics, you're a list maker, taking great delight in marking off the completion of each task.

This type of rigid thinking is typical of workaholics who hold tightly to their unrealistic expectations of themselves and others. Some experts say that the workaholic's to-do lists become a tight girdle instead of a flexible guide: "One woman allots a certain amount of time each day to spend with her children. If the children are not willing or available between three o'clock and five o'clock, they get no time with their mother. The list is a link to our stash. It tells us what we have accomplished and what is left to be done. The problem, for the work addict, is that the list is never done. There is always another list."[2]

Instead of thinking, "What can I realistically accomplish?" your workaholic mind-set says, "What would be so great an accomplishment that everyone (myself included) would see how valuable I am?"[3] The attorney tells herself that winning one more case will put her on top. The writer believes she will be revered after just one more book. The construction worker will have all the money he needs after building just one more house. When part of a compulsive pattern, all these acts convey similar messages: "Look at me: I am worthy; I have value."

Are You Leading Your Life with Confidence?

How confident are you? To find out how you stack up, take the confidence quiz on my website: www.bryanrobinsononline.com. Click on "Books" and look for *The Art of Confident Living*. Click on "How Would You Rate Your Confidence?" After you take the quiz, click on "show results," and view your confidence report card in seconds.[4]

The Impostor Syndrome

It was January, and snow covered the ground. Inside my office, Lois was having an anxiety attack because she feared she would not be able to succeed in the highly competitive real estate field in which she had worked day and night for several years. She believed it was only a matter of time before her incompetence was revealed and she would lose her job. The paradox was that she had just received an award and a bonus for being the top salesperson in her company the previous year. I was puzzled at the contradiction. I saw her as bright, friendly, and obviously capable and accomplished. She said to me: "At first I felt good about it, but that only lasted for about twenty minutes. Then I realized it was a fluke, and I'll never be able to pull it off again. I feel like I'm going down the tubes this year."

Distorted workaholic thoughts can make you feel like an impostor. You've been able to fool people that you're competent, even though you're not convinced yourself. You think if people really knew you, you'd be discovered for the fake you truly are. You're afraid of failure and success at the same time, and these fears motivate you. Your rigid beliefs about yourself tell you that you have to work even harder to keep up the charade. One financial consultant said: "I want to achieve everything there is to achieve in my profession. I am humble in the spotlight, but I am afraid of not being in the spotlight."[5]

The fear of failure drives you to produce more and more to ensure your worthiness. You take on mountains of work even when your professional and personal life is already overloaded. You set yourself up for failure because your standards are so high that no one could ever meet them. Lois described the sabotage of her workaholic mind-set: "I feel like people judge me on what I do —on what I accomplish, achieve, and on what products I produce and what effect I have on the world. And if I'm not doing the best job I know how, I feel like a failure. And because I can't possibly be doing the best job at everything, I feel like a failure most of the time. Any time I set a goal for myself that I can actually achieve, I think, 'That wasn't worth it; that was nothing.' So I create a higher goal that I can't possibly reach."

If you're a true workaholic, your thinking is rigid and distorted, much like an anorexic looking in the mirror, seeing herself as fat although she weighs just eighty pounds. You have negative feelings because your rigid beliefs tell you that you have to do more and more to be worthy. Although you exceed most people's expectations, you can't seem to meet your own because your standards (not unlike the anorexic's) are unrealistic. You're doomed to fail. On the inside you might feel like the small child who never does anything right, judging yourself harshly for the most minute flaws. When you eventually do make a mistake, you kick yourself for your shortcomings.

The organizational management expert Gayle Porter suggests that workaholics struggle with low self-esteem to such an extent that they have distorted patterns of working with others, because they focus on how interactions enhance their self-esteem, not on how they can enhance the quality of the task itself:

> The good of the organization, the department, or the work team is secondary to choosing the task or method that will protect the workaholics' self-concept and possibly highlight their efforts. . . . When choices are available, workaholics may redirect effort in a way that does not risk damage to self-esteem. The job outcome is secondary to ego protection. The most common response to any problems will be to work more hours. It would also be important that the ego be protected from any possible connection to lack of results to accompany those added hours. This requires finding a way to assign external blame when the work does not go well rather than focusing on genuine efforts of problem resolution.[6]

Tanya refused to see her own father when he showed up at the office without an appointment with her. Her employees complained that she wouldn't train them because she didn't want them to function without her: "If you're given a project to do, you automatically go under her microscope. Whatever you can do, she can do it better, and nobody gets complimented for a good job. If there's a problem, she'll find it, and if she can't find it, she'll create one to find, because she gets off on that type of superiority."

Your workaholic mind tells you that you're the only one who can solve a certain problem at work, when the truth is that the work could be delegated. The belief that only you can do it in the specific right way or at the speed necessary gives you a sense of superiority and bolsters your self-esteem. Being able to handle heavier loads more swiftly than your coworkers makes you think you measure up to the performance of others. But, of course, when you have to denigrate others to prove your own adequacy, it only calls more attention to your insecurities.

When you stay at the office past five o'clock, after everybody else goes home, you often quietly fume or smugly demand that coworkers and subordinates put in equal time. The thing people applaud you for most, your work ethic, is also the thing people close to you dislike the most. Despite your superior attitude, you're often surprised to learn from office surveys that business associates don't admire you for your abusive work habits. You're shocked to discover that you're viewed as narrow-minded, difficult to work with, and lacking in vision.

The World through Workaholic Eyes

Your workaholic beliefs keep you stuck in an addictive cycle. Most people enter situations with a mind-set that doesn't necessarily fit with the actual situation. After a three-week trip to China, I returned to my job at the university unaware of having a new mind-set. I remember walking into another faculty member's office and noticing a book on her sofa, only half of which I could see. I thought the title of the book said *Tea Ching* and thought at the time that she too had an avid interest in the Orient.

As I came further into the room and examined the entire book cover more closely, I saw that the actual title was *Teaching in the Elementary Schools*, and I chuckled to myself. My Asian frame of reference caused me to view that situation differently than I ordinarily would have. Usually, when we expect a situation to be a certain way, that's the way it will turn out, because we think and behave in ways that make our thoughts come true.[7]

The human mind works in such a way that you believe what you learn about yourself as a child. Then you collect evidence in your adult life to support this belief. Perceptual studies conducted with animals have implications for the workaholic mind. In a laboratory experiment at Cambridge University, in England, the visual field of baby kittens was restricted to horizontal lines (——) from birth. They were never exposed to vertical lines (|) while growing up. As adult cats, they could recognize horizontal lines but not vertical ones. They could jump up on horizontal table tops, but they consistently bumped into vertical table legs. Vertical lines were not part of the adult cats' perceptual reality because they had never experienced such lines as kittens. Another way of putting it is that because of their restricted past, the cats had a restricted view of the world.

As a human, the way you think about yourself was formed early in life and depends to a large degree on the cultural norms and daily experiences with which you grew up. The words you hear and the attitudes, feelings, and actions of parents and other significant adults define how you view yourself.

If you're a workaholic, chances are that you were held to high standards that you couldn't reach (see chapter 5). These repeated failures restrict your beliefs about your capabilities, so what you see as an adult is set in a certain direction, like the cats' difficulty with vertical lines. If you believe you don't measure up, you develop a mind-set that tells you you're inadequate, defective, inferior, undeserving, unworthy, and unlovable. In adulthood you're driven by the belief that you're not good enough, and you unwittingly collect evidence to fit with this belief. You're looking for the horizontal line, because that's the template that was shown to you. You devote your thoughts and actions to disproving your inadequacy and proving your worth by overcompensating, overdoing, overcaring, overachieving, and generally going overboard with work. But the consequence is the opposite—you prove to yourself that you're inadequate, because that's what you believe.

Try this exercise. Ask a friend to spend one minute looking around your office or whatever room you're in right now. Ask the friend to list mentally as many items as he or she can that are blue—perhaps the carpet, wallpaper, bindings on books on shelves, curtains, the sofa. After a minute have the person close his or her eyes and name out loud all the items he or she can remember that are yellow. Most people go blank and cannot remember any yellow items. Your friend might look at you strangely, wondering what kind of prank you're pulling, and say something like, "I didn't see any yellow, because you told me to look for blue." However, if you had instructed the friend to see yellow, he or she would have seen yellow items. Even if there were only a few of them, the friend would have blocked out everything else to focus on whatever yellow objects were in the room.

The point of this exercise is to demonstrate that the mind sees what it expects to see. Essentially, your workaholic outlook makes present experiences coincide with your mind-set. You verify your unworthiness by unconsciously proving how inadequate you are. You get a 98 on an exam and condemn yourself for not making 100. You receive a promotion, but it's still not high enough up the corporate ladder. You're named salesperson of the month but still didn't break the all-time sales record. You get the bronze medal, but you should have won the gold.

When feedback from people around you conflicts with your perception of yourself, you change it to fit with your belief system. In other words, you turn positive situations into negative ones. If you think you're inadequate (let's call that the blue), you frame each experience through that belief system and collect evidence to fit with it. Any situation that contradicts the belief that you're inadequate (call that the yellow) is ignored, discounted, or minimized or is not taken in as part of your personal experience. In these ways, you continue to look for blue, despite the fact that you're confronted with a veritable rainbow every day. Compliments sail over your head. You tell yourself that your triumphs are accidents, and your failures are proof of who you are.

You're constantly looking for the blue, and you find it because you see what you expect to see. Your rigid beliefs tell you that you must earn the right to be. And when you believe you never achieve enough (the blue), perfect is never enough. So you're usually feeling bad about yourself; striving to disprove your negative ideas about yourself; pushing yourself to try harder; working longer hours; neglecting yourself and loved ones, and going deeper into performing, achieving, being out of control, attempting to feel better, and hoping to be the best. Elaine said, "If I wasn't accepted, I had to excel, I had to keep pushing to keep working, to prove myself to somebody out there so they would recognize me and think that I had a brain and thought I had something on the ball."

Twelve Workaholic Mind Traps

You can see how easy it is to get swept away by addictive thinking patterns that distort your work pace and habits. What you say to yourself under the duress of work pops up with such lightning speed that you might not even notice. Work addiction is kept alive by the exaggerated conclusions you draw, most of which are distorted. And you continue to draw wrong conclusions because you keep falling into mind traps—rigid thought patterns that blind you to the facts. Most workaholics don't realize they're stuck in a mind trap, worsening their addiction. Once you identify the traps you keep falling into, it helps you recover from your addictive thinking. Following are twelve mind traps that feed work addiction, present in workaholics to varying degrees. Put a check mark by the mind traps that snare you when you're working.

1. *Perfectionistic thinking.* Things have to be perfect for me to be happy, and nothing I ever do is good enough.

2. *All-or-nothing thinking.* If I cannot be all things to all people, then I'm nothing. I'm either the best or the worst; there is no in-between.

3. *Telescopic thinking.* I always feel like a failure because I focus on and magnify my shortcomings and ignore my successes.

4. *Blurred-boundary thinking.* It's hard for me to know when to stop working, where to draw the line, and when to say no to others.

5. *People-pleasing thinking.* If I can get others to like me, I'll feel better about myself.

6. *Pessimistic thinking.* My life is chaotic, stressful, and out of control; I must stay alert, because if I take time to relax, I might get blindsided.

7. *Helpless thinking.* I am helpless to change my lifestyle. There is nothing I can do to change my schedule and slow down.

8. *Self-victimized thinking.* My family and employer are the reasons I work so much and am stressed and burned out. I am a victim of a demanding job, a needy family, and a society that says, "You must do it all."

9. *Resistance thinking.* Life is an uphill battle, and I must fight to force my way, resist what I don't want, and cling to keep things as they are.

10. *Wishful thinking.* I wish I could have the things I cannot have because the things I have are of no value. If only my situation would change, I could slow down and take better care of myself.

11. *Serious thinking.* Playing and having fun are a waste of time because there's too much work to be done.

12. *Externalized thinking.* If I work long and hard enough, I can find happiness and feel better about myself. It's what happens to me in the external conditions of my life that will determine my happiness.

Perfectionistic thinking tells you to bite off more than you can chew—an action that leads again to feelings of self-defeat and failure, which then leads you back to where you started: self-inadequacy. You engage in *all-or-nothing thinking*—thinking in extremes instead of seeing the shades of gray. You think you can either spend time with your family or work to support them, but not both. You think something's wrong with you if you can't give 100 percent to every area of your life, motivated by such cultural maxims as "I must be all things to all people or I'm a failure," "If you cannot do a job right, don't do it at all," or "If I can't do it all, I might as well do none of it."

Even when you succeed, your critical inner voice says you've failed. *Telescopic thinking* is when your workaholic mind acts like a telescope, blind to anything that raises your self-worth, and zooms in on and magnifies the negative. This distorted thinking pattern often starts with critical parents in childhood, as in this example from Stephanie: "I won a writing contest and sent my dad a copy of the story. He said, 'They must not have had too many entries to pick yours.' So I have this real sense of needing to prove something." Telescopic thinking is carried into adulthood where you're perceived as outstanding by others but you continue to berate yourself, overlook your accomplishments, and focus on your shortcomings.

With *blurred-boundary thinking*, you show a lack of clear boundaries. What others consider excessive, workaholics like you consider standard. It's hard for you to see that you're biting off more than you can chew, because you don't realize it. And like Kathy, you find it difficult to say no because you don't know where to draw the line. You sacrifice your own needs, giving into other people's demands as Kathy did in her job. You're so used to doing what others expect that you don't know what you really want or need. This type of thinking leads to self-neglect, putting your needs at the bottom of the list until you crumble from burnout or uncontrollable resentment.

Sometimes what others believe about you becomes more important than what you believe about yourself. You saw this with Kathy, whose *people-pleasing thinking* caused her to be indecisive and overly agreeable, using the opinions of others to gauge her actions. You figure if you can get others to approve of you, you'll feel better inside. It's impossible to please everybody, and when you try, your opinions change with the wind. You lose your self-respect and become unsure of what you believe without someone else to tell you.

When you get praised by friends or coworkers, your *pessimistic thinking* discounts the praise, and you continue to feel unworthy and unfulfilled. You unconsciously filter out the positive aspects of your life, allowing only negative aspects to enter. This bad habit of selecting the negative over the positive eventually leads you as a workaholic to believe that everything is negative. You believe you live in a world where sooner or later the worst will happen. At the core of this fear is shame. No matter how successful you are in the outer world, you attribute your success to luck or accident and believe it's only a matter of time until failure is imminent. Your fear of failure can become a self-fulfilling prophecy, driving you so hard that you unintentionally sabotage your own success. It ruins your physical and emotional health and cripples your relationships with coworkers, families, and friends.

Many workaholics feel helpless and unable to change their lives. When you engage in *helpless thinking*, you view your life as determined by high-pressured lifestyles, how much you accomplish, and how much praise you get. As a result, you externalize your responsibilities and blame other people and situations for your problems—the job, your family, or the economy.

Believing that problems and solutions are outside yourself, you engage in *self-victimized thinking*. You characterize yourself as a victim by blaming such outside forces as corporate downsizing, a relentless economy, an impossible boss, or the need to support a family. A common form of denial is the messiah myth—"Honey, I'm doing all this for you and the kids"—to which there is little a spouse can say in rebuttal. The more victimized you feel, the more your resentment builds and is expressed through bitterness and cynicism about a lifestyle in which you feel trapped.

Resistance thinking causes you to perceive life as a struggle. You structure your life by wearing too many hats and doing too many things, pushing yourself beyond human limits. Determined to do it all, you straitjacket yourself into a lifestyle that has no spontaneity or flexibility. As you forfeit relaxation and serenity, you fight harder to be more perfect, trying to cram forty-eight hours' worth of activities into twenty-four hours, to make life's schedule conform to your self-created one. You get frustrated in traffic jams or become annoyed with people who move too slowly. You get impatient in long, slow-moving lines.

You waste a lot of emotional energy getting mad at the conditions of your daily life, instead of accepting them and living your life within those limits.

Your workaholic mind-set causes *wishful thinking*—based on lack and discontent—wishing that you had more of something or someone to make you more complete. This type of thinking fans the flames of work addiction to gain more. You want what you cannot have and devalue or ignore what you already have, simply because you have it. Focusing on what's missing keeps you in a state of feeling empty and incomplete, which encourages more working to fill up the hole.

Serious thinking tells you that life is mostly struggle and grim determination, that fun and joy are taboo. This rigid belief causes you to think of life as serious business and keeps you from laughing at yourself and seeing the humorous side of things. Perhaps you didn't get to enjoy the carefree world of childhood and had to grow up as a little adult. You look on laughter and fun with contempt because they conflict with the single-minded goal of getting the job done. You consider relaxation to be wasteful and view people who fritter time away by playing and having a good time as frivolous and foolish.

Your *externalized thinking* is reflected in the need to have a concrete product to show for your efforts. Your value is attached to what you can do, not how you feel. The more you produce, the better you feel because the more worthy you are. You look outside yourself for your self-worth and put more value on what you accomplish and what people say or do in regard to your accomplishments than on your inner personal opinions and human qualities.

Thinking That Black Cloud Away

Elizabeth, once a dispirited wage earner, was able to stop blaming the workplace and accept responsibility for her job choices: "I have picked high-pressured jobs for my last three jobs. I wasn't aware of it going into them, but now I see that I am doing that. Nobody's doing that to me."

Sometimes critical messages blink in your mind like a neon sign. Perhaps you stew over mistakes, worry about things you can't control, and expect the worst in each situation. In adulthood, the childhood messages continue to remind you of who you are through mental dialogues you have with yourself. Much of what you think and do is still dictated by your refusal to let go of that inner dialogue. The critical voices of parents and other significant adults from the past continue to drive your workaholic pattern. Your addictive thoughts are so automatic that you hardly notice them unless you make an intentional effort to pay attention to them.

Jason's father used to tell him that he'd never amount to anything. That

Outwitting Your Workaholic Mind Traps

If you're a workaholic, you can outsmart your mind traps by making an intentional effort to notice them and naming the addictive thoughts that have become part of your inner dialogue. Once you've changed your perspective, you can commit to changing your work habits, instead of blaming your family, the media, society, the job, the economy, or the dog. The way to change is to change your perspective. Here's an exercise to help you identify your mind traps:

Think about what you say to yourself right before, during, and after a workday. Then answer the following questions:

1. Which of the mind traps do you fall into the most?

2. What conclusions do you draw about your work and yourself?

3. Are your conclusions accurate, compassionate, and helpful?

4. If you were on the outside looking in, how would you evaluate the conclusions you make?

5. What would you say to a loved one who thinks this way about his or her work?

critical voice, echoing in his head, reminded him that nothing he ever did was enough, driving him deeper into work addiction. Today, he knows that his father's criticisms, although directed at him, were a reflection of his dad's inner frustration, low self-worth, and deep unhappiness.

As you recognize where your critical messages come from, you can give them back to whomever they belong, instead of carrying them around. Jason was able to give his father's critical messages back to him by silently saying, "Dad, I'm letting you have your feelings back. I know you felt like you never amounted to anything. Now I know those feelings are yours, not mine."

Tips for Clinicians

Recovery from work addiction is not something clients can dash through like a commuter rushing to catch the 5:00 train. Most of us have spent a lifetime developing our work habits, and changing them requires a reversal of our mind-set. As a clinician, you can help clients get in touch with the beliefs that drive their workaholism, make appropriate changes, and begin to set realistic expectations. After you help them understand that their self-worth is not tied to what they do, they can begin to adopt an internal instead of an external focus.

WRITTEN EXERCISES AND BEHAVIORAL TECHNIQUES

A pencil-and-paper exercise may bring to the surface the catastrophic, all-or-nothing thinking that lies behind some workaholic patterns. One man said to me, "I can spend time with my family or provide for my family financially, but not both." Another client, a successful, thirty-eight-year-old heart surgeon, had not gone on a vacation in ten years because he was convinced that if he took even a week off, his multimillion-dollar business would crumble. I asked him to draw a line across a sheet of paper and write his two extreme beliefs on each end. He put "I must work nonstop to build my business" on one end and wrote "If I take a vacation, my business will crumble" on the opposite end.

This helped him externalize and dispassionately examine the unspoken assumptions that had driven his financially successful but lonely and harried life. I asked him to consider an option and write down a new phrase at the line's midpoint: "It is possible for me to take a week's vacation and for my business to continue to grow." I call this simple process "accessing the graydar," because it helps clients get in touch with their internal radar, attuning themselves to shades of gray rather than extremes.

Sometimes I teach simple behavioral techniques to stop work thoughts from elbowing their way into every waking moment. Once, for example, I taught a financial planner who worried obsessively about his job to compartmentalize his intrusive thoughts by mentally placing each one in a box, putting a lid on the box, and setting it on a storage shelf in a basement or attic. He was to take the thoughts off the shelf and out of the box only when he planned to give them his full attention. I also suggested he wear a thick rubber band around his wrist and if an intrusive work thought got loose, to snap the band and say, "Stop!" in his mind.

You would have thought that this simple rubber band was a miracle cure. He proudly wore it to each session, proclaiming the dramatic changes in his life. Combining these simple strategies with an antidepressant and basic relaxation and breathing techniques, the planner slept better, was more present with his wife and young son, and tackled work problems with greater clarity and energy.

COGNITIVE PSYCHOTHERAPIES

Cognitive psychotherapies are excellent approaches to treat work addiction, because they capitalize on the workaholic's reliance on thinking and cognition rather than on feelings and intimacy.[8] These techniques help clients get to the core of the workaholic cycle and change their incorrect beliefs about themselves. As these beliefs begin to change, the motivation to overwork subsides. By helping workaholics change their rigid belief systems, you also help them develop a more flexible, balanced perspective on themselves that automatically translates into a healthier, more balanced, and more flexible lifestyle.

In your clinical work, you can help clients make a mental shift to get them out of the workaholic cycle by following these four steps:

- ❖ *Step 1:* The first step in modifying incorrect beliefs is for clients to become more aware of them. Start helping clients identify their negative thoughts by suggesting that they pay attention to and keep track of their self-referencing, negative thoughts for a one-week period. Tell them to notice each time they have critical dialogues with themselves and write down the negative thoughts, without censorship, in a daily log.

- ❖ *Step 2:* Once the log has been generated, ask the clients to look it and star the criticisms that occur more than once. They may be surprised at how often they call themselves names such as "stupid" or "unworthy," use shame-based words such as "should" or "must," and otherwise downgrade themselves. Next, have clients write beside the thought whether or not the belief is true (these thoughts are almost always untrue). For example, are they really losers? Is it really true that no one loves them, or that everything they do is wrong?

- ❖ *Step 3:* Have them get a sheet of paper and draw two lines down the page, making three columns. In the left column have them list each negative thought. In the middle column, have them identify the mind trap in each statement, using the list in table 4.1, or explain why that addictive thought is not true.

- ❖ *Step 4:* In the right column, have clients rewrite each addictive (or exaggerated) thought by substituting a truer statement, more rational thought, or positive affirmation about themselves. For example, if they had thought, "I'm a loser," a more honest replacement might be "I'm competent and capable" or "I'm a worthy person." Positive statements usually represent a more accurate view of the workaholic and the perspectives of others. Table 4.1 presents a few examples.

The positive statements, more than the negative ones, tend to be accurate portrayals of how clients are viewed by others. The positive statements can become affirmations that clients repeat silently to themselves from week to week. The more they use these positive statements, the more they come to

TABLE 4.1

Addictive Thought	Mind Trap	Positive Statement
"I must be competent in all tasks I undertake or else I'm worthless."	All-or-nothing and perfectionism	"Achievements do not determine my worth; I'm capable and competent and can learn from my mistakes."
"I should get approval from everyone."	All-or-nothing and people-pleasing	"My worth doesn't depend on people liking me; no one gets 100% approval. Many people approve of me."
"If only things were perfect, then I could be happy."	Wishful thinking and perfectionism	"People, myself included, aren't perfect. I accept myself as I am, with my strengths and shortcomings."

believe that they are true. The use of positive affirmations, repeated silently during the day, before the morning mirror, or written in a journal, helps strengthen the nurturing voice so it can trump the self-critical voice.

Written affirmations can be put on mirrors, refrigerators, desks, or even telephone answering machines. You can suggest that clients keep a bulletin board with all the affirming letters, notes, gifts, and sayings that loved ones, friends, and business associates send them and look at them often as reminders of their inherent value.

HELPING CLIENTS CONNECT WITH THEMSELVES

Exploring and learning to validate the existential, authentic self becomes an important therapeutic task for workaholics in recovery.[9] Clinicians can confront clients with questions about how they honestly feel about themselves and their lives, what they value, what their sources of validation are, and whom and what activities they have been neglecting because of their work addiction. You may find opportunities to explore ego-threatening feelings such as loneliness, ennui, insecurity, and hopelessness.

As you help clients reframe how they think about themselves, you'll notice that their feelings and behaviors automatically start to shift. The shift starts as they redefine themselves, not by what they have or do but by who they are on the inside. This shift takes them from an external, quantifiable focus to an internal, quality-based, process-oriented focus: they become beings, not just doers. When you can help clients connect with their true selves this way, they learn flexibility and how to live in the process rather than exclusively quantifying their lives through products that they can point to with pride.

Breaking out of the self-destructive cycle of work addiction comes with time for renewal, rest, pampering, contemplation, a time where workaholics intimately connect with that deeper personal part of themselves. You can share the following tips with clients so that they can develop an internal relationship with themselves based on self-compassion instead of self-judgment:[10]

❖ *Change how you think about yourself.* Good health and self-esteem are part of a state of mind. Henry Ford once said, "If you think you can or you can't, you're right." The starting point is to realize how exaggerated, addictive thinking undermines your health and self-esteem and how an optimistic outlook can change that. See yourself honestly by recognizing your accomplishments along with your defeats, your strengths as well as your faults. The more you look for the positives, the better you will feel about yourself.

❖ *Learn to identify your feelings and to accept the fact that you're angry or frustrated.* Listen to yourself. Pay attention to your thoughts and feelings. Attune youself to your feelings and get in the habit of writing them down in a journal. Ask yourself what you're using your activities to escape from. What are you afraid of facing? What resentments or hurts are unresolved? Face your feelings and feel them completely. Ask yourself where the voice came from that tells you that nothing you do is ever good enough. Is it your voice, or is it the voice of a critical parent or another adult figure from your past? Learn to stand up to the critical voice and take charge of it, instead of letting it take charge of you.

❖ *Give yourself pep talks.* Replace the critical voice with one that nurtures and encourages you. Whether you're asking for a raise, making an important presentation, starting a new job, or struggling with parenthood, doubt and lack of confidence can flood your mind. When addictive thoughts pop up like burned toast, ask, "What would I say to my best friend or child if she thought she couldn't do something?" You wouldn't say, "Of course you can't do it. You might as well give up." Your confidence in her ability would lead you to encourage her. Value yourself enough to be your own best friend by giving yourself the same encouragement that you give to others. Pep talks bring self-reassurance and ultimate success. Tell yourself, "Yes, I can do this, and I can do it well." Use a mirror as you send yourself positive, encouraging messages. Imagine the best of outcomes, instead of the worst, before you get into a situation. Encourage yourself just as you would your best friend. Tell yourself, "You can do anything you set your mind to, and you can do it well."

❖ *Please yourself instead of pleasing others.* When you trim yourself to suit everybody else, you whittle yourself away until there's nothing left. Learn to let go of other people's opinions and form your own. Develop solid values and beliefs and stand up for them instead of being a chameleon. Keep company with people you respect who mirror your positive worth.

❖ *Learn to accept your human limitations without feeling flawed.* Learn to admit and accept your shortcomings, to value yourself in spite of them. Your ability to acknowledge and accept your limitations is strength of character, not a flaw. Treat yourself as a human being with emotional needs instead of a machine that can be driven nonstop. Make a mental shift and begin seeing your limitations as normal instead of as a drawback. Acknowledge those human limitations and value them, instead of trying to push yourself beyond them. Make it a goal to stay away from relationships that drain you, instead surrounding yourself with people who support, love, and affirm you.

❖ *Recognize that less is more.* Lower your standards, simplify your life, and be more realistic about what's possible. You can relax your standards and still do a stellar job. Instead of asking yourself what additional commitment you can make, ask yourself what obligations or chores you can eliminate. Instead of taking on more work tasks, decide which ones you can delegate, sell, or give away. Instead of juggling three or four tasks at once, choose to do only one at a time and focus on it.

❖ *Work smarter, not longer.* Make your schedule work for you, instead of working for it. Avoid overscheduling your life and leave gaps in your calendar for something spontaneous and unexpected to happen. Consider assigning errands and chores to others whenever you can, at home, work, or play. Rely on outside help to get the windows washed, the lawn mowed, the house painted, and rooms cleaned. Tell yourself you don't have to do it all. Get up earlier or go to bed later to have extra time for yourself and loved ones. Remember, it's your life. You can be in charge of it, instead of letting it be in charge of you.

5

Childhood and the Making of a Workaholic

We're so engaged in doing things to achieve purposes of outer value, but the inner value, the rapture that is associated with being alive is what it's all about.

—Joseph Campbell

Gloria and Me

The first time I spoke with Gloria Steinem, we both said, "I feel like I know you." Although our lives were very different on the outside, the way we experienced them was much the same on the inside. The following accounts of the childhoods of two self-professed workaholics, Gloria Steinem and me, illustrate the connections that can lead two adults of different genders, ethnic backgrounds, and geographic regions who have never met to say, "I feel like I know you."

I, Bryan, could have been the workaholic poster child, living in an alcoholic home where I was caretaker of a younger sister and overly responsible for the emotional tone of an out-of-control family. My upbringing led me to use housework, homework, schoolwork, and church work as groundwork to my adult work addiction.

My stomach turned as the jolt of my father's drunken outbursts hit me like a jackhammer. I quaked in my bed late at night as I heard him stagger up the porch steps and fumble around for his house keys. Lights came on all over the house, and everyone was in an uproar. I'd jump out of bed to control the scenario, closing doors, windows, and drapes so that neighbors wouldn't see and hear, hiding lamps and breakables so that the house wouldn't be destroyed, and no one would be killed or sent to the hospital. It was not a role I chose; it was one that I took by default, out of necessity and out of a will to survive. I had become the one who ran the show: the protector, the peacemaker, the referee, the judge, the general. I was nine years old.

On many nights, my father abandoned me and my little sister at the movies. And although I was learning to read and write, I still had to get us home. Underneath the big-screen excitement of James Dean and Marilyn Monroe lurked my fear and worry. Sometimes when we stood in the dark street not knowing what to do, my sister would cry, and, although I wanted to cry too, I had to make her think I was in charge of the situation. I was scared and mad because of the cold and the dark, empty streets. Sometimes the police would take us home, and other times we walked the three-mile trek in the dark, dogs barking and chasing after us.

In high school I wrote and directed the church Christmas play, single-handedly designed and built the sets, and acted the role of lead character. I didn't know it at the time, but doing everything gave me immense feeling of control and a sense of stability that served as an anchor to my rocky home life. Paradoxically, accolades from teachers, neighbors, and relatives who admired and rewarded my disguised workaholism only drove me further into misery, feelings of inadequacy, and an addiction to work that would stalk me into adulthood.

Schoolwork helped me feel good about myself, and, later, the working world gave me the same sense of what I thought was fulfillment. It provided an escape so I didn't have to deal with the many feelings I had buried since childhood. I covered my pain with a cheery smile and hard work, both of which concealed the problem, kept me disconnected from people and intimate relationships, and gave me something intimate with which I could connect safely. With the sense of total control that work gave me, I'd found my drug of choice. I transformed my long hours of college study into long hours of career building, on weeknights, weekends, and holidays.

By the time I was forty, work addiction had invaded every tissue of my body. I was hooked. I was a chain-smoking, caffeine-drinking, one-man production line. Like an alcoholic without a bottle, I felt restless and became irritable when I spent more than a few days away from my desk. Even when I lounged on a tropical beach, my thoughts centered on my next project.

I hid my work as my father had hidden his bottle. I slept off work highs in my clothes, just as my father slept off his alcoholic binges in his clothes. As an adult, I came to realize that I had cultivated the use of work to conceal emotion and my true self instead of expressing them. Believing my family's problems were unique and shameful, I strove to gain control and approval by excelling in school and the world outside my home.

Gloria

On the surface, there seemed to be no similarities between Bryan's childhood and my own. Unlike his father, mine had been a kindhearted and gentle man who took care of me more than my mother did. Because her spirit seemed to have been broken before I was born, she was often a figure lying on the couch, talking to unseen voices, and only able to make clear that she loved me and my sister. There was no violence in my house, and I grew up with the sureness that my parents were treating us as well as they treated themselves. That not only satisfied my need to feel loved and therefore lovable, but also the sense of fairness that seems innate in children.

Nevertheless, as I read Bryan's account of his feelings, I felt deep parallels. He had felt ashamed of his home and parents—and so had I. A house filled with dirty dishes, stacks of unwashed clothes, and a "crazy" mother had made me fantasize about a normal home where I could invite my friends. He had adopted cheerfulness and competence in school as a way of concealing the shame of sad feelings and "differentness"—and so had I.

I realized that Bryan had turned to the more rational and controllable world of first school and then work as a way of escaping emotions he did not want to feel—and so had I. I had even denied my need for vacations and periods of introspection, just as he had done. Though I had been lucky enough to find feminist work that was a direct way of helping myself and other women —and an indirect way of helping my mother—I had sometimes carried on these efforts at the expense of my own writing and as an anesthetic for buried childhood emotions.

Only when I, like Bryan, was forced by one too many episodes of burnout to uncover those childhood sadnesses did I begin to see work as an irreplaceable part of my life, but not the whole of my life. And only then did I begin to focus on what I was uniquely able to do instead of trying to do everything —thus beginning to be far more effective as a worker.[1]

Early Origins of Work Addiction

Now that we have explored the inner workings of the workaholic mind, we turn to the workaholic's childhood to get a better understanding of the template that shapes the distorted thinking and feelings in the family of origin.

Once grown, children who were primed for workaholism in childhood often have an emotional bond with each other that is stronger than any more obvious demographic characteristics. As was the case with Gloria and me, the early lives of many workaholics share an emotional blueprint: isolation, pain, loss, fear, and sometimes embarrassment. We are comrades of the soul bound together by common childhood wounds.

TWELVE GOING ON TWENTY

Many workaholics, I have found, grew up in homes dominated by parental alcoholism, mood disorders, or other problems that forced the children to take on adult emotional and practical responsibilities. They became grave and serious little adults and first forgot how to play when they were still young. We call this early induction into adult life *parentification*—parentified kids carry grown-up emotional burdens bigger than they are without the emotional scaffolding to bear them.

At age seven, Carol stood on a chair in the kitchen to make homemade biscuits. She ironed the family's clothes and did most of the housework. She already had learned to write money orders so that the electric bill would get paid. Both her parents were alcoholics. Nobody told her to take on the grown-up responsibilities; she did them as an intuitive way of bringing order and security to her young life. At twenty-eight, Carol is a workaholic.

Studies show that work addiction is a consequence of family dysfunction in childhood and that it contributes to continued family dysfunction in adulthood.[2] In childhood it is natural to try to make sense and order out of your world as you grow, learn, and develop. When everything around you is falling apart on a prolonged and sustained basis, your natural inclination is to stabilize your world by latching onto something predictable and consistent—an anchor to keep you afloat amid the chaos, turmoil, and instability. Out of your confusion and desperation, you begin to seek control wherever and whenever you can find it.

Work addiction develops more frequently in kids who get a roller-coaster ride through childhood than in those whose bounces and jostles are buttressed by steady parental hands. Imagine if you were propelled as a child into the adult world and expected to cope, even though you were unprepared and lacked an adult's emotional and mental resources.

Examples of family situations that can cause kids to become hooked on work are a parental separation or divorce in which children are placed in the middle of a tug of war; the death of a parent, shattering family unity and promoting the child to "the man (or woman) of the house"; devastating unemployment, creating an economic see-saw for the family; a traumatic move that uproots the child's life; parental substance abuse, throwing family roles and expectations off kilter; parental schizophrenia or other mental illness that sends the child conflicting Dr. Jekyll and Mr. Hyde messages; and emotional incest, in which one parent is physically or psychologically absent (because of workaholism, depression, or other factors) and the other parent elevates the child to replace the absent parent emotionally. Lacking the emotional equipment to meet these unrealistic expectations, you instinctively grab onto any life raft you can find to carry you through the storm. You might find security in caretaking, schoolwork, housework, homework, church work, or perfectionism.

THE BREEDING OF WORK ADDICTION

Families that breed work addiction operate in the extremes and can be placed into one of two categories: the perfect family on one end of the continuum and the chaotic, imperfect family on the other. They either have rigid rules or hardly any, boundaries that are too thick or too blurred, and lifestyles that are overorganized and perfect or disorganized and confusing. These families are often characterized by open or subtle conflict, poor communication, and lack of nurturance.

In perfect families, looking good and putting up a happy front are unwritten family rules. The message is clear: say and do the right thing, pretend everything is okay even when it isn't, don't talk about your feelings, and don't let people know what you're like on the inside. Being in control, being perfect, and doing what others want are some of the character traits reinforced in workaholic kids from these families.

In imperfect families, inconsistency and unpredictability are often at the root of childhood work addiction. The common theme is a lack of psychological insulation during your vulnerable childhood years. Although no child's life is completely carefree, children have a basic need to receive psychological protection from their caregivers, who keep them safe and separate from the adult world. When your childhood security is breached, you learn that you cannot depend on adults to protect you. You conclude that you must have absolute control over people and situations in order to survive psychologically and physically. Constant disruptions require you to take charge of a life that feels like it's crumbling under your feet.

As a workaholic child, you learn to take control of your surroundings to keep your world from coming unglued, overcompensating for the confusion. And you eventually bring these qualities to your adult job. While your carefree friends played, your childhood was marred by serious, adult problems. Your outward competencies concealed deeper problems of inadequacy and poor self-esteem. Underneath, you were an overly serious child who browbeat yourself into perfectionism, judging yourself unmercifully so you could survive the chaos. See the section titled "Portrait of a Workaholic Child."

Portrait of a Workaholic Child

If you were a workaholic child, you . . .

❖ Put more time into schoolwork than playtime

❖ Had few friends and preferred the company of adults to that of other children

❖ Showed signs of health problems related to stress, such as chronic exhaustion, headaches, or stomachaches

❖ Took on such adult responsibilities as keeping the household running smoothly, cooking, cleaning, or caring for a younger sibling

❖ Strove for perfection in most of the things you did

❖ Remained serious much of the time and carried the burden of adult worries on your shoulders

❖ Spent little time relaxing, playing, fantasizing, having fun, or enjoying childhood

❖ Had precocious leadership abilities in the classroom and on the playground

❖ Sought constant social approval from adults by striving to be a good girl or boy

❖ Demonstrated compulsive overachievement in church work, schoolwork, sports, or other extracurricular activities

❖ Got upset or impatient easily with yourself for making even the smallest mistake

❖ Showed more interest in the final result of your work than in the process

❖ Put yourelf under self-imposed pressures

❖ Frequently did two or three things at once

❖ Had trouble asking for and receiving help

Dysfunctional Childhoods and Self-Regulation

Most of the workaholics I've studied in my twenty-plus years of research had dysfunctional childhoods, characterized by *Global High Intensity Activation* (*GHIA*)—a condition in which the central nervous system is overwhelmed because of a massive shock to an individual's body and mind.[3] This massive shock can create a sense of disintegration and fragmentation that is coupled with intense emotions such as rage and terror. This was true of my own childhood in alcoholism, where the seeds of my work addiction were planted. Looking back, I realize that my writing was a way for me to regulate my feelings of anxiety in a chaotic household beyond my control. At age nine, I instinctively fled to my bedroom and wrote stories about characters I made up so I could control the outcome of their lives—a great comfort to me.

My upbringing is an example of how chronically stressful childhoods are often at the root of workaholism. Incessant working is often the limbic system's red-alert reaction (your stress response) to current work pressures, much as if you were in physical danger. Thus, constant control, while providing the workaholic limbic system with protection and safety, also keeps the *sympathetic nervous system* (your fight- or- flight response) in high arousal, trumping the *parasympathetic nervous system* (the rest- and- digest response). This is why many off-duty workaholics say that it's difficult for them to relax and do nothing. I discuss the workaholic nervous system in chapter 9.

For many workaholics, early stress is severe enough or repeated early in development before the parasympathetic nervous system (PNS) is well established, and GHIA consumes the workaholic's response even with minor triggers. Cooper, now a forty-seven-year-old workaholic, recalls his frequent futile attempts as a child to escape his parents' loud, heated yelling matches: "There was no getting away from the shrill voices and harsh tones, so I hid in my bedroom closet, curled up in a corner. The hanging clothes would muffle the yelling, and I would push my fingers into my ears as hard as I could to block out the screaming bouts and fists pounding the kitchen table on the other side of my bedroom wall. Mom would drive off in the car. And Dad would head back into the garage and tinker on a car or lawnmower. I was left physically untouched but injured by the verbal onslaught."

The existence of this GHIA pattern is supported by personality research showing that major traits of Type A people are anxiety, hostility, and anger.[4] That research also supports the evidence that children who grew up in dysfunctional or alcoholic families often find early work (schoolwork, after-school jobs, or housework) to be a stabilizing force in their lives. Gloria Steinem, who describes herself as a workaholic, has chronicled her attempts to stabilize her childhood by caring for an invalid mother who alternated between wandering the streets and sitting quietly: "I remember so well the dread of not knowing who I would find when I came home: a mother whose speech was slurred by tranquilizers, a woman wandering in the neighborhood not sure where she was, or a loving and sane woman who asked me about my school day. I, too, created a cheerful front and took refuge in constant reading and afterschool jobs—anything to divert myself (and others) from the realities of life."[5] There's an old saying among neuroscientists that "neurons that fire together, wire together." This is certainly true of workaholics.

Carried into adulthood, the stabilizing force that gave children early control in a sea of chaos becomes a compulsive stabilizer that they depend on to regulate their lives in the present. In other words, constant working reduces unpleasant feelings such as anxiety or worry. This relief acts as a reward to the nervous system, causing a dopamine release (an adrenaline high) that creates feelings of safety, enjoyment—even a worker's high—that motivates workaholics to continue overworking. Many workaholics describe the addictive feeling of this neurophysiological payoff as similar to the sensation of a drug rushing through their veins.

If you're a workaholic, chances are that GHIA has been embedded in your nervous system, and you're "stuck on high." It's as if your nervous system is a constant idling engine running inside you. This engine can be triggered into overdrive when you're deprived of constant working. The aftermath of prolonged childhood stress is a lack of safety in your own physical body. To avoid this feeling, you get stuck in future thoughts, are jittery in present situations where you must relax, and unwittingly employ constant overdoing and overworking to regulate a nervous system stuck on high.

Parentified Kids: Little Adults with Big Burdens

Chances are that if you were parentified, you became a little adult at a young age, emotionally and mentally. You might've been a child caretaker of younger siblings or of an emotionally dependent, alcoholic, or mentally and physically disabled parent. If so, your role might've required you to become overly responsible at a young age, before you were fully constructed.

It's not unusual for adult family members whose own needs were not met in childhood to turn to you, the chosen child, to satisfy those needs. You might have been made into a confidant or an emotional caretaker or required to live out a parent's dream, even if it went against your desires and best interests, examples of emotional incest.[6] In order to keep your family balanced, perhaps you established family justice by providing your parents with whatever they didn't get from their own upbringing. Or maybe you were engulfed in molding your identity to fulfill the needs of parents or other adults: "Parentified children take care of their parents in concrete, physical ways by comforting them emotionally, and also by shaping their own personalities to meet the expectations of the parents, thereby increasing the parents' self-esteem."[7]

Parentification can take two routes: you are shaped to be Mom or Dad's "Little Helper" or inducted to live out a "Parent's Dream."[8] If you were the "Little Helper," you developed a caretaking, self-defeating character style, the mode of adaption that offered the best possibility for achieving proximity to your parents.[9] If you were the parent's "Dream Child," you were more likely to forfeit your self to serve your parent, falling short of self-development, which left you with a narcissistic character style. Either path can lead to careaholism and workaholism, a sacrificing of the self in favor of another person or a task. Many parentified children become careaholic grown-ups, feeling compelled to take care of others, seeking out and finding people to help in professional or personal situations.

Are You a Parentified Careaholic?

A Methodist minister and therapist to his flock believed that every person who came into his life was sent by God. Even when he was overloaded with congregation members, hospital visits, and pastoral counseling, he had difficulty saying no because his guilt told him it was God's will that he help every person, even when his phone, mounted on the headboard of his bed, rang in the middle of the night.

At 2:00 one morning, after a full and hectic week, he got a call from one of his parishioners who had lost a family member. He told the caller he would come to the hospital immediately, rolled over for what was to be a brief second, and reawakened at 7:00 a.m. By the time he got to the hospital, the family was furious. Guilt ridden and overburdened, the pastor took ten years to recover from his feelings of failure and inadequacy.

Compulsive caregiving in adulthood is another form of work addiction veiled in noble intentions—the result of parentified attachment bonds in childhood, where children are expected prematurely to care for their parents emotionally. In such cases, children deactivate and renounce their need for comfort, protection, and reassurance from parents, because their best shot at gaining emotional attachment is giving emotional support to a needy parent: "The structure of a person's interactions with the parent is carried forward into adulthood and serves as a template for negotiating current relationships. Deference and subjugation of self to others is assured to be the price exacted by attachment. The compulsive caregiver thus develops affectional ties along old relational lines: playing the role of the caregiver is the vehicle through which relational proximity is sought and maintained."[10]

Careaholics have great difficulty in asking for and giving help to themselves. The psychologist John Bowlby explains why: "The person showing it [careaholism] may engage in many close relationships but always in the role of giving care, never that of receiving it . . . the person who develops in this way has found that the only affectional bond available is one in which he must always be the caregiver and that the only care he can ever receive is the care he gives himself."[11]

The relationship between the helper and the helped is potentially destructive when carried too far. There are many people who are more than willing to entrust their lives to another person; when they give their power to another, they keep themselves helpless. Careaholism can keep people dependent on a caretaker and unable to move forward with their own lives.

Are you a careaholic who was parentified as a child? Take the test in "Are You a Careaholic?" to find out.

If you're a careaholic, you might not sit behind a desk or in front of a computer. It's more likely that you're tending to the sick, caring for the young, advocating for the needy, or saving the souls of the lost. The helping and health professions are bulging at the seams with grown-up parentified children— workaholics who bring into the workplace their needs to caretake, fix, make peace, and carry others' burdens.

Twelve-year-old Katie became mother's Little Helper when her father died. Her mother had to take two jobs to support Katie and her younger brother, and she was gone from early morning until late at night. Katie was only twelve, yet her little brother became what she called "her baby":

I got him up every morning, made sure that he got his breakfast, had his lunch, and learned to read when he came home from the first grade every afternoon. I helped him with his *ABC*s, made the beds, and cooked meals. Mother would come in at supper time, tell me I had made a good meal, and go to her second job. My world was falling apart around me, and by grasping onto those duties, I was able to gain control over my life. I could take care of my brother, clean the house, make cakes, and do a multitude of chores that would make my world stable. And I have been doing this all my life.

The tacit family contract here was that Mom would fill the father's role as breadwinner, while Katie moved into the mother's role as partner to Mom and mother to the "baby." Katie's hectic childhood contributed to a stressful bout with work addiction and a broken marriage by the time she was fifty, at which point she was working day and night as a nurse administrator:

My husband complained about me working in the evening. So I bundled up all this work, took it home, and closed myself in my bedroom to work on it into the wee hours of morning. I'd fall asleep with work piled on top of me. My husband would come to bed and find his side covered with ledgers. Finally, he quit coming to bed and slept on the sofa.

It was two years before I realized anything was wrong. When we separated, I wondered why I was crying about the bed being empty on the other side. I'd tell myself how dumb it was because he had been on the sofa for the last year

Are You a Careaholic?

Read the following twenty-five statements and grade how much each one pertains to you, using the following scale: 1 (never true), 2 (sometimes true), 3 (often true) or 4 (always true). When you're finished, add the numbers in the blanks for your total score.

____ 1. I get overly involved by taking on other people's problems.

____ 2. I feel overly responsible when bad things happen and feel that it is my role to make them better.

____ 3. I overidentify with others by feeling their emotions as if they were my own.

____ 4. I have an ongoing urge to take care of other people.

____ 5. I neglect my own needs in favor of caring for the needs of others.

____ 6. I take life too seriously and find it hard to play and have fun.

____ 7. I have a need to solve people's problems for them.

____ 8. I have not dealt with a lot of painful feelings from my past.

____ 9. I feel unworthy of love.

____ 10. I never seem to have enough time for myself.

____ 11. I criticize myself too much.

____ 12. I am afraid of being abandoned by those I love.

____ 13. My life always seems to be in crisis.

____ 14. I don't feel good about myself if I'm not doing something for someone else.

____ 15. I don't know what to do if I'm not caring for someone.

____ 16. Whatever I do never seems to be enough.

____ 17. I have dedicated my life to helping others.

____ 18. I get high from helping people with their problems.

____ 19. I have a need to take charge of most situations.

____ 20. I spend more time caretaking than I do socializing with friends, on hobbies, or on leisure activities.

____ 21. It is hard for me to relax when I'm not caring for others.

____ 22. I experience emotional fatigue and compassion burnout.

____ 23. It is hard for me to keep emotional boundaries by saying no when someone wants to tell me about a problem.

____ 24. I have developed health or physical problems from stress, worry, or burnout.

____ 25. I seek approval and affirmation from others through people pleasing and by overcommitting myself.

SCORING: The higher your score, the more of a careaholic you are. Use the following key to interpret your score: 25–49 means you are not a careaholic; 50–69 means you are mildly careaholic; and 70–100 means you are highly careaholic, and chances are that you were parentified as a child.

anyway. I'd find myself almost falling off the bed, rolling over trying to find him there. I purposely started leaving books and stuff on his side of the bed so there would be something there for me to cuddle with.

Stolen Childhoods

As I became my sister's father, as Katie became her mother's husband and her brother's mother, and as Gloria Steinem became her mother's mother, we forfeited our childhoods in return for the adult jobs of being overresponsible and overdoing. We grew into adults who believed that we couldn't count on anyone else and that our emotional, financial, and physical survival required us to do everything ourselves. These qualities provided us and other workaholics with the psychological insulation of certainty and security that we had to manufacture early to survive childhood.

If you, too, are haunted by these workaholic traits, your refusal to ask for help or inability to delegate can put you at risk for compassion burnout. Paradoxically, the insulation from your parentification becomes your isolation. As an adult, it's difficult for you to become fully involved in an intimate relationship. You're suspicious and unforgiving of people who procrastinate or who fail to follow through on commitments. Having renounced your own early need to be cared for in order to attend to a family member, you carry the pattern forward into adulthood where you pay the price, subjugating yourself by attending to your work above all else.

Tips for Clinicians

Workaholic kids are able to detach themselves emotionally from their stressful surroundings through the escape that their achievements and accomplishments provide. Along with this self-distancing comes a greater sense of emotional insulation, independence, and a more objective understanding of what's going on around them. Their early family misfortunes, instead of destroying their intellectual and creative potential, help motivate them, and in adulthood they often become high achievers in their careers.

DON'T LET THE GAME FACE FOOL YOU

If you're like most clinicians, you might have overlooked workaholic kids because they are high functioning. Be sure to exercise caution in labeling chil-

Preventing Emotional Bankruptcy

If you're burning the candle at both ends, you could be headed for emotional bankruptcy or COMPASSION BURNOUT—the physical exhaustion and depletion of emotional energy brought on by the stress of caring for and helping others at the expense of taking care of yourself. Fortunately, self-care can recharge your batteries if you're facing burnout.

Think of yourself as a bank account. When overworking or caretaking is withdrawing more than self-care, it's time to make some deposits toward your well-being. Practice setting limits on the demands placed on you, leaving yourself elbow room to stretch and breathe, as well as time to look out the window or take a walk around the block. Set aside fifteen minutes to an hour each day to relax, exercise, play, meditate, pray, practice deep breathing, or just watch the grass grow. Eat nutritious foods instead of fast food on the run and get ample sleep. Then look inside yourself and examine your motivations for helping. Do you believe fixing others will fulfill a greater need in you than in them? Respect other people's refusal of your help. If you end up helping someone, make sure you're in the habit of showing them how to fish instead of feeding fish to them. Sometimes the best way to care for others is to care for yourself first. So before embarking on a helping campaign, help yourself in the same ways you tell others to care for themselves.

Think of these practices as building investments so that your daily deposits equal the withdrawals that work makes from your personal account. Ask yourself if you made a "to-be list" alongside of your "to-do list," what you would put on it. One item on mine is sitting outdoors listening to the sounds of nature. Jot down a few of your items and check a few off in the next twenty-four hours.

dren who appear to be high functioning, since their resilience can also be the source of deeper feelings of inadequacy and poor self-esteem. I recommend not discounting the burdens of workaholic children simply because they are functioning better than less competent children in the family. Workaholic children may, in fact, be in greater need than those who can reveal their vulnerability. The invulnerability could be a disguise for an inner misery that workaholic children feel compelled to hide. As a clinician, you can best help these over-functioning children by making sure that, while developing their talents and skills, they get a chance to add the maximum balance possible to their personal lives.

MOURNING A CHILDHOOD LOST

The workaholic's defenses are strong. The unresolved hurt and pain of a lost childhood are buried under piles of ledgers, sales reports, and computer print-outs. Here's where you can employ inner-child work and family-of-origin work. They pinpoint how and why work became a sanctuary from a dangerous world. By introducing self-nurturing techniques, you give clients tools other than overwork to soothe themselves. When this work is done in the presence of the workaholic's partner, it can give the relationship some breathing room, as the spouse sees clearly that the work compulsion has ancient roots and is not a personal rejection.

Once I uncover the childlike vulnerabilities, I teach clients ways to access their own nurturing abilities so that they can consciously protect and nourish the childlike parts that they had to disown and leave behind. Clinically, we know that psychotherapy, organized around the completion of mourning, allows clients to master the consequences of role reversal in childhood. You can assist clients in coming to terms with their childhood losses by helping them complete a delayed mourning process. Missing out on a magical and joyful childhood, one that is free of adult concerns, is good reason to grieve. As clients recognize their parents' failure to nurture and emotionally protect them and to provide a strong, wise, and loving model for them, they uncover the feelings of anger, bitterness, sadness, despair, and sorrow that they have internalized. As they respond over time to the realization that their childhoods are lost to them forever, they often travel through the predictable stages of grief and loss that parallel the loss experienced by people mourning the death of a loved one.

In a way, the period of mourning, which usually lasts from several months to several years, can be thought of as a grief process for the workaholic's lost childhood. The grief framework of the physician Elisabeth Kübler-Ross can guide your therapy with clients so that they see their progression through the stages of mourning and their emotional movement forward.[12] The grieving process can help them remove their uptight, inflexible masks and embrace the spontaneous, playful, and joyous child within—a part of themselves that they had disowned.

Inner-child work and the learning of self-parenting and nurturing skills are integral parts of the recovery process for careaholics and workaholics. Deep within each workaholic and careaholic is a wounded child whose needs were neglected. It's difficult for workaholics to access those inner feelings, and their barriers might be difficult for you to penetrate. Through the self-parenting process, clients learn to give to their inner child what they never got as children. This experience, in turn, leads them to allow others to give to them. You can encourage grief work around the loss of the safe and secure childhood, supporting clients as they work out their anger, sadness, and hurt and get in touch with their playful inner child by learning to relax, play, and have fun.

HELPING CLIENTS DEVELOP AN INTIMATE RELATIONSHIP WITH THEMSELVES

Clients may believe that self-care and attention is selfish, wasteful, and counterproductive, but the fact is that the more they take care of themselves, the more they have to give others and the more efficient they can be. Balancing the need to stay busy with a rich internal life can heal stress and burnout. You can encourage clients to get to know themselves, to be their own best friends, and to treat themselves with the same respect and kindness with which they treat others. One useful metaphor is to have clients think of themselves as a bank account, as I discussed above. They can use the time in the account or newly deposited time daily in any way they choose—to go inside and do a body scan, collect their thoughts, stay in touch with who they are, or nurture themselves.

Here are some examples of ways you can help them get in tune with themselves: have them write their feelings down in a journal; listen to soft music with their eyes closed, letting all thoughts go; reading daily devotionals; getting a facial, massage, or manicure; grooming themselves; soaking in a hot bath; going for a walk. The goal is to have them get away from their work-related thoughts or to-do lists and activate their resilient zone, where they can relax and renew themselves (I say more about the work resilient zone in chapter 11).

Clients might feel boredom, restlessness, or agitation at first. Or they might want to sleep because of tiredness, and that's okay, too. It's natural for the body and the mind to resist attention when they're not used to getting it. You can encourage clients to feel the boredom and restlessness, instead of medicating it with something to do. Have them sleep, walk, sit, or stare into space—whatever feels right. Have them recognize the symptoms and experience them, and be aware of what their thoughts, feelings, and body are saying to them. Remind them to take it gradually, one step at a time.

PARTICIPATING IN LIFE'S CELEBRATIONS

Many workaholics refuse to break for birthdays, holidays, or even funerals. This pattern has the effect of reinforcing their feelings of inadequacy: "I don't deserve to indulge myself." I suggest helping clients reestablish the rituals and celebrations in their lives that have fallen by the wayside. Without such rituals, people can feel separate, isolated, and disconnected from life. Taking time out to acknowledge rituals helps people realize the passage of time and the markers on the road of life.

A child's recital or graduation or a loved one's birthday is a marker of time that needs acknowledging. Rituals can help workaholics to appreciate the here and now—what is rather than what will be. Have clients determine the value they put on birthdays, graduations, anniversaries, reunions, and weddings in their lives. Emphasize the importance of taking time to recognize and celebrate their accomplishments and those of their loved ones and friends with vigor and enthusiasm.

FAMILY-OF-ORIGIN WORK

Family-of-origin work is essential for clients to fully understand work addiction. You can help clients identify their childhood family roles (for example, hero, mascot, lost child, or scapegoat) and see how fulfilling these roles functioned as survival behaviors in a dysfunctional family system.[13] By using a family systems approach to treatment, you can help workaholics examine more deeply the family-of-origin wounds that led them into work addiction. It's important to examine the etiology of the depression, anxiety, and anger that often drive the work addiction and then help your clients find constructive outlets for the expression of these feelings. Drawing a *genogram*—a diagram of the family tree—can help clients understand the intergenerational nature of addictions and trace the origins of their own low self-esteem, difficulty with intimacy, perfectionism, and obsessive control patterns.

6

Spouses and Partners of Workaholics

*Americans generally spend so much
time on things that are urgent that
we have none left to spend on those
that are important.*

—Henry Ward Beecher

Loretta

The simple fact is that my husband's work addiction was stronger than anything else in the family. And we're now an unkept statistic. My children and I carry the oh-so-common legacy of pain that lies in the wake of every soul-destroying obsession. For Ron a normal workday lasted eighteen hours, six days a week. Sunday was only a twelve-hour day. In the busy season, there were twenty- to twenty-four- hour days for weeks on end. Ron's need for sleep has been his lifelong enemy. It's amazing he hasn't had a heart attack yet or an accident.

My eyes were opened late one night when I was alone with the baby in our isolated farmhouse and two drunk men began pummeling on the doors, running around to each of the windows, trying to break in. When I called my husband half a mile away, he was too busy with paperwork to come home. Instead, he called the police. I spent forty terrifying minutes crouched with a knife in front of my son's bedroom door until the police came. Ron's response to my upset? "What's your problem? The doors were locked. You weren't in any danger."

I became ill when my son was one year old, but even that wasn't enough for Ron to find time to come home from his work. I locked the baby in a bedroom with me so that if I passed out, he wouldn't get hurt. I could make it into the bathroom if I crawled. It worked, but I managed to piss Ron off when there was no food prepared for him when he flew in for one of his stopovers.

During his ten-day business trips, I never knew which state or city he was in. To contact him, I'd have to call one of his business partners to find out where he was. Although we never knew when he'd be home, we were lucky to have him there for a meal once a week. Even then we were lucky if we got twenty minutes of him before the phone rang, and he never once told anyone to call back after supper. The house and yard were wired so that he could hear all three phone lines no matter where he was. A two-way radio was perched in the kitchen, volume on high, so that he would hear and contribute to conversations between all employees and his business partners. I was forbidden to lower the volume even when he wasn't in the house, and he expected me to keep up with who said what to whom and when.

At one point, I was hospitalized for three days with a serious infection. He dropped me at the emergency-room door, and I didn't see or hear from him again until the medical staff called him to come get me. Foolishly, I believed him when he said his commitment to us was the only thing keeping us from starving. And I always felt guilty putting an extra burden on him when I was sick. I watched other husbands in amazement when they'd ask their wives and children, "How are you doing?" or "What can I do to help?" Then I told myself that if I worked harder, was more patient, more supportive of him, that one day I would also enjoy a relationship like that.

I envied single mothers who shared parenting by dropping the kids off at their dad's for the odd weekend. I was the one to teach both children to ride a bike, swim, play ball, paint a room, hammer a nail. He was too busy. He never put a single present under the Christmas tree for me. But if I complained, he would chastise me for being selfish. One Christmas my nine-year-old daughter looked up at me from her pile of gifts and said, "Gosh, Mom, it would be awful to be you." She was right. It was.

Ron spent holidays with laptop, cell phone, faxes, and day trips to research more of his projects. He saw it as an opportunity for his family to prove our love for him by joining him full time in the delight of his work. In public, he would work the room, the plane, the subway, the traffic jam. In one trip to the Caribbean that we were supposed to have to ourselves, he hammered away at his laptop. He never spoke to me the entire day, leaving the computer only to go to the bathroom. He didn't need me because he had his fix.

After I began reading about work addiction, I asked him what the best thing in life was. His eyes lit up and his immediate reply was, "Doing a deal. There's nothing like it!" That's when I knew no matter how hard I tried, I couldn't compete with the rush a deal could give him. Because drugs and alcohol had always kept a stronghold on the men in my life, I had looked for a sober, drug-free man to father my children. When I met Ron, I had congratulated myself on having eliminated addiction from my life. But the insidious monster in my house had a life of its own. It grew an arm here or a leg there based on how I was situating myself in the relationship.

In the aftermath of my family's disintegration, I drove away for the last time from the community where I had spent my marriage and raised our children. I stopped and looked at the memories I was leaving behind. There was the hospital where the kids were born, the schools they attended, the swimming pool, the community center where I alone watched them play soccer. But not one building or place housed a memory I had with my now ex-husband. No restaurant or bar where we socialized, no mutual friends where we'd been entertained, no dance hall. Nothing. Ron was too busy for a social life unless it was work-related, in which case he would buy me a drink and disappear for the evening.

The night we separated, Ron carefully entered me into his address book, last name first, followed by a comma and my full first name. I watched him do it, frozen in disbelief. The main thing that stuck with me was that at least he got the spelling right.

Married to the Job

You have seen how the childhoods of workaholics predispose them to being more object-focused than people-focused. You also have seen how the workaholic mind-set is outer-directed, geared almost exclusively toward task completion, to the point where workaholics neglect the emotional needs of themselves and their loved ones. This chapter illustrates how workaholic neglect can negatively affect commited relationships with spouses and partners.

WHAT'S OUT OF WHACK?

Loretta's painful story of living with a work-addicted husband follows a pattern common among partners of workaholics, who feel alone and isolated. She may have felt alone, but she isn't alone. My colleagues and I studied a random sample of 326 women, asking them to fill out questionnaires on their husband's work habits and the state of their marriage.[1] The 22 percent who reported being in workaholic marriages also reported far more marital estrangement, emotional withdrawal, and thoughts of separation and divorce than those whose partners were not workaholics. The workaholic husbands worked an average of nine and a half more hours a week than the nonworkaholic husbands. And only 45 percent of the women married to workaholics were still married, compared to

84 percent of the women married to nonworkaholics. The spouses of workaholics also felt more helpless: they were more likely than the partners of nonworkaholics to say that external events controlled their lives.

We repeated this study with a random sample of 272 men, asking them to rate their wife's work habits and the state of their marriage.[2] We found that the more husbands perceived their wives as workaholics, the more likely they were to say the women worked longer hours and to report their marriages as having greater incidences of marital estrangement and negative feelings. Together, these two studies suggest that the strength and cohesion of a marriage is associated with the presence or absence of a spouse's workaholism.

ISOLATION AND VILIFICATION

Has your partner failed to appear at family gatherings too many times because of work? Has she promised to spend more time with you and not delivered because work comes first? Has he said, "I'll quit tomorrow," but tomorrow never comes? Or has she stood you up or kept you waiting because of work? If you answered yes to these questions, your partner may be suffering from work addiction.

Trudy complained that her workaholic husband had been away from the family for so long he'd grown a beard and mustache. When he showed up after six months, his two children didn't even know who he was. Melinda was so chained to her bank job that on school holidays she took her three children to work with her, leaving them in her car in a parking deck. She justified her actions by insisting that she had to finish a report and said that she went down to check on her kids every hour.

After Seth arrived home from a hard day's work, his wife asked where he had left their son, whom he had taken to work for the day. Searching the car, Seth freaked out, exclaiming, "Oh, my God! I forgot and left him at work!" The common theme in all these real-life examples is the workaholic's emotional and/or physical absence from intimate relationships.

If you're the mate of a workaholic, like Loretta, you probably feel alone as a partner and parent, as if you've been left with the responsibility of holding the family together. You feel unimportant and minimized, even innately defective, because you get so little attention from your workaholic partner.

You might even harbor feelings of anger, resentment, sadness, and guilt. Or you may live under a distinct set of unwritten and unspoken rules, dictated by your mate's work habits: Handle everything at home. Don't expect anything from me, because I have enough on my plate at work. Put me at the center of your life and plan the household and family and social life around my work schedule. I'm depending on you to do your best, be perfect, and not let me down.

Perhaps you describe the intimate, isolating times within the confines of your house and family as maddening. In rare cases, this isolation has led to violence, as shown in this report: "Earl D. Rhode, 28, a bright executive climbing the ladder of success, fell victim to a national aberration—workaholism. He returned to his suburban home in Washington, D.C., one evening after a long day at the office, with a briefcase bulging with work. The executive secretary of the Nixon administration's Cost of Living Council rested on the living room couch as his wife approached and then calmly put a bullet in his head. Then she killed herself. A newspaper story quoted neighbors as saying she had been complaining about her husband's seven-day workweek."[3]

Although most workaholics die from stress-induced illnesses, this rare case exemplifies the frustration many partners feel. Some, perhaps even you, say life with their mates is a nightmare, because they have little support from the mental health system, relatives outside their nuclear family, friends, and, least of all, the workplace. If you have a workaholic partner, chances are that he is extolled by friends and society as a superachiever, dedicated worker, and good provider. So what do you possibly have to complain about? You have to watch your step in how you express your concerns.

Along with the general acclaim for the workaholic and the shaming from friends and clinicians in response to any complaints, many spouses blame themselves for their gut sense that something is wrong. Karen, the wife of a New York lawyer, said: "I know how pathological it sounds, but my feelings of rage, confusion, and abandonment are such that I often wish my husband would bruise my face or break my arm. That would enable me to say to myself and everyone else, 'See, he really is hurting me. He's doing something terrible to this marriage, and it's not my fault.'"

Karen's relatives looked at her expensive townhouse and European vacations and couldn't understand what she was complaining about; she had tried couples counseling, only to be told by the therapist in the first session that she'd been reading too many pop psychology books. Without support from her family or friends, she tucked her feelings neatly away inside and tried to fix some faulty aspect of herself that she couldn't put her finger on.

Stella also said she gets vilified: "To everyone else, my husband is perfect. I feel like I'm one of his employees, even at home. He denies there's anything wrong and gets hostile if I confront him about his workaholism. Our friends always want to know why I'm always complaining. I have become the bitchy wife in the eyes of our friends, but they don't understand what it's like being alone."

'Til Death Do Us Part

My research has shown that couples in which one spouse is a workaholic are more likely to divorce than couples without a workaholic member. In addition, a survey by the American Academy of Matrimonial Lawyers cited preoccupation with work as one of the top four causes of divorce. It makes sense that workaholic families would experience problems similar to those of alcoholic families, because of the similarity between the two addictions.

The lawyers' group surveyed four hundred physicians about their observations of workaholics as marital spouses. What follows is a summary of how the physicians would have described your partner, had he or she been a workaholic patient:[4]

1. Devotes an inordinate amount of time and effort to work for the following reasons, in descending order of frequency: inferiority feelings and fear of failure, compulsive defense against strong anxiety, need for approval, fear of personal intimacy, and sexual inadequacy

2. Tends to choose spouses with more dissimilar than similar personalities

3. Has higher than normal expectations for marital satisfaction

4. Is much more demanding of achievement in the children

5. Fills leisure time with work activities

6. Avoids confrontation and marital fights with passive-aggressive maneuvers such as silence and sulking

7. Engages in extramarital affairs more than his partner

8. Engages in marital sexual relations less frequently than other couples

9. Is more prone to alcohol abuse than nonworkaholic peers

10. Frequently has the following sexual problems, in descending order of frequency: emotional detachment, lack of sexual desire, routine and unvarying practices, inhibition of arousal, and inhibition of orgasm

An Office Affair

Sometimes partners feel jealous, even suspicious that their workaholic mate is having an affair because of the long and late hours he or she spends away from home. *Exec* magazine surveyed the work habits of three thousand men, one-third of whom said they'd been accused of having an affair due to their long hours on the job.[5] The survey also found that spending excessive time at the office can wreak havoc on family life. Eighty-six percent of the men surveyed said their personal relationships were marred by work-related stress. Similar findings were reported in a survey by *McCall's* magazine, in which 80 percent of the readers said their husbands worked too much.[6] The phrase "wedded to work" illustrates this condition, and it knows no gender boundaries. Spouses of workaholics are not always wives. When women are addicted to work, men become the suffering partners, as Elizabeth confessed: "I remember my ex-husband saying to me, 'I feel so lonely. You're here in this house and I feel so lonely.' At the same time he was saying that, I felt lonely, too. And we couldn't come together. Work was what was filling us up. He wanted me to fill him up, and I couldn't."

Profile of Partners and Spouses of Workaholics

If you're a spouse or partner of a workaholic, chances are you . . .

❖ Feel ignored, neglected, shut out, unloved, and unappreciated because of your spouse's physical and emotional remoteness

❖ Believe you're carrying the emotional burden of the marriage and parenting, which makes you feel lonely and alone in your relationship

❖ Think of yourself as second to work, because family time is a low priority, dictated by work schedules and demands

❖ Perceive yourself as an extension of your workaholic mate, whose addiction demands to be center stage

❖ View yourself as controlled, manipulated, and sometimes rushed by your partner, who calls the shots

❖ Use attention-seeking measures to get your partner to see you or agree to conversations and activities related to work in order to connect with the workaholic

❖ View your relationship as serious and intense, with a minimum of carefree time or fun

❖ Harbor guilt for wanting more out of the relationship, while your partner is applauded by colleagues and society for accomplishments

❖ Have low self-esteem and feel defective, in some way unable to measure up to your spouse, who is often put on a pedestal

❖ Question your own gratitude and perspective when faced with the accolades bestowed on your workaholic partner

Another feeling frequently expressed by partners of workaholics is reflected in Eric's comment: "I feel like one of her employees, that the only way to be close to her is to join her in her work." And that is exactly what many do. Tears in her eyes, Valerie expressed her struggle with intimacy and work addiction:

> People think that the workaholic doesn't love them, and that's absolutely not true. It hurts me more than anything that my friends and family would think they're not important to me. Work addiction is like alcoholism, and workaholics have unfulfilled needs that they're trying to fill. It's sometimes uncontrollable. It just takes me over and carries me away. So family and friends need to be patient and need to educate themselves. That will help them understand the person they're with and care about. Work addiction is self-destructive, but it's also destructive to the people around you, if you're not careful.

Intimacy Problems: Romancing the Grindstone

There is a common misperception that workaholics must enjoy their jobs to be addicted to work because they spend so much time with their nose to the grindstone. In fact, workaholics work for the sake of working. Regardless of work conditions or salary scales, they are willing to do whatever it takes and go the extra mile to get the job done, even when the company doesn't reciprocate with material rewards.

The reason they are accused of "romancing the grindstone" is not necessarily that they love their work. What they love is the escape from intimacy that the work gives them, and its accompanying boosts of self-esteem. Immersion in work feels safe and secure for workaholics, whether or not the work itself is satisfying.

THE GREAT ESCAPE

Workaholics tend to be what family therapists call minimizers in their couple relationships.[7] Minimizers withhold and minimize their feelings and are emotionally detached and withdrawn. In a marital argument minimizers are tight-lipped, cold, uncommunicative, and unfeeling. Intimate feelings are difficult for them because their emotions are frozen. Constant work keeps workaholics numb, with their feelings buried in the deep freeze, and emotionally disconnected from loved ones.

Workaholics handle intimacy issues by wishing them away, putting them off, or ignoring them altogether. They preserve their own space by keeping their thoughts and feelings to themselves, making it difficult for their partners to know what they think or feel.[8] When workaholics share anything with their partners, it's more often about their work or logical and rational thoughts rather than feelings. A request for closeness feels like a demand to a workaholic, a distraction from his or her goal-directed job. Workaholics often feel hounded by well-meaning loved ones who say, "Why don't you just cut back?" and who don't understand that cutting back isn't as easy as it sounds.

MARS AND VENUS

If your partner is a workaholic, chances are that the two of you are coming from totally different emotional worlds, caught in the pursuer-distancer interaction style—a dynamic in which the workaholic wants distance and you want closeness. So you pursue your workaholic mate for emotional closeness and affection, while he or she retreats, feeling threatened by this desire for closeness, and throws himself into his job or makes herself emotionally unavailable through preoccupation with work. The more you pursue, the more your workaholic partner flees. This interaction, which becomes circular, was shown in the Smith family by the stereotypical—but true—nature of Dorothy's nagging and Jack's withdrawing (see chapter 3).

As the mate of a workaholic, you more than anyone else feel the shield that your loved one uses as protection from closeness and intimacy. The barriers are hard to penetrate, and workaholics have few or no friends. Their tools of trade are their best friends, because they don't have to worry about disappointing their computer screen, falling short of their iPad's standards, or hurting the feelings of their day-at-a-glance planner. They immerse themselves in their jobs, which are structured, predictable, and controllable—a process that is safer for them than immersing themselves in slippery intimate relationships. Workaholics who excel at work but not at home are more likely to engage in areas where they feel most competent. In the past, these behaviors were encouraged and supported by our culture, which idealizes the remote, controlled, rapid-fire-paced image of men.

Perhaps your workaholic treats your relationship like he treats his job, because that's what he's best at doing. He uses the same control and hard-driving perfection to relate to you and other family members that he uses with coworkers. Dictating and organizing, workaholics run their households like a work camp. Like Loretta, you might feel treated like an employee on work detail. Your teenage son's ballgame with his father must be scheduled, and you might be expected to share intimacy on command.

Your workaholic probably forgets, ignores, or minimizes important family rituals and celebrations, such as birthdays, anniversaries, or children's recitals. He might be unable to stop work long enough to participate fully, because such events represent a distraction from his commitment to work—even in emergencies, as a terrified Loretta found. Accomplished in his field, the workaholic might still have few social skills and few interests outside work, often remaining disengaged in social conversations that don't pertain to his work interests.

WET FALLEN LEAVES

Japanese wives use the derogatory term *nure-ochiba* (a wet fallen leaf) to refer to retired workaholic husbands who don't know what to do with themselves when they're not working and who hang around the house expecting their wives to plan their spare time: "They follow their wives around, like unwanted, wet fallen leaves which are stuck to the bottom of one's shoes. Thus, competencies developed at work are not necessarily transferable to a post-retirement lifestyle. The wife has lived all these years without her work-immersed husband's support, and has achieved emotional independence and ego-identity. She possesses appropriate skills for social survival and networking. On the other hand, the husband may lack such skills. He is like a fish out of water, becomes dependent upon his wife, while the latter feels annoyed with him who constantly disrupts her routine and demands her attention."[9]

Many Americans report that their workaholic partners experience a sense of lostness or helplessness that is especially noticeable during down times like vacations, holidays, and retirement. On their trip across Europe, Wendy handled all the details of the plans, keeping Tim's wallet and passport and arranging their daily trips to museums, tours, and sightseeing. Tim dutifully followed her lead from Scandinavia to the Mediterranean, almost as if they had an unspoken bargain: "I'll traipse all over the world with you and indulge your every whim, but I expect you to let me work without interruptions or complaints." In this way a tacit contract gets played out in ways that couples don't usually realize. Some workaholics bargain to win release from family obligations by telling a spouse, "I'll go with you to the wedding next weekend if you'll keep the kids out of my hair today and tomorrow so that I can finish the sales report." Promises to cut down on work or spend more time with family are more often broken than kept. As the weekend approaches, there's more work to be done, accompanied by an apologetic refrain: "Sorry, honey. Looks like you and the kids will have to go without me."

Work Infidelity

You might've noticed that your workaholic doesn't tolerate obstacles to working. If someone stands in her way, she takes either an aggressive approach of blowing up or a passive-aggressive approach of sneaking to her stash. This concealment and deceit is known as *work infidelity*.

Work goes everywhere the workaholic goes, regardless of what family or friends say: in briefcases or luggage, under car seats, in glove compartments, in car trunks, beneath spare tires, in dirty laundry bags, stuffed inside pants or a skirt, and, in at least one case, hidden in a secret compartment of another person's suitcase, unbeknown to that person. Once workaholics start bootlegging their work compulsions, you might as well admit it: they're desperate; they must get their fix at all costs, even if it means being deceitful and dishonest, even if it hurts the ones they love the most.

If your partner is like most workaholics, she caves in to your demands by concealing work in an effort to please you and avoid criticisms, much like an alcoholic who hides beer bottles.[10] Your workaholic might hide memos or files in a suitcase, pretend to rest while you're off at the grocery store, or feign going to the gym and working out at the end of the day in order to sneak in an extra hour or two of work.

Mildred committed work infidelity to deal with the stress and anxiety caused by her husband's expectation that she be home with him by 5:00 p.m. She told him she'd enrolled in an aerobics class after work. Her husband was thrilled that she was finally taking an interest in activities outside work. But the truth was that Mildred was working two hours overtime, changing in her office from business outfit to aerobic garb, tousling her hair, and dampening her tights with water—all to convince her husband that she was coming around.

In his book *Working*, Studs Terkel describes how the broadcast executive Ward Quaal concealed his working from his family:

> I get home around six-thirty, seven at night. After dinner with the family, I spend a minimum of two and a half hours each night going over the mail and dictating. I should have a secretary at home just to handle the mail that comes there. I'm not talking about bills and personal notes; I'm talking about business mail only. Although I don't go to the office on Saturday or Sunday, I do have mail brought out to my home for the weekend. I dictate on Saturday and Sunday. When I do this on holidays, like Christmas, New Year's, and Thanksgiving, I have to sneak a little bit, so the family doesn't know what I'm doing.[11]

Kate's work obsession became like a weekend lover. She lied to her family so she could rendezvous with work at the office: "I'd tell my family I was going shopping on a Saturday and I'd end up in my office working. Or I'd tell them I was going to my girlfriend's house. After calling my girlfriend's and not finding me, they'd call the office and say, 'I thought you were going to Dottie's.' I felt like I'd been caught with my hand in the cookie jar."

The New Normal

Have you put your life on hold because of a workaholic mate? If so, you could be enabling the very addiction you wish to erase from your life. Many partners and spouses build their lives around the workaholic because they want to feel connected and supportive. That's natural, right?

But as with any addiction, molding your life around a workaholic spouse only leads to disappointment and enabling. The key to avoid enabling, when you're desperate to spend time with your workaholic partner, is to stop postponing your life. For example, if you plan a trip to the zoo with the kids and the workaholic cancels (for the umpteenth time) because of last-minute demands at the office, go without her. When your workaholic promises to be home in time for dinner and never shows, consider eating on time without him and, instead of putting dinner on the table at midnight, let him fix his own meal.

You can refrain from such activities as bringing your loved one work when he goes to bed sick, making alibis for her absenteeism or lateness at social functions or family gatherings, and leaving the responsibility for explaining with the workaholic. You can also stop assuming your workaholic's household duties, returning phone calls for him, or covering for her by lying to business associates on the telephone—all because the workaholic is too busy working.

Although it's important for you to include your workaholic in your plans and let him know he was missed and how disappointed you were by his absence, you don't have to continue putting your family's lives on hold. Here's a real-life example: "My husband used to be late for everything—parties, dinners, movies—because he always worked overtime. Then one night, our friends came to pick us up, and as usual, he wasn't home yet. So I left without him, but I wrote him a note that read, 'You're always late, and it's embarrassing. We're at the restaurant. I hope you get home in time to join us.' He's been much more considerate ever since. He even gets home early enough on Fridays to take me to the movies!"[12]

Your workaholic might comply with pressures to curb work by the "white-knuckling approach"—going through the motions of being at a cocktail party or on a Caribbean vacation, attending a child's ballgame or recital. Although present in body, in her head she's back at the office working. Cynthia described her husband's inability to let go and be present: "It's really difficult to pull him away from any of his work activities. He gets really anxious when he's not working, and then I feel guilty if I try to get him to do something with me other than work. I wind up feeling as if I have deprived him of something."

Concealment serves the purpose of lowering tensions in the couple relationship. Once the truth is revealed, though, partners often feel betrayed and mistrustful, and relationships suffer severe, sometimes irreparable, damage because of the deceit. Once workaholics have entered the lying and concealment stage, it indicates their desperation and inability to say no. Professional help is often required at this juncture for workaholics and their partners.

Tips for Clinicians

If you're a clinician, you can provide counseling for couples whose marriages have been damaged by work addiction. Change, however, doesn't come easy or fast for workaholic couples, and change is necessary for all family members if the damage is to be repaired.

ADDRESSING THE CHICKEN-EGG CYCLE

When family members expect workaholics to change, they also must examine the reaction patterns they've built in response to the workaholism and be prepared to change as well. They may have gotten into the habit of complaining or being cynical about the compulsive working, and workaholics may have withdrawn into "vital exhaustion"—total shutdown and detachment from the relationship.

If you work with couples to restructure the family system, be prepared for resistance on both sides. The parent who has single-handedly raised the kids, for example, may become resentful when suddenly the work-addicted partner decides to take a more active role in parenting. Reversing these types of patterns can evoke anger and hurtful feelings, leading to turf battles and questions like "Where were you ten years ago?" Family members may be sending the workaholic mixed signals by complaining about his or her absence and then, as the workaholic begins to move back into the family system, complaining about his or her attempts at reintegration.

You can also make family members aware of the double bind they create by complaining about the work addict's overworking in one breath and making unreasonable financial demands in the next. In some cases, they must be willing and prepared to sacrifice financial advantages in return for the workaholic's increased presence and participation in the family and less time spent working.

You can take several clinical approaches to help workaholics and their loved ones—who, not unlike alcoholic families, are entrenched in denial. Outwardly, workaholic families appear immune to the effects of the hard-driving, compulsive behaviors of the addict. Workaholics in particular mask their anxiety,

depression, or fear of not being in control by demonstrating resiliency, perfectionism, overresponsibility, or self-reliance to the point of having difficulty
asking for help. Family members often are reluctant to come forward for fear
of being branded ungrateful for the material rewards generated by the workaholic lifestyle. Typical workaholic families avoid acknowledging this issue, leading to tension and resentment. By helping couples identify and express their
feelings about the problem, you can reduce their tension and prepare them for
further work.

IDENTIFYING THE PURSUER-DISTANCER DYNAMIC

During the therapeutic process, try to be aware of the troublesome pursuer-
distancer dynamic and take steps to help couples identify and correct it.
When you name the pursuer-distancer interactional style in therapy sessions,
you help couples recognize it and give them something concrete to work on
in their daily interactions. You can help couples understand the transmission
of their respective roles from their families of origin, which can foster their
taking responsibility as a couple for their relationship, instead of blaming
each other.[13]

Workaholics often "check out" during therapy sessions, and when they do
you can gently prompt them to invest more of themselves to effect change. The
family therapist Stephen Betchen cautions you, the clinician, to not enlist or
enable pursuers to play cotherapist, which often unconsciously happens. If you
align with a pursuer, the workaholic spouse will feel ganged up on and withdraw even more. Because pursuers often take responsibility for their part in
the relationship plus that of their spouse, Betchen recommends the following
approach: "Clearly, the pursuer is the overfunctioning, overresponsible spouse,
and I often tell her that she overworks her relationship. I let the underrespon-
sible distancer know that when he abdicates responsibility in his relationship,
he is more likely to be controlled by his spouse—something I know he is
deeply concerned about."[14]

When working with couples affected by work addiction, I have observed
that the more one spouse pursues, the more the other retreats. I often use this
analogy with clients: "When it's hailing [the pursuer], the turtle pulls its head
in its shell [the distancer]. And as long as it's hailing, the turtle is not going to
stick its neck out." To break this cycle, I suggest that pursuing spouses consciously and deliberately pull back or take a vacation from working the relationship. This strategy gives workaholics the space to take more responsibility
for their part by becoming the pursuer. Each party must embrace part of the
role of the other. You can recommend that pursuers change by ceasing to offer
unsolicited advice, no longer expecting distancers to join them at social events,

no longer pushing for physical contact, or ceasing to constantly ask distancers if they love them. You can encourage distancers to express their intimate feelings, create romantic dinners with candlelight and flowers, invite the pursuer to special social events, and initiate conversations by asking their partners about their day.

The effect of having pursuers withdraw is that it gives distancers the psychological space they need to take more initiative in the relationship. As distancers increase their interest in and attention to the relationship, pursuers ultimately get the closeness they have been seeking, and the couple is able to meet at an emotional halfway point. Other clinical evidence documents that distancers move closer to their partners when pursuers reduce their pursuing.[15]

NOURISHING THE OVERWORKED RELATIONSHIP

Typical twenty-first-century couples overwork their relationships. After spending all day at the office, couples spend evenings cooking meals, attending to children, and, in some cases, preparing work for the next day. Busyness and doing infiltrate the relationship to the point that intimate relationships are replaced with business relationships: discussing financial concerns, hassles at work, headaches with the kids, problems with day care or school; juggling family schedules and children's activities; and preparing meals for the next day. Eventually, couples in these overworked relationships start to show the same signs of stress and fragility as the individual workaholic: irritability, tension, and exhaustion. In problematic relationships, couples may have shut down completely and not talk at all, in which case television or late-night work often becomes a replacement for companionship.

Relationships need attention to stay vital. You can assist workaholic families in negotiating boundaries around the amount of time they spend working together, talking about work, or discussing family business or scheduling issues. These boundaries can be tailored to the unique schedules and lifestyles of each couple. One possibility is to eliminate work after a set evening hour and to carve out a set time every evening (without the Internet or television) for intimate conversations about matters not related to work. Mealtime is a great time to put these boundaries in place; another possibility is to set aside the time immediately after the partners have both arrived home.

Couples can learn to not let work dominate their conversations, but still discuss work frustrations and successes as all healthy couples and families do. They can set boundaries, making weekend working the exception rather than the rule and barring work from vacations. Establishing appropriate boundaries around work is essential in today's intrusive wireless world to protect fragile relationship intimacy.

You can guide couples through a couple-care plan to achieve balance in their relationship by using the procedures for the self-care plan outlined in chapter 2. Using the categories of (1) couple relationship, (2) family, (3) play, and (4) work, couples can separately and together compute their scores for each area and then name three or four activities or goals for each area to bring healthier boundaries and greater balance into their relationship. The content of the couple-care plan can make for lively discussions and invigorate an otherwise neglected or overworked relationship.

HELPING PARTNERS COMMUNICATE

As the family unit shifts its dynamics, you can tackle additional goals such as effective problem solving, better communication, more clearly established family roles, greater affective responses, more affective involvement, and higher family functioning in general—all of which are frequently cited problem areas within the workaholic family system.[16]

Tension builds in families whose members have refused to acknowledge and discuss their problems. Angry outbursts occur over trivial events that have little to do with the real problem. Here's another area where you can help families talk about their problems and feelings. You can provide a communication structure such as active listening or the couple's dialogue, the framework used in Imago Relationship Therapy to ensure that listening, understanding, and empathy are reciprocal.[17] Imago Relationship Therapy is an excellent approach not only to building communication among couples but also to helping them understand how their family-of-origin experiences get recast in unconscious ways, causing problems in their current relationship (see the appendix for more information on Imago Therapy).

By facing these problems and getting their feelings out in the open, families can reduce tension and address the real source of conflict. Treatment issues address intimacy problems as they're manifested in the present family and social functioning of the workaholic. The most common clinical observation is that workaholics hide behind a psychological shield to avoid closeness with their families. You can help workaholics identify when and why they dissociate and to learn to stay in the present and communicate with loved ones. In addition, you can facilitate the process for partners of workaholics, helping them express to the workaholic their feelings of isolation, abandonment, anger, resentment, guilt, hurt, and sadness. This allows partners to share their hopes and dreams for, as well as disappointments with, the relationship. They can share their fears of drifting apart, how it feels to be kept waiting or stood up, or what it's like living with a stranger who escapes into work. With the right help, partners of workaholics can develop compassion for the difficulty their companions have in controlling work compulsions without making themselves doormats to the abusive work habits. Bibliotherapy resources for family members are often helpful in this regard (see the appendix).

INTERVENTIONS

You can assist family members with interventions when work addiction becomes life threatening. Forgetfulness, chronic fatigue, grouchiness, mood swings, and physical ailments related to stress all indicate that the body is burning out. Families can lovingly share their concerns about their workaholic's health and encourage him or her to consult a physician. They can ask the addicted family member to go with them for counseling and, if the addict refuses, get help for themselves through a support group or continued individual therapy.

In severe health cases, a family intervention might be appropriate. Family interventions with workaholics are similar to those used with alcoholics. The workaholic is lovingly confronted by family, friends, and significant colleagues (for example, employers, supervisors, or employees) under the supervision of an experienced family therapist. Each person tells the workaholic how it feels to watch him or her deteriorate and explain what the intervener plans to do about the relationship (threats are never used) unless the workaholic gets help with the problem.

7

Children of Workaholics

My child arrived just the other day,
came into the world in the usual
way, but there were planes to catch
and bills to pay; he learned to walk
while I was away.
                              —Harry Chapin

Charles

My father had two loves: work and bourbon. He also, of course, loved his two children but we learned at an early age that being close to our father required entering his world of ambitious interests and endless cycles of working, drinking, sleeping. Our house ran on our father's energy. When the phone rang, as it frequently did just as we sat down to an already delayed, late-evening family dinner, it was usually a graduate student or colleague calling for my father. "Oh, damn!" he'd say, jumping to his feet, racing from the dining room into his study. Sometimes I'd groan as he made his quick exit, but usually my mother, brother, and I would just sit in silence, staring and continuing to eat until he returned with the latest tale of upheaval in the department or of the almost nervous breakdown his advisee was having over an oral comprehensive exam.

My father's life seemed exciting, passionate, and important. By comparison, everyone else's life seemed less so. Childhood pleasures like the state fair, shooting basketballs through hoops, picnics, going fishing or to the pool, learning to ride a bike without training wheels, or carving the Halloween pumpkin were all scheduled around Dad's work and often were simply endured by him in a state of irritation or, worse, exhaustion after long hours "at the office." It was clear from the start that family life and "traditional" family activities came second and were actually rather trivial compared to the adult world of work, politics, ambition, collegiality. Even vacations to the beach involved taking along favored graduate students. If students couldn't come with us, my father would make contacts with colleagues and former students in a nearby town, asking them to come visit. Over shrimp and beers, they'd give him the latest scope on the local school system or reminisce with him about his early years as a bachelor high- school chemistry teacher in this same nearby beach town.

My father's (and thus also my mother's) friends were his students and for- mer students. I realize now that his mentoring of these young, admiring pro- fessionals occupied his time and energy and left me, his older child, competing with handsome, bright male graduate students for his love and attention.

When he brought home his favorite students or colleagues to drink and "talk shop" late into the evening, he was at his best: happy, lively, and eloquent. As a small boy on these nights of discussion and drinking, I would run ram- bunctiously in and out of the living room where he was holding forth. In child- ish ways, I'd compete for his audience's attention or actually for his attention by asking questions, making noises, or hiding and jumping out from behind the sofa to scare everyone. Usually Dad would just give me a hug and then firmly direct me out of the room to find Mom (who was sequestered in her bedroom) so that she could give me a bath and put me to bed, usually well past the des- ignated hour. These were the fun nights in the house filled with my father's business company, their laughter, their serious and meaningful conversation. I remember nights like these throughout my entire childhood and adolescence.

As I grew older, I learned to sit quietly and listen, watching Dad as he related to his students and colleagues. If I was quiet and didn't interrupt I could stay in the same room with him, and this was very important to me since it was often the only contact I would have with him for days at a time, except when he would sleepily drive me to school (almost late) the following mornings.

As I grew still older, I learned to enter into these conversations about phi- losophy, politics, child development, educational curriculum, John Dewey, Martin Buber, and other topics of interest to my dad, and thus topics I too attempted to read about and understand. I did my ninth-grade English project on existentialism. I learned to make strong percolated coffee and serve it to him in his study when he would write until two, three, or four in the morning. My bedroom was next door to his study. I loved to try to stay awake reading as late into the night as his light was still on. And I'd get out of bed, go to his study door, and see him sitting, focused intensely, at his desk wearing his black horn-rimmed glasses. It seemed as if I was constantly interrupting him and distracting him from something very important.

My father was always "at work," at the office, hovering over his desk at home, or entertaining his students and "talking shop." When I was very little, I'd beg him to play with me in the evenings when he would come home from his office without his students. "Daddy's tired," he'd say, as he slumped in a chair. I'd grab his arm and pull him to get up to play cowboys with me, which at times he would agree to do, grudgingly. Then in a less than enthusiastic tone, he would respond to my piercing war cries with a distracted "bang, bang." Even then I remember feeling mad at him for being so tired and uninterested in my child-hood fantasies and dramas.

I was always the little warrior in our family. I raged and cried at canceled camping trips, at my father's out-of-town consulting jobs, which took him away for days, and at his sleeping till noon on the weekends when I wanted him up to be with me.

At a very young age I followed him to his university office on Saturdays and Sunday afternoons to play alone in the science lab with the hamsters and gaze at anatomy books while he labored in a nearby office. It was lonely, but it was a way to be near him, so I always behaved and was trusted fully to take care of myself and not interrupt him too often. When he'd take a coffee break, we'd walk to the soda shop across the street. I'd get a vanilla ice cream cone and, on our way back to the office, I would ask him to "Watch!" as I balanced myself walking along the ivy-covered stone wall beside the sidewalk. I was happiest when I was with my dad, even if it meant learning the importance and priority of his work over my childish whims and wishes.

When I cried and yelled at him for "always working," my little brother just sucked his fingers and watched quietly. Mom was depressed and often in her bedroom or even hospitalized for extended periods with what later was diag-nosed as manic depression. Manic depression, I now think, was an appropriate illness to have in my family. If she was to have a mental illness, manic depres-sion certainly complemented her husband's waxing and waning energies. Dad's work cycles of all-night writing binges, teaching, and long hours with students at home or at the office were always followed by periods of intense exhaustion when he would sleep for long periods or sluggishly mope around the house, relax with his bourbon, and sleep more.

Dad had his first heart attack at forty-two. In my fifteen-year-old eyes he seemed so old, even fragile. His doctors told him to quit smoking his four packs per day, stop drinking caffeine, and stop eating the New York strip steaks he loved to cook and serve generously to his protégés during those late-night sessions after bourbon rendered them ravenous at ten o'clock, when they'd gone without dinner. His doctors also told him to exercise more, work less, reduce stress, and consume no more than two alcoholic beverages daily. In other words, at forty-two my father was told to change just about every aspect of his life that had been so much the source of his greatest success and plea-sure: hard working, hard drinking, smoking, and late-night talking and din-ing. Although then, in my usual fashion, I was so angry at him and his failed attempts to reform himself, I realize now how very sad it was to watch his feeble efforts to smoke less, drink less, and be with his students less.

In the year before he died, I remember he would sometimes spend an entire weekend in bed or in a recliner reading a novel. In my early twenties, when I would return to my parents' home for visits, the students didn't come to the house as much, and I didn't hear anymore about his dreams of starting experimental schools or becoming president of a university. He was at home more, less busy, quieter, sadder. I didn't realize then what was happening. I thought he was just getting older—after all, he was almost fifty. He died at fifty-one of a coronary after a full day at the office. My grandmother, his mother, said my father would have wanted it that way—to have worked fully every day of his life until he died. I was twenty-four when he died. I'm now forty-two, and fifty-one doesn't seem all that old.

Sometimes I go to professional baseball games and watch the fathers with their sons and daughters. The kids are so excited, and the fathers buy them things, hold them on their laps, and talk to them about the game, pointing, whispering in little ears, and the kids jump up, arms waving, with loud joyous cheers. I don't really like ballgames now; they're boring, no fun, and a waste of time. But when I was a child, I wanted so much for my father to take me to ballgames like other dads. But he was either too busy or too uninterested in sports and the heroes like Mickey Mantle and Roger Maris whom I, as an eight-year-old, adored. Who knows? Maybe if he had taken me to some of those games before the age when my stodgy boredom set in, I would know how to enjoy baseball now.

When I watch those children with their dads at ballgames, I get a glimpse of what it means to have lost the moments childhood offers us all, however so briefly, to know pure excitement over something simple and playful. My father worked through most of my childhood. And he hasn't been around for any of my adulthood.

Carrying the Legacy of the Best-Dressed Addiction

In 1983 Janet Woititz wrote a small book that became a best-seller, called *Adult Children of Alcoholics*. The book sold millions of copies and started a movement among legions of adults who had been damaged growing up in alcoholic homes. During the 1980s a lot of research on adult children of alcoholics was published, showing this population to be at risk for a variety of problems.[1] Parental alcoholism was linked to low self-esteem in children and, in adults, to a higher external locus of control (which means they believe that they are controlled by external circumstances instead of by their own internal fortitude), depression, and anxiety. Adult children of alcoholics came to realize that they carried an insidious legacy that affected their current mental health, their intimate relationships, and, in some cases, their careers. The Woititz book, credited with starting the recovery movement of the late 1980s and early 1990s, opened the floodgates for other popular books on codependency, dysfunctional families, and the inner child.

This chapter is about a parallel problem with workaholism and how it damages children—the addiction that looks so good on parents, it's also pretty on their children. Despite the abundance of studies on children of alcoholics, the research on children of workaholics is sparse. Clinical reports suggest that, while attempting to medicate emotional pain by overworking, workaholics suffer some of the same symptoms as alcoholics.[2] My early clinical observations suggested that children in workaholic families were subjected to subtle yet harmful influences, yielding coping problems similar to those of children of alcoholics.[3]

Children of Workaholics under the Microscope

Still, near the turn of the twenty-first century, not one scientific study had been conducted on children of workaholics. This sad state of affairs prompted my university research team to launch the first study on children of workaholics to use the same methods that scientists had employed to study children of alcoholics. We gave a battery of tests to 211 young adults (their average age was twenty-four).[4] Using the WART, we asked them to rate their fathers on workaholic tendencies. On the basis of the ratings, fathers were categorized as either workaholics or nonworkaholics. We also asked the young adults to rate themselves on depression, anxiety, and locus of control. Adult children of workaholic fathers had statistically higher levels of depression and anxiety and believed events outside themselves controlled their lives, compared to adults from homes where fathers carried an average workload.

Our findings showed that children with workaholic fathers carry their psychological scars well into adulthood, as Charles did. These scars manifest themselves as an outer-directed reliance on others for decision making and a lack of inner confidence that is associated with greater anxiety and depression than in the population at large. These results match similar studies on adult children of alcoholics, compared to adult children of nonalcoholics.[5] Two studies replicated our findings with two different populations. One, conducted at the California Graduate Institute, surveyed a sample of 107 working nurses.[6] The other, conducted at the University of South Australia, tested 125 first-year university students.[7] Both studies found that children of workaholics, compared to children of nonworkaholics, had significantly higher depression and anxiety levels and more incidences of obsessive-compulsive tendencies, rated their families as more dysfunctional, and were at higher risk for workaholism themselves.

In another study, my colleagues and I wanted to see if there was a difference in psychological adjustment between children of workaholics and children of alcoholics. So we tested 207 young adults (average age twenty-five). Those who reported growing up with a workaholic parent had higher depression levels (as measured by the Beck Depression Inventory) and higher rates of parentification (as measured by the Jurkovic Parentification Questionnaire) than a control group of adult children from alcoholic homes. And children of workaholics reported that their parents worked significantly more hours than did parents of children of alcoholics.[8]

Picture-Perfect Childhoods? Really?

These statistics match the stories I've received from readers far and wide—people who describe patterns of failed marriages and anxiety and depression with no obvious causes, yet who seemingly came from picture-perfect childhoods. If your father drank too much, you could point to the bottle; if your mother was strung out on pills, the drugs might explain her unusual mood swings. But if you grow up in a workaholic home, there's no tangible cause for your feelings of confusion, guilt, and inadequacy. Besides, the American work ethic prevents us from faulting a parent for hard work and from viewing workaholism as a bad thing. So if you're the offspring of a workaholic, you examine your supposedly picture-perfect life and conclude that "something must be wrong with me." After all, workaholic parents are usually highly successful and responsible and may even hold leadership positions in the community. Their overachieving is sanctioned by society, the community, and, often, the church.

So you silently reprimand yourself for complaining when your workaholic parent is an upstanding contributor to society. When you acknowledge the problem, it can bring up feelings of guilt and disloyalty. After all, your family is perfect, which makes you the unappreciative bad guy. This scenario is why workaholism is called the respectable addiction, and why I say it's the best-dressed of all the addictions.[9]

Dana told how she carried the legacy of the pretty addiction into her own adulthood:

My dad was such a workaholic he got his thank-you notes out the day after Christmas. He does it right and holds those same standards for everybody. If he could do it, then everybody else ought to be able to do it and should do it. Wasting time was not allowed in my family, and both of my parents were always busy and doing. And there was no obvious dysfunction to point to as a reason for my discontent, emptiness, and frustration. My parents were avid churchgoers, civic leaders, a good family who worked hard to send us to summer camp. They wanted to be Ozzie and Harriet, and they tried real hard to be. They were so perfect that the logical conclusion was that there must be something wrong with me for wanting to have intimate, feeling conversations and relationships and for feeling like I wasn't loved or accepted. If I had children, the biggest thing I would hope to do would be to promote an atmosphere of intimacy, of being the kind of mother who would want to hear how your day went and to talk more about how I felt and how my children felt.

When Relationships Feel Like a Death Sentence

If you're the grown-up child of a workaholic, you're likely to either shun intimacy altogether or become enmeshed to the point of reinventing yourself to accommodate to your partner. On the inside you feel trapped in a lifelong legacy of personal emptiness, disappointment, and depression, much of which materializes in your adulthood. You might have a pattern of getting involved in long-term relationships with people whom you're constantly trying to please, who are emotionally distant, and whom you're always disappointing. In other words, you become intimately involved with someone who reminds you of your workaholic parent.

Helen is example of the many adults I have seen in my practice who suffer from having grown up in a workaholic household. Her first marriage ended on a bright sunny day during a vacation in Yosemite National Park. Relishing the sunshine on her face, the smell of the clean fresh air, and the breathtaking natural beauty, she turned to share the experience with her husband—who was on his cell phone with someone in Argentina and who grunted and kicked the dirt. He'd just lost a huge business deal. The loneliness Helen felt in this marriage paralleled the loneliness she had felt with her father, a physician who was physically and emotionally absent during her early years.

Now, as she and her second husband sat before me, their marriage was on the rocks, partly for the same reasons. Huge tears ran down her cheeks faster than she could dab them away. Her guilty conscience said that she should stay in the marriage and make it work (even though she didn't want to) and sacrifice her needs. Another part of her was desperately trying to figure out who she was. After all, she'd spent both marriages pleasing her husbands. From the age of five, she'd been taught that performing, being perfect, and accommodating the needs of others was her life's work. Never mind what she wanted, needed, or felt. Play the role, produce, achieve. Both husbands had been emotionally vacant, and she felt disconnected and emotionally sterile living with them. The distance felt familiar to her because it echoed the painful loneliness she had felt growing up with her workaholic father.

This scene is repeated over and over in therapists' offices around the country. There is no label for it. But millions of adult children of workaholics are confused and in pain and don't understand why. In some cases, they're unaware that their parents were workaholics or that parental work addiction insinuated itself into their lives at an early age, let alone that it continues to play a role in their adult mental health. They are fumbling badly in relationships and are self-critical, anxious, depressed, and willing to accommodate whomever they are with at the moment. Most of what we know about children of workaholics is based on case studies, clinical observations, and a handful of scientific studies. Although embryonic, this information is insightful.

Profile of Adult Children of Workaholics

If you're an adult child of a workaholic, you might fit the profile of this group:

- ❖ Outwardly focused conformists
- ❖ Self-critical
- ❖ Self-disparaging people who feel unworthy and incompetent for not being able to meet others' expectations
- ❖ Prone to depression
- ❖ Approval seekers striving to make up for self-inadequacy
- ❖ Performance-driven perfectionists who judge themselves by their accomplishments, rather than by their inherent worth
- ❖ Overly serious people who have difficulty having fun
- ❖ Prone to feelings of disloyalty and guilt for acknowledging a problem in their picture-perfect family, which, on the surface, has provided them with everything
- ❖ Angry and resentful
- ❖ Prone to generalized and performance anxiety
- ❖ Unsuccessful in adult intimate relationships
- ❖ Chameleons with an undeveloped sense of self

The section "Profile of Adult Children of Workaholics" is painted from this small body of literature. Does any of it ring true for you?

"Daddy Gone": Growing Up with a Workaholic Parent

Case studies indicate that workaholics are physically and psychologically unavailable to their kids, that they generally don't take an active role in their children's development, and that their offspring become resentful of their emotional absence.[10] According to one management consultant, "it is easier for him [the workaholic] to be a mentor than a parent, because there is more distance. I have heard workaholics talk in glowing terms about students and subordinates and yet never speak with such delight about their own offspring."[11]

In interviews, adult children of workaholics have revealed that they had four major concerns regarding their parents' work addiction.[12] *Preoccupation* was the most significant concern. The second was *haste*, because their parents were always rushing around. The third was *irritability*: the parents were so deeply involved in their work that it made them cross and cranky. The fourth concern was that children felt that their work-addicted parents took work too seriously, lacked humor, and showed *depression* about work. All four signs were present in the case of Charles.

Desperate for love and attention, Charles pulled every antic his child's mind could dream up to get his father to notice and spend time with him. Such futile quests, that made him a lonely and angry child and an empty adult, are a common refrain among children of workaholics. Tom said: "The second words I learned to say were, 'Daddy gone.' That indicates to me that I was missing my dad at a very young age, and it shocks me that I am doing the same thing to my kids."

Children like Charles, hungry for attention from their psychologically absent parents, complain about their parents' mental absenteeism. But their natural way of handling the disappointment is to defer their emotional needs by joining in the workaholic pattern to get their parents' approval. If this were you, you'd work alongside your workaholic parent or accompany him or her to the workplace in hopes of stealing a few moments of attention, the way some children of alcoholics let themselves be propped up on the counter at the corner bar in order to have time with Daddy.

At thirty-five, Nell smuggled memos and contracts into her dying father's hospital room. "It was the only way I could be with him," she said, fighting back tears. "The only time he'd pay attention to me was around the subject of his work." Desperate to connect with the unavailable workaholic parent, children unwittingly enable the working parent by helping him or her. Nell's father died working, a pen in his hand. Now she lives with the guilt of hastening his death.

A Deck Stacked against You

When workaholics do actively parent, it's often to make sure their children are living up to their perfectionist standards. Workaholic parents push achievement and accomplishment over unconditional acceptance of their offspring. Their love and approval are unwittingly doled out on the condition that a standard is reached—one that, from the child's perspective, is often unattainable.

At the age of forty-three, Pat remembered how difficult it was living up to her workaholic mother's expectations: "In some ways growing up with a smart, hard-working mother was hard. I've never felt like I could measure up to her success in either of the domains of running a family or having a career. And while I have never competed directly with her, I know that working extra, extra hard and being successful is the only real way to feel good about my efforts. I worked hard but never felt like I'm successful because I could've done more."

Chances are that if you were the child of a workaholic, you felt loved only if you did well. Because of a perpetual fear of failure, you might have had performance anxiety about challenges at school, in work, and even in relationships. Perfectionism is your lifelong and haunting companion. Being good and doing well become the standards to which you conform.

Marsha's workaholic mother ran the household according to the motto "Your best is always better yet." The mother believed that no matter how hard you work, you could work harder, earn more, do better. Marsha shudders at the memory of traveling home after her high- school graduation—not just because there'd been a late spring snow and it was cold outside, but also because of her mother's chilly attitude toward her. Despite the fact that Marsha had been honored for having the second-highest grade-point average among two thousand students, her mother had been distant and unenthusiastic all day long. As tires crushed the ice on the road beneath them, Marsha's mother broke the ice inside the car. "Why couldn't you have been number one?" she demanded.

Something Must Be Wrong with Me

The message you take away from a workaholic parent is, "I can't measure up" or "I need to be someone other than who I really am." With parental expectations out of your reach, you internalize failure as your own inadequacy. The anecdotal literature suggests that like many children of workaholics you're apt to carry the same best-dressed legacy of your workaholic parent: you become other-directed and approval seeking, trying to meet adult expectations. Or you go in the opposite direction: you see measuring up as a hopeless task, give up trying, and act out your frustrations, anger, and hostility. You might become an underachiever or behavior problem at school, where you displace your anger and aggression.

Scientific studies support many of the clinical observations: families where parents have high achievement expectations or evaluate a child's performance on the basis of others' performance promote the development in children of such Type A behaviors as competitiveness, aggression, and hostility, as well as decreased self-esteem and perceived control.[13] In addition, an unsupportive family climate and a lack of positive familial affiliation are linked with children's anger and hostility.[14]

Four hundred physicians, polled on their views of workaholics, supported the clinical reports. Asked if workaholics are more or less demanding of achievement in their children, 88 percent of the physicians responded "more demanding." The study concluded that because workaholics regard their spouses and children as extensions of their egos, family conflict is inevitable. As children of workaholics learn that parental love is contingent on their perfect performance, they react with resentment and become hostile and rebellious.[15]

They learn to measure their worth by what they do rather than by who they are. When they ultimately do fail, they internalize the experience as a lowering of self-worth. They feel incompetent, as if nothing they do is good enough. They often feel inherently defective for being unable to meet parental expectations, and they feel like failures even when they succeed.

Dana describes how she was caught in this no-win cycle:

There was little open conflict in my family. Everybody was always trying to do everything right—anticipating anything that could create trouble before it happened. We operated from the avoidance of conflict. My dad didn't get angry; he got cold and sarcastic. I learned early that the wrongdoing around my house meant freeze time, an awful, tangible chill! I'd rather have been beaten. It was worse than a slap across the face. I always feared that if I didn't meet my parents' expectations, they would withhold their love and abandon me emotionally. That had a big effect on my self-esteem. The way to have self-esteem was to be good, to be right, to do well, to be perfect. I never felt a sense that my parents were people to talk to or to turn to when I was in trouble. I didn't feel loved and accepted, even though I know my parents were well-intentioned. They were always the last people on earth I wanted to know my business, because there was no history of that kind of intimacy. There was a focus on the belief that "you are what you do."

The Making of a Chameleon

When Dana was a child, her dad gave her a dollar every time she read Dale Carnegie's *How to Win Friends and Influence People*, a book that she internalized:

> It emphasizes the people-pleasing stuff—tuning in to others and making them feel important. Underneath all that manipulation is the need to control how others feel about me. That's how I can feel okay about myself. As an adult, I still struggle with whether it's okay for me to be different from others. It's been okay for other people to be different from me, but the issue of my being different from them is based on a security within myself that I'm okay even if others don't like me. Being accepted and understood has been one of my own coping devices, being a good girl, a good daughter, doing all the things you're supposed to do. I often laid myself open too much and too soon and ended up hurt and resentful in my adult relationships with a lot of self-doubt about not being smart enough on how to discriminate who to trust and how much.

If you're a child of a workaholic, you might have learned to conform and become an approval seeker, searching for the acceptance you never had. Chances are that you learned early in childhood that doing "right"—which often means doing what others want—is more important than being who you really are. You learned to mold your attitudes, emotions, and behaviors around the wishes of others, usually the dominant workaholic parent.

Whose Drum Do You Dance To?

What about you? Have you disowned your true self and tried to measure up outwardly, becoming whomever and whatever it took to get the approval you craved? If you're like many children of workaholics, somewhere along the way, you lost touch with who you are on the inside, becoming a chameleon yet viewed as accomplished and held in high regard. You developed an outward focus (or an external locus of control), an undeveloped sense of self, and a lack of differentiation. Simply put, this means you became other-centered and perceive yourself as being "at effect" instead of "at cause" in your own life. People who have an external locus of control tend to be more pessimistic and to respond more negatively in general to the vicissitudes of life. As a result, they are at risk of being victimized by life rather than empowered by it, and of having codependent relationships as adults.[16]

Case studies of adult children of workaholics confirm that, in order to gain

Making Amends

There's almost always unfinished business between workaholic parents and their children, whether kids are twelve or twenty. As a parent, you might not have the luxury of quitting your job to mend damaged relationships. Nor do you need to. But if you're a workaholic, part of your Twelve-Step recovery is to repair tense and broken relationships. Step 8 says: "We made a list of all persons we had harmed and became willing to make amends to them all." And Step 9 says: "We made direct amends to such people wherever possible, except when to do so would injure them or others."

Sound advice comes from an interview with Bill Smith, who suggests that workaholics use the tools of their trades as a way to revive closeness: "Write a love note to your son or daughter or wife telling them how much they mean to you. Pull out your DayTimer and make appointments to meet with your children one by one. No one on their deathbed wishes they'd spent less time with their family."[17]

Think of special activities you can initiate with your children, such as long walks and heart-to-heart talks. Take an active interest in their lives by listening to what they have to say, finding out what they've been up to, and paying attention to how you interact with them. Everybody has bad days, but try to avoid coming home in foul moods or unloading your anger on family members. Focus on the positive things your children do instead of harping on the negative.

Save newspaper reading or work until young children are asleep. Consider carving out quality time with youngsters, perhaps helping them with homework, playing games, scheduling weekday or weekend family outings, or conducting family projects. Preparing meals together and having pleasant mealtime conversations (with the television and all other electronic devices turned off) is another way to restore family rituals and celebrations that have disappeared. Practicing daily rituals is the glue that holds your family together. This glue is neutralized when workaholics forgo the bedrock ritual of nightly dinners. Family members become virtual strangers, losing track of who's doing what and how each one is feeling about his or her life. Research backs the idea that rituals keep loved ones stabilized and help them fare better amid the chaotic juggling of each day's diverse activities. So make it a point to celebrate birthdays, holidays, and anniversaries.

If you're like many adult children of workaholics, no matter how hard your parent tries to mend past mistakes, you feel that the divide is too great, that your workaholic parent's overtures are too little, too late. If that's the case, consider discussing your natural resentment with a trusted counselor to see if it's possible for you to work toward reconciliation with your workaholic parent.

parental attention, the children learned to gauge their emotions and behaviors according to the expectations of their high-achieving parents, as George described:

> Everything I did as a kid was based on accomplishment and goals. I tried hard and got awards for everything: outstanding academic scholarship, top awards in band and choir, captain of the football team. But the one award I never won was my dad's love and attention. He was always working. Oh, yeah, he would come to my games and criticize what I did wrong. He *always* looked for a better way to do things. His way was the right way. What about all those things I did right? "I'm proud of you" would've been nice. I just wanted him to play catch with me or hit me on the head with a pillow and say, "How ya doing?" To this day it's hard for me to sit in a room without having a project or a product. I guess something in me is still trying to grab my dad's attention.

You must be perfect to receive love, so you try to please, even if it means being someone you're not. And you often don't think for yourself or venture outside a safe comfort zone for fear of ridicule. In attempting to please, you gauge your emotions and actions by those of your workaholic parent. In short, you learn to dance to the beat of your workaholic parent's drum instead of your own.

Tips for Clinicians

As a clinician, you will be called on to work with children of workaholics who have a variety of needs. There's almost always unfinished business in family relationships on the part of parents, their children, or both. You might work indirectly with children through their workaholic parents—children struggling to alter their lives to accommodate their families. Or you might work directly with young children or, retrospectively, with adult children of workaholics.

REPAIRING WORKAHOLICS' RELATIONSHIPS WITH CHILDREN

Workaholics' self-care plans usually address how they can put more thought, care, and time into their often-neglected relationships with their children. This is an important area for you to explore with workaholic clients. Understanding the nature of the parent-child relationship and setting goals to repair damaged relationships are essential parts of the workaholic's individual psychotherapy.

Your workaholic clients will benefit from knowing that investing in relationships is a good use of their time. After assessing their view of relationships, you can help them set aside time to rebuild damaged relationships and make time for the people they're with at the moment.

Explore the importance of family time with workaholics. Research shows that families are not as close when they eat on the run or in shifts as when they sit down together for a meal. Households where holidays are observed and birthdays and anniversaries recognized and celebrated have stronger relationship bonds than homes where life's markers are ignored. Rituals such as a family dinnertime provide an anchor when loved ones are caught in the whirlwind of today's fast-paced society. Together time heals tensions and teaches kids the importance both of togetherness and of having plans and seeing them through. Rituals provide stability and dependability and make family members feel they have something to count on. When families value and practice rituals, they generally have less anxiety and fewer signs of stress related to burnout. You can explore with clients what rituals they can put back in their lives to restore family cohesion and heal tensions in relationships.

WORKING WITH PERSONALITY PARTS

One of the most effective ways to help workaholics rebuild relationships is working with their subpersonalities or parts.[18] A *subpersonality* is an aspect of your personality or a part of you that shows up on a temporary basis to help you cope in different situations. You can be forceful at times, yielding at others. Sometimes you're in the mood for a burger; other times you prefer a salad. Isolating and working with the workaholic part helps clients see that they are multidimensional—more than they think of themselves as being.

This approach gives them room to explore their disowned parts, embracing aspects of themselves that their workaholism unwittingly eclipsed. Most workaholics have highly developed manager parts—the part of the character that brings home the bacon, focuses on goals, and exercises the virtues of strength, persistence, decisiveness, self-denial, and determination. Individual counseling shows clients how to develop the other aspects of themselves that form connections to others, love fun, and are calm, centered, confident, and compassionate.

Reese, the forty-six-year-old president of a large computer company, had built a business from the ground up with the determination and perseverance that had taken him from poverty to great wealth. But his workaholic part's singular focus on goals had led to communication problems that caused disgruntled employees to leave in droves. His workaholism left his wife fed up and produced teenaged children who, feeling they could never meet their father's impossible standards, used drugs and got into trouble at school. Labeled the tyrant workaholic at work and the Nazi parent at home, he had a genuine desire to change.

I encouraged Reese to continue to value his determination and hard-working parts but also to get in touch with his wise, creative inner elder who helped him slow down, see the magic of process, stay in the present moment, smell the flowers, and enjoy each instant of life as he moved toward his accomplishments. The wise elder helped Reese control less and delegate more, trusting his employees to be creative and find their own ways to get the job done.

I also helped Reese get in touch with his compassionate self, which allowed his caring and love to flow, as well as his passion and commitment. The compassionate self helped Reese be more accepting of all people, especially his employees, wife, and children. It helped him recognize human frailty when his workers made mistakes or revealed weaknesses. He used this part to listen, show genuine appreciation for his employees' hard work, and praise them for good work, which his workaholic part had often failed to do. The compassionate self also pulled out his iPhone, scheduled date nights with his wife, and carved out special moments to be with his children.

Reese also made contact with his clown—the fun-loving and playful part of him—to restore the joy and freedom he had forfeited in order to complete tasks. The clown helped Reese see the lighter side of life at home and work, as well as to enjoy laughing and being with people. He started planning trips with his family and instituted birthday celebrations and employee picnics to boost morale at work. He became less serious about financial security, less perfectionistic, less explosive, and more lighthearted.

YOUNG CHILDREN OF WORKAHOLICS

Professionals who work with children often fail to assist those who come from workaholic homes because, as we have seen, these children appear to be immune to the effects of the parent's hard-driving approach, competitiveness, and perfectionism. As adults, these children are usually well liked and accomplished, and they excel in their careers. Their low self-esteem, anxiety, or depression are often masked by resiliency, overresponsibility, and exaggerated self-reliance. You can look underneath the veneer to see if young and adult children of workaholics are driving themselves for approval, providing the following tips to workaholic parents or directly to children of workaholics:

❖ Be on the lookout for "overly competent" children who appear to be functioning at their maximum. It's important to mention that not all successful or competent children are suffering in the way described in this chapter. When you find children with an *overdeveloped* sense of accomplishment, responsibility, and perfectionism, you can make sure that they get as much attention as other children who may find it easier to show their needs or ask for help.

❖ Insist that children of workaholics do not sacrifice or forgo potential benefits derived from activities, experiences, or interactions because they are too busy putting others' needs before their own.

❖ Avoid being overly critical, comparing the child to others, overencouraging him or her or setting unattainable goals, and overcommitting the child to activities without evidence of a natural interest or consent.

❖ Continue to present children of workaholics with challenges that match their developmental abilities, but help them learn not to take on too much. Avoid having unusually high expectations and burdening these children with adultlike responsibilities, even when they are eager to accept and capable of accepting them.

❖ Let children know that it's okay to relax and do nothing. Reassure them that they don't always have to be producing to please someone else, that it's acceptable to please themselves—which can include doing nothing.

❖ Encourage youngsters in their successes and enjoy their accomplishments with them, but let them know that it's also acceptable to fail and that they don't have to be perfect in everything they attempt. Encourage significant adults in their lives to let youngsters see them fail and handle failure in a constructive way.

❖ Affirm children, and provide them with unconditional support for who they are, regardless of their achievements. Let them know they're valued even when they're not producing, that they're accepted regardless of whether they succeed or fail. Be there for them in case of a big failure or letdown. Help children understand that success is built on failure.

❖ Encourage children to identify their true feelings and to express them often in conversations or through creative outlets.

❖ Provide children with guidance as they make difficult decisions that parents have left up to them, such as how and where to spend their after-school time.

❖ Provide children with opportunities for noncompetitive games so they can enjoy the sheer fun of play and enjoy their childhood with other youngsters their age, rather than spending all their time with adults in adult activities. Welcome laughter, giggling, and even silliness by building in funny stories or experiences during the day, and suggest activities that are creative and here-and-now to balance out the focus on products and future-oriented activities.

ADULT CHILDREN OF WORKAHOLICS

Children of workaholics often grow into adults who are envied by everyone: responsible, achievement oriented, able to take charge of any situation. At least that's how they appear to the outside world. Inside, they often feel like little kids who can never do anything right, holding themselves up mercilessly to standards of perfection.

You can screen for work addiction in the families of origin during the intake process with any client, just as you would for alcoholism and other addictions. When you identify work addiction, you can use this information to implement a therapeutic plan for adult clients. In cases where adult clients identify living or having lived with a workaholic parent as the presenting problem, you can help them learn how to avoid enabling parental work addiction. You can inform clients of the potential damage of joining in the compulsive work habits out of their need to spend time with their parents and of bringing them work to do when they go to bed sick. You can help clients refuse to make alibis for their parents' absenteeism or lateness at parties or family get-togethers and let their parents be responsible for explanations. Consider pointing out the importance of not enabling workaholics by refusing to assume their household chores, return phone calls or fulfill family obligations for them, or cover for them at a business meeting or social gathering. It's important for the children to understand that building their lives around the workaholic's busy schedule only sets them up for further hurt and disappointment.

Try helping adult children of workaholics lower their perfectionistic standards to set more reachable goals and delegate tasks in the office or at home. Help them to be less self-critical and to strengthen their inner, nurturing voice, and teach them to affirm themselves for who they are and not just for what they do. Providing unconditional support for themselves as individuals —not just measuring their worth by what they produce or achieve—can be a major step forward for people who have spent their lives measuring their value according to the standards and approval of others.

You can teach stress-relief exercises or refer adult children of workaholics to workshops or special classes where they can learn yoga, meditation, and other relaxation techniques to help them live more in the moment. Show them how to develop flexibility by building in spontaneous, spur-of-the-moment activities and welcoming fun and laughter, perhaps by deciding to go to the beach at the last minute or walking barefoot and umbrelialess in a summer rain shower.

Consider encouraging clients to deliberately do something imperfectly—to go for a week without making their bed or to find a process-oriented activity or hobby that they cannot measure by a standard of perfection so they are free to be imperfect, such as painting their feelings on a canvas or engaging in activities like learning a new dance that permit them to make and learn from mistakes.

8

Risky Business

Work Addiction in the Company

The rung of a ladder was never
meant to rest upon, but only to
hold a man's foot long enough
to enable him to put the other
somewhat higher.

—Thomas Huxley

Margo

I got my first job at fourteen, not out of necessity but out of want. I went to school to finish my senior year in the morning and at noon to work in a grocery store, where I worked for forty hours a week. I bragged about what a great work ethic I had, but little did I know that that was just the beginning. I went to college and found myself studying and usually working some kind of job —always busy, working too many hours.

The real workaholic came out when the pace I kept landed me in my first deep depression. During the day, I was driven to succeed in the wholesale manufacturing firm that I worked for as general manager. It was a $3.5-million company that produced twenty-four hours a day, six days a week. Plus, I enrolled in a university to study business management at night. I had a wonderful husband who supported my efforts and a beautiful baby boy.

I continued this regimen until I graduated with a bachelor of science in business management, and then I continued school during the summers. I took two courses while still running the company, which had grown to a $5-million business. The last semester I took three courses while working over forty hours a week. I made almost all *A*s and won the President's Award for the best-managed plant—twice. As you may have noticed, my family hasn't been mentioned. My husband still supported me, and by now my son was ten years old. But my relationship with both suffered because of my not being there. I was constantly working at my job or doing school assignments at the university. I was obviously gone on weekends and many nights during the week.

I thought I was superwoman and succeeded at everything. Although I had a lot of guilt where my son was concerned, I tried to be the best mother I could. In reality, I was on a collision course and didn't have any idea how to relax. I hit a wall at age thirty. Even though I had graduated, I missed college. I was still in the same position, making a lot of money but no longer fulfilled by the job. I felt like I was eighty years old. I hardly listened to the radio for pleasure, read only educational books, and felt miserable if nothing was planned for every second on a weekend. I was used to being busy every second of my life and hated slowing down.

My marriage was suffering, I was having horrible mood swings, and I was angry at everyone and everything. Through therapy I came to realize that I was going through a major depression brought on by years of workaholism. So what did I do? You guessed it. I went back to work. I enrolled in an MBA program and took two graduate classes each semester. I poured myself back into school and immediately felt better, or so I thought. I was doing what my father had done: when things get tough, work harder. I was withdrawing from my husband more and more and, regrettably, expected perfection from my son, just as I did myself.

In addition to classes during my last year of graduate school, I taught a night class at the local community college and ran the manufacturing plant. I knew I needed to slow down but didn't know how. After I received my master's degree, I found the perfect job. My plan was to slow down, relax, and enjoy. It was hard to leave the company because my employees were my family. I had given my heart and soul to that job for almost twelve years. But I managed to walk out the door for the last time as the "boss."

I knew my life was unmanageable when one Friday afternoon I called a local mental health hospital. Feeling desperate, I was ready to commit myself. I would have done anything to stop this all-too-familiar roller-coaster ride. I cried for two solid weeks for no apparent reason. My life had slowed to a snail's pace, which would have been great for most people but not for a workaholic like me. In desperation, I emergency-beeped my therapist, whom I had not seen for some time. I was now willing to try anything, and I shamefully took the new antidepressants that I had refused to take before. How could I stoop so low? Why couldn't I just work harder and fix everything? I had finally found one thing I couldn't fix.

Thank God It's Monday (TGIM)!

Everything you have read about workaholics up until now is about America's obsession with work. These days you might be thinking you'd be happy simply to have a job over which to obsess, but that's another story. For those who are workaholics, the barriers I have discussed so far are carried over into the workplace: your rigid thinking, compulsive work habits, neglect of your family, ways of relating to coworkers, even your family-of-origin issues. In this chapter I show how—because the workplace is often a replication of the family of origin —some adults have a higher tolerance for stress and chaos and seek out high-stress jobs, unwittingly reenacting unresolved family- of- origin issues in the form of rampant work addiction.[1] After a certain point, these work habits and patterns hurt both workaholics and companies.

Many of us dread facing a new workweek after a relaxing weekend, but if you're a workaholic, chances are that you white-knuckled your way through the down time and cannot wait to get back to the office on Monday. While your coworkers have the Monday-morning blahs, you're revved up and ready to go. You're probably not a team player, and your need for control makes it difficult to solve problems cooperatively and participate in give-and-take situations. You believe your approach and style are best, and you cannot entertain less perfect solutions. When your narrow perspective prevails on the job, spontaneity and creativity are diminished. Because of these problems, some management experts have gone so far as to say that the best advice for any workaholic is to work alone or only with other workaholics.[2]

As a workaholic, you feel different from your coworkers because excessive work isolates you, setting you apart. You feel that your colleagues don't understand the significance of the volume of work you accomplish. You may not understand other workaholics because of their diverse work styles.

Working on Shaky Ground: Workaholism in the Company

While I was conducting research on workaholics and family dynamics, Gayle Porter, an organizational psychologist at Rutgers University, was studying the impact of workaholism in the workplace. Her findings paralleled those of my research with families. While corporate America failed to focus on the problems resulting from workaholism and extolled its virtues, Porter continued to emphasize that workaholism leads to inefficiency and erodes trust throughout the organization.[3] She insists that it's not uncommon for workaholics to generate a crisis and then to get attention and praise for resolving it: "During a crisis, everyone's attention goes to its resolution. Rarely is time taken to reexamine the history of decision points at which the crisis might have been averted, but the cost of meeting crisis conditions is significant. All organization members should be concerned about the possibility that someone in their midst may contribute to or create crisis. Indeed, managers focus on praise for those who function well during that time. The same person could be playing both roles, and this person may be a workaholic."[4]

Porter also describes how, eventually, the amount of effort that savoring workaholics put into their jobs exceeds their level of productivity:

> The important distinction, when talking about addictive behavior maintenance, is that a workaholic seeks to maintain a high level of involvement in the work even when the task could be accomplished with less involvement. This is the person who convinces himself that working on Saturday is necessary and spends time carefully lining up tasks that would not be completed without doing so. In comparison, another worker exerts extra effort during the week, asks for help, or finds more efficient ways to approach the task in order to have the weekend off. Both accomplish the required task. However, the first worker has devoted more of the week to doing so. To some, that person would appear to be more involved in the job, or appear to be the harder worker, but the motive was not to do better, only to keep doing.[5]

Are You a Shooting Star?

As you continue to overinvest in your job, fatigue sets in, and errors and accidents increase. You become less efficient than your coworkers who put in fewer hours planning and working toward a job goal. In contrast to you, the workaholic, your optimally performing coworker has warm, outgoing relationships and a good collaborative sense, and has mastered the art of delegating.

A nationwide study of 1,500 people in numerous careers revealed a major difference between workaholics and optimal performers in terms of their success.[6] Workaholics are not the high-level performers that management perceives them to be. In fact, the study showed that workaholics hurt the company because they are addicted not to getting results, but to the process of working. They tend to be motivated more by fear and loss of status than by high-level motivations, such as the desire to make a creative contribution, and they are more reluctant than optimal performers to take necessary risks in the organization to achieve positive, creative outcomes. Table 8.1 shows the characteristics that distinguish optimal performers from workaholics.

TABLE 8.1

Profile of Optimal Performers in the Workplace

Optimal Performers Are:	Workaholics Are:
Good collaborators or delegators	Unable to delegate work or work as a team; they work best alone
Socially gregarious	Employees with few or no friends
Employees who enjoy the process and outcome of work	Employees who work for the sake of working
Motivated by intrinsic needs and the desire to make creative contributions	Motivated by fear and loss of status
Efficient; they see the whole picture as well as the details	Inefficient; they get bogged down with details
Creative risk takers who stretch beyond customary bounds	Reluctant to take chances to achieve creative outcomes
Masters of self-correction; when they make mistakes, they learn from them	Unable to tolerate mistakes; they try to avoid them or cover them up

The national study also found that the career trajectories of workaholics are predictable: they tend to be flashes in the pan. Like shooting stars, they burst onto the scene, are viewed as "up and coming," rise quickly on the basis of their initial big splash, and then level off, consumed with managing the details of their careers. The leveling off tends to start at midlife, and it is accompanied by cardiovascular disease, psychosomatic disorders, alcoholism, drug abuse, and marital problems.

When the Workplace High-Fives Work Addiction

Workaholics and work addiction could not survive without the workplace. In the past, the corporate atmosphere has encouraged work addiction by perpetuating a work ethic and promoting loyalty to the company at the personal expense of its employees.

Mary described her experience living with a spouse in a high-pressured job:

"My husband is working for an Internet company and is expected to be on call virtually seven days a week. His lack of balance and my hard worker tendencies have put a severe strain on our marriage. We live in this fast-paced high-technology area where one hundred hours a week at Microsoft is the expected work week. All the other dot-com companies use this as the standard. We simply cannot keep up the pace."

A global survey by *World Business* revealed that 49 percent of workers said overwork was encouraged and applauded by their company. More than 70 percent said they worked weekends, and 14 percent admitted they'd be proud to be called a workaholic.[7] Workaholics are often attracted, consciously or unconsciously, to these types of work environments because they are looking for a lot to do. So companies must take some responsibility for enabling and promoting work addiction.

Changing Tires at Eighty Miles Per Hour

Many companies operate from top to bottom through a workaholic structure. In contrast to slogans that condemn drug use, like "Just Say No" or "Just Don't Do It," the message that rings loud and clear—sometimes subtle, sometimes direct—in the workaholic organization is "Don't Go Home without It." As I travel far and wide and in my own clinical practice, I hear more stories of corporate threats. One woman told me in her case the threat was subtle: "Oh yeah, I could take all of my earned vacation. But if I do, I won't have a job when I get back. They may say it's okay, but believe me it isn't!"

Other workers say they're afraid to take lunch breaks for fear of how they'd be perceived by management. There comes a point where these work environments hurt employees, whether or not they are workaholics. Organizations that actively recruit workaholics and promote work addiction tend to attract more workaholic types. Nonworkaholic types, however, do not fare as well in these jobs. Many organizations have stripped management layers in order to remain competitive and now make a habit of employing four people to do the work of five.[8]

The philosophy of one major US bank is, *We expect you to change tires going eighty miles an hour.* An executive at this bank told me that at meetings, six or seven managers typically sit around a table discussing issues, each one constantly checking her Blackberry as it goes off. The consensus is that to survive in this culture, employees can no longer afford to just focus on one thing at a time. Multitasking is an essential lifeboat to keep from drowning in a sea of work.

Is Multitasking a Waste of Time?

You might consider multitasking to be an essential survival tool in a 24/7 work culture that expects immediate results. But if you think multitasking is the ticket to more productivity, think again. Experts say juggling e-mail messages, phone calls, and text messages actually undermines your ability to focus and produce, fatiguing your brain in the process.[9] University of Michigan researchers report that when you're bouncing between several tasks, you're actually forcing your brain to keep refocusing with each rebound, reducing productivity by up to 40 percent. They conclude that multitasking undermines productivity, efficiency, and quality of life and results in several half-baked projects that leave workers overwhelmed and stressed out.[10]

Studies from Stanford University confirm that heavy multitaskers have more stress because of trouble focusing and shutting out irrelevant information.[11] In an effort to handle the overload from prolonged multitasking, scientists say, your brain rewires itself, causing fractured thinking and lack of concentration. As a result, if you're a multitasker, you waste more time taking longer to switch among tasks and are less efficient at juggling problems than people who don't multitask.

Corporate Exploitation and Abuse

Gayle Porter and her colleagues fear that the combination of information technology and excessive corporate demands carries the risk that companies will exploit workers, who feel they must be available 24/7.[12] If career advancement depends on 24/7 connectivity, it becomes more difficult to distinguish between a worker's choice to work and an employer's manipulation. The prevalence of information technology raises many questions about the future of corporate responsibility: Have organizations set their expectations so high that addiction-level work involvement is a requirement for many jobs, and can employers be held liable for employees' addictions to information technology?

Another example of increasing corporate demands is the disappearance of company picnics, which used to be a family affair. Replacing them are what is proudly heralded as "power picnics"—the traditional company picnic serving double duty to get more work squeezed in during the annual event. During 2006 Chicago's Windy City Fieldhouse—which hosts company picnics—reported a 20 percent increase in company events with an added work dimension, such as two-hour brainstorming sessions before the celebration.[13]

Companies are making sure that they get a greater bang for their buck, that every dollar spent contributes to the company's growth. This shift in corporate emphasis has begun to show up in sobering ways: "As PowerPoint presentations replace softball, the guest lists are changing. Business partners, vendors and potential customers are being invited and families are getting nixed."[14]

Are you overworked? Micromanaged? Have you been downsized? Or are you overworking, micromanaging, or downsizing others? Today, even if you're not a workaholic, you're probably under the gun to work more because of a declining economy, downsizing, fear of job loss, or job insecurity resulting from takeovers. Employers foster work addiction by limiting neither the hours employees work nor the amount of work they take home, by discounting the importance of family life, and by applauding those who work tirelessly rather than those who have balanced lives. Some companies send mixed messages to employees (itself a trait of the workaholic personality). They say they don't want workaholics, but they scrutinize time records or put subtle pressure on employees to log more hours. An alarming 46 percent of professional workers claim they have too much stress and pressure in their jobs.[15] In 2012 job pressures were the second cause of stress, after financial worries.[16]

Some companies have been accused of deliberately manipulating the darker sides of workers' consciousness for profit. They set tight deadlines that are impossible to meet, hint at nonexistent competitors, and tell employees that clients are dissatisfied when in fact they're not. Such corporate tactics create paranoia, stress, and a prolonged adrenaline rush among the workers; employees never know for sure which crises are real and which are fabrications. The label "cultures of sacrifice" has been applied to those organizations that manifacture crises as a ploy to keep pressures on employees to produce:

In a culture of sacrifice, people are driven by feelings of responsibility to the company. This is particularly true for those who link loss of performance with loss of self-esteem. These people become the company workaholics. Workaholics get caught up in a never-ending mission to gain control by devoting more and more time to work, to the exclusion of virtually everything else. If they slow down or relax, they worry they will be seen as slackers or incompetents. In their quest to be "good enough" they draw themselves and others into a working frenzy that focuses on quantity rather than quality, aggressively pushing the company and fellow workers to the point of collapse. . . . Failure is inevitable in this culture. These companies operate on the assumption that the company is more important than its workers, and they are prepared to sacrifice excellent workers to prove the point.[17]

The Addictive Organization

Organizational experts charge that many businesses encourage the denial of work addiction and actually promote it as acceptable because it seems to be productive.[18] They suggest that corporate America functions like an individual addict by denying, covering up, and rewarding dysfunctional behaviors among its employees. They also say that dysfunctional managers and those in key corporate positions negatively affect the organizational system and the employees of that system by perpetuating work addiction at every level. They offer six characteristics of companies (described below) that promote work addiction on the production line, in the boardroom, or in sales meetings.[19]

Do you toil in a workplace where the human element is overshadowed by the details of the workload? Check out the following characteristics and see if any of them ring true of where you work:

1. *The mission of the organization is denied, ignored, or forgotten.* You're so preoccupied with being productive that you forget why the organization exists. You lose sight of the overall mission of your work because you're pressured by the economics of the business.

2. *Corporate survival reigns supreme.* Corporate survival is the top priority, and you're viewed as a commodity to be used up and then discarded. Stress management is offered to keep you and your coworkers productive. The business survives as employees drop like flies.

3. *Profit is the driving force of the workaholic company.* Your company seeks short-term, immediate gratification instead of deferred, long-range solutions, results, and profit. The integrity and mission of the organization, as well as your mental health and that of other employees, are better served by a long-term focus at the expense of immediate profit.

4. *The workaholic environment is self-centered and has no boundaries or respect.* You're expected to carry your workload home on weekends and glue yourself to your laptop, e-mail, and iPhone on weekends and holidays to perform adequately. With its lack of boundaries, your company doesn't respect and honor your personal life. It's selfish, greedy, and demanding. You're constantly at the disposal of the organization, regardless of your personal or family needs. The workaholic organization makes you dependent on it through perks and benefits. It buys your loyalty, even though you're miserable and officewide morale is low. Quitting isn't a viable option for you.

5. *Crisis management is the norm in workaholic organizations.* Crisis shifts the focus of the organization away from emphasizing your needs and

welfare to solving the crisis. When businesses are organized to respond to problems without forethought, they're perpetually putting out fires. This keeps you and your colleagues hyped up, with your adrenaline flowing, your attention focused on the needs of the organization, and your emotional and mental health needs on the back burner. There's less attention devoted to long-term planning; when it does exist, it's often cursory.

6. *Intimacy does not exist in the workaholic environment.* You feel like a cog in the corporate machine. Your work environment is cold and impersonal. Socializing and close relationships are minimized or even discouraged. Your company operates on the premise that employees are dispensable, like machine parts, and, once used up, you will be replaced by someone else.

If you're a workaholic, you're at risk of being attracted to and thriving in jobs that have any or all of these six characteristics. You might even insinuate your way into the ranks of management, fostering work addiction throughout the company. But if you're an efficient worker, you're less willing to sacrifice your whole life for unreasonable work demands. In some cases you're able to make drastic changes in your work life, such as downshifting into less stressful jobs and simplifying your personal life.

Do you work in a job that promotes work addiction or one that nurtures its employees? See the next section and grade your workplace on work addiction.

How Would You Grade Your Job?

Are you in a win/lose work culture? Do you work in a job that promotes work addiction, stress, and burnout? Or are you fortunate enough to work in a company that considers human factors and nurtures its employees? Test your workplace to see how it rates on corporate abuse by answering yes or no to the following questions:

_____ 1. Is your job rapid paced, with little time to casually talk with coworkers or supervisors?

_____ 2. Does your work environment feel cold, sterile, or devoid of the human touch?

_____ 3. Does your work environment thrive on crisis, chaos, and pressure?

_____ 4. Do you work for a company that emphasizes production and profit above the welfare and morale of its employees?

_____ 5. Does success in your company hinge on putting in overtime on weekdays, weekends, or holidays?

_____ 6. Do you think your company fosters work addiction?

_____ 7. Are you constantly in a hurry and racing against the clock on your job?

_____ 8. Is it necessary to juggle many activities or projects at one time in order to keep up in your job?

_____ 9. Does your company put you under the gun with short notice of high-pressure deadlines?

_____ 10. Have you had any stress-related illnesses caused by this job?

_____ 11. Do you work for a company that puts the welfare of its employees above profit and production?

_____ 12. Does your company have a nurturing attitude toward workers who have concerns about family and personal time or who experience stress and burnout?

_____ 13. Is your job environment relaxing, evenly paced, warm, and friendly?

_____ 14. Do you feel like a human being more often than a commodity on your job?

_____ 15. In your job, can you limit the amount of work you bring home and have weekends and holidays for yourself and loved ones?

_____ 16. Do you think your company has a long-term, vested interest in you as a human being, as opposed to a short-term interest?

_____ 17. Does your company promise celebrations—including of birthdays and holidays—or other socializing as an integral part of the work schedule?

_____ 18. Do you work with colleagues who are cooperative and supportive and with whom you can communicate?

_____ 19. If you have a problem in your job, can you talk with someone who will listen and offer you support?

_____ 20. Does your job give you personal satisfaction, meaning, or purpose?

SCORING: Start with 60 points. Subtract 2 points for each yes answer to questions 1 through 10. Add 2 points for each no answer to questions 1 through 10. Subtract 2 points for each no answer to questions 11 through 20. Add 2 points for each yes answer to questions 11 through 20.

YOUR JOB'S REPORT CARD:

Scores	Grade	Interpretation
0–59	F	Poor. Consider a healthier workplace. You may already have the signs of stress and burnout or other physical symptoms that lead to bad health.
60–69	D	Below average
70–79	C	Average
80–89	B	Good
90–100	A	Excellent. Stay put. Sounds like you've hit the jackpot of a non-workaholic, healthy workplace.

The Boss from Hell

Does your boss wail at the clock and shake a fist at the heavens because there's never enough time to do everything? Is your boss someone who rushes around moaning about the shortage of time and creating crises for everyone in his or her path? Is your boss the sort who sets short deadlines, overloads you with more to do than is humanly possible, and then breathes down your neck? If so, your boss could be a workaholic.

Working under a workaholic boss can be a nightmare. Andrea worked for a major East Coast newspaper. Her boss, she says, was a workaholic who routinely awakened employees in the middle of the night and on weekends to get an obscure fact from the West Coast for a next-morning deadline. "Naturally everything was closed, so there were times when I ended up calling Tokyo at 3:00 a.m. to get the information he wanted," she said. "It was always one crisis after another!"

Workaholics are often rewarded for their attempts to change and control other people by being promoted into management positions. Although many bosses are blatant in fostering work addiction, some are much more subtle. Their overresponsibility, poor communication skills, and inability to express feelings usually make them ineffective managers. Managers who are out of touch with their emotional lives are likely to be insensitive to the needs and feelings of their subordinates. If they are uncomfortable expressing feelings, they are less likely to provide positive feedback, praise, and appreciation.

RULING WITH AN IRON FIST

Instead of seeking advice, asking for input, or showing humility, workaholic bosses usually rule with an iron fist, using intimidation as a defense against their own insecurities and unwittingly undermining—rather than supporting—subordinates to reinforce their own, more powerful position. They tend to pressure employees to match their own inhuman standards of long hours and frantic pace. Employee morale nosedives and burnout skyrockets under such autocratic control. Countless millions of people become anxious at the thought of facing a new week with a work-addicted manager, supervisor, or employer. See the "Profile of a Workaholic Boss."

Alcoholics like nothing better than a drinking buddy. Workaholics feel contempt for slackers, preferring instead to surround themselves with people who can match their crisis-oriented pace. Workaholic supervisors and managers spread work addiction by setting impossible and incredibly high goals and then pushing employees to replicate their own frenetic work patterns, often against the employees' natural work pace: "One of ITT's former presidents set a companywide precedent for work weeks of sixty hours or more and more late-night meetings. Some CPA firms send a memorandum to all their employees just before tax season reminding them that a fifty-hour workweek is considered the minimum. These pressures impose feelings of guilt on all

Profile of the Workaholic Boss

- Constantly watches over employees' shoulders to monitor their work, while refusing to delegate
- Constantly pushes and hurries employees to the point where they feel undue stress and burnout
- Makes unreasonable demands in terms of work hours, workloads, and deadlines
- Has unpredictable, erratic moods, so employees never know what to expect
- Creates a climate of frenzy, urgency, and tension without respect for the feelings or personal lives of employees
- Manages time inefficiently because of overscheduling and overcommitting
- Judges himself or herself and employees without mercy as they struggle to hit impossible targets
- Tends to be overly critical and intolerant of even the most minor employee mistakes

executives who do not work the same number of hours others are working. As a result, employees feel insecure about their jobs unless they spend Saturdays at their desks."[20]

DR. JEKYLL / MR. HYDE

Workaholic bosses are overly critical, overly demanding, and unable to tolerate mistakes. They become roadblocks to productivity and quality in the workforce, causing disharmony, absenteeism, tardiness, mistrust, and conflict. Their leadership style lowers productivity and morale and destroys team playing and creative brainstorming in the workplace. Judith shared the difficulty she had working under Susan, the district sales manager at a multimillion-dollar computer company:

> Susan's addictive work habits make it unbearable for her sales reps. She's in the office by 7:30 a.m. and doesn't get home until eight or nine o'clock. Her obsession and constant driving leave no time for family life, and her social life includes only people within the company. She won't leave the sales representatives alone to do their jobs. She can't delegate and wait until a task is accomplished and is burning out trying to keep her hands in everything they do. She's always breathing down our necks by phone or e-mail. She's afraid that nobody's going to do the job as well as she would do it if she were there. The morale of the sales reps is rock bottom. The sales force doesn't function as a team. Their spirits are shattered, and they're constantly frustrated that they are not accomplishing enough in a time frame to satisfy Susan. Some of my fellow workers try to respond to everything she wants, and they're getting as crazy as she is, just constantly working. I've seen people come into the office with bloodshot eyes, completely drained. They look as if they haven't slept in three or four days. She's like Jekyll and Hyde—tough to read—constantly flying off the handle and jumping down people's throats. When she notices you're under the pile [of work], instead of offering support, she'll start harping on what you're doing and then she'll jump you.

If you're an employee, no matter how hard you try to please, you can never satisfy your boss's perfectionist standards. You get little positive feedback for your work efforts, and you end up feeling resentful. As the moods of a workaholic manager or foreman swing from high to low, you try to satisfy him or her by swinging back and forth as well. You're never sure what to say or do, and you waste enormous amounts of energy trying to second-guess your boss.

Willa, an office manager for a prominent attorney, said her boss is a "grouchaholic" with giant-size mood swings:

One day he's happy, the next day he's snappy. He works day and night and hardly ever talks to the other people in the office. He comes in, walks into his office, shuts the door, and stays there all day long. Everybody walks on eggshells and has learned to steer clear of him for fear of becoming the target of his anger. The tension is so thick, you could cut it with a knife. When he's grumpy, I feel like I've done something wrong and spend half the day worrying and feeling guilty because maybe it's my fault, or I try to get him out of his bad mood. Although part of my job is to inform him of problems that need to be addressed for the good of the business, I am afraid to tell him some critical things he needs to know because I'm afraid he'll blow up at me. When I do have meetings with him, I have to measure each word to make sure I don't use the wrong approach or sound too negative, because if I do, it will set him off.

Workaholic managers are notorious for making and breaking promises because the unrealistic deadlines they set cannot be met. So a new plan is substituted. The work climate is unpredictable and inconsistent, just like the climate in an alcoholic's home. Apprehension, fear, and insecurity are normal reactions for employees in unpredictable job positions.

As a result of the stresses and strains of a work-addicted environment, your emotions run the gamut from fear, anger, confusion, guilt, and embarrassment to sadness and depression. In order to cope, you might guess at what your boss wants and find yourself making stabs in the dark. Emotionally battered and bruised, you might limp through your career. Poor self-esteem, lack of control over your career, poor coping skills, and problems in interpersonal relationships can all result as you try to meet demands from the dysfunctional powers that be. Rather than focusing on quality production, you concentrate your efforts at work on covering your tracks, distorting the truth, and watching your back.

Many workers get revenge by passive resistance. One man said that his way of getting back at his boss was to do as little as possible and that his productivity would increase dramatically if he worked under someone else. Instead of benefiting companies, workaholics are costing them money in terms of personal injury lawsuits and workers' compensation and medical insurance claims —all related to the stress and emotional burnout of work addiction. In 2006 it was estimated that workaholic employees cost businesses over $160 billion a year because of absenteeism, diminished productivity, and stress-related illnesses such as high blood pressure, heart disease, abdominal problems, and a host of mental health problems such as depression and anxiety.[21] Heart disease caused by job stress alone is responsible for an annual loss of 135 million workdays. Workers' compensation costs rose from $23 billion in 1982 to $60 billion in 1990, due to increased claims for psychological and mental stress. If you have a workaholic boss breathing down your neck or toil in an abusive workplace, check out the "Tips for Clinicians" section at the end of this chapter for your options before calling it quits.

Do You Quit or Commit?

No one can tell you to quit your job without knowing the intimate details of your work and personal life. That's your call. But if your current position is all you can find, even if you're not thrilled with it, you wouldn't want to trade one problem for another by being unemployed in today's economy. And if your job is tolerable and pays the bills, you have to weigh the financial advantages in light of your job's negative aspects, plus the other factors in your life such as the people who are dependent on you and your amount of debt. So if you're debating whether to quit or stay put, before you throw in the towel make sure your emotions aren't biasing your decision. And think it through thoroughly.

Making a U-Turn in the Workplace

In the past, the corporate world believed that having ranks of workaholic employees would guarantee greater production. But corporations are finding they can achieve more creative results and greater revenues from a more balanced workforce. Salespeople who have achieved balance in their lives, for example, are more likely to attract potential clients than obsessed, high-pressure salespeople, who are more likely to turn clients off and drive them away.

How can corporate America take all the problems of work addiction and convert them into dollars and cents? That question is being asked more and more. Many businesses are taking a stand against work addiction and structuring more humane working environments. A former head of Caterpillar was a pioneer in insisting that employees lead balanced lives:

> I don't want workaholics working for me. . . . One of my predecessors called that "living on the square." . . . One side of the square represents our work life, one our family life, one our spiritual life, and one our community life. I believe we're healthier, happier—and more productive—if we live on all sides of that square.
>
> I doubt that such people [workaholics] can be effective managers over a lifetime. I question whether they've learned how to delegate, if they've sought ways to become more efficient, if they've learned how to set priorities.[22]

Finding cost-effective ways to help employees balance career with family, recreation, and self-care needs are major concerns for employers nowadays.

More companies are starting to hire socially balanced employees and to institute work-break aerobics and meditation workshops. In some cases, bosses are telling employees, directly or indirectly, to slow down. General Mills is among a growing number of companies that insists workers use their vacation time. Susan's boss rejected one day she "took off" for vacation because she had left him electronic messages that same day. He told her: "You weren't on vacation because you sent me a message, so take another day of vacation. Get away from the office and forget about work for a while."

The Changing Tide

More companies are realizing that work addiction is a major health and safety issue, that it's to their advantage to promote healthy employees and work environments. More Fortune 100 companies are finding that meditation, chanting, and yoga benefit both payroll and personnel. Mark Bertolini, the CEO of Aetna Health Insurance Company, discovered that yoga helped him with lingering pain from a skiing accident. So he put in place a stress-reducing mindfulness program for Aetna's workers and had Duke University scientists study the results. The findings showed that with one hour of yoga classes a week, there was a 33 percent drop in workplace stress.[23] So far over three thousand of Aetna's workers have completed the program, saving Aetna $2,000 in annual health care costs for people who moved from the highest-stress group to the lowest-stress one.

Both Google and Dow Chemical have established onsite mindful meditation classes (see chapter 10 for more on mindful working) to reduce workers' stress levels.[24] Other companies have destressed work environments by using natural light, indoor gardens and plants, and relaxation rooms with trickling fountains.[25] Still others have instituted stress reduction policies such as flextime, job sharing, and paid paternity leave.

Tony Schwartz, chief executive officer of the Energy Project, created a business around the concept of "energy renewal," which promotes the idea that energy is finite but, unlike time, is renewable.[26] The energy that employees bring to their jobs is far more important in terms of the value of their work than is the number of hours they work. By managing energy more skillfully, it's possible to get more done in less time, more sustainably. Schwartz's ideas have helped organizations such as Coca-Cola, Green Mountain Coffee, Google, the Los Angeles Police Department, Genentech, and the Cleveland Clinic. His company has dedicated space to a "renewal" room in which employees can nap, meditate, or relax. There's a spacious lounge where workers hang out together and snack on healthy foods. The company encourages workers to take renewal breaks throughout the day and to leave the office for lunch. The workday ends at 6:00 p.m., and nobody is expected to answer e-mail messages in the evenings or on weekends. In addition, employees receive four weeks of vacation starting in their first year at the company.

Other companies can raise employee awareness of workaholism and balance by establishing "healthy work" days, in conjunction with Earth Day, with posters and special seminars featuring the components of a healthy work environment. Organizations can present the information by using outside speakers so that all workers learn about the effects of work addiction on the job in a nonthreatening way.

If you're a company administrator, you can assess the degree to which your organization promotes work addiction. Using the six characteristics of the workaholic company and the workplace report card in the section titled "How Would You Grade Your Job?" as criteria, company officials can objectively evaluate the work environment at their organization to determine what needs changing to improve the welfare of workers first and the profit of the organization second.

The removal of work addiction from the workplace can dramatically reduce burnout and stress, health problems, poor communication, and low morale. It would save businesses billions of dollars a year and provide both a better work climate for employees and a better product for consumers. It's a win-win for employers, employees, and consumers—everybody benefits.

Tips for Clinicians

If you're a clinician, consider asking yourself what type of work environment you have established for yourself and your clients. Is the atmosphere rushed and frenetic, or is it serene and relaxed? Grading your work environment with the test in the "How Would You Grade Your Job?" section can help you evaluate your work space to see what kind of example you're setting. It's important to be a positive role model by creating a positive work environment for workaholics and their families.

THRIVING INSTEAD OF SURVIVING IN A WORKAHOLIC COMPANY

You can help workaholics or just plain hard workers who are trying to survive in a workaholic culture. The following tips can even help them thrive instead of just survive:

❖ *Know where to draw the line.* Don't wait for your company to decide what's reasonable for you. Evaluate your job and life and decide for yourself what's reasonable. How far you are willing to go to meet your boss's unreasonable demands? Be prepared to put your foot down when you believe your employer oversteps those bounds. There are many occasions on the job when you have a choice to stay late or work weekends. You may be reluctant to say no. But feeling overloaded and saying no without feeling guilty or disloyal is a healthy practice.

❖ *Keep your own balance.* Each of us is responsible for maintaining our work-life balance. Consider taking ten or fifteen minutes in the middle of the day to walk or meditate to release bottled-up stress and become more clear-minded. Take an aerobics class, a meditation workshop, a stress-reduction class, or an exercise program during work breaks to sidestep stress and burnout. Striving for balance in your personal, social, and family life may be a high-wire act, but it ensures greater harmony within yourself, at home, at work, and at play and makes it easier for you to survive in a workaholic company.

PERFORMING OPTIMALLY INSTEAD OF WORKAHOLICALLY IN THE WORKPLACE

Flashy, dramatic bursts of working often draw attention from supervisors and colleagues, but consistency and moderation are the redeeming traits of optimal performers. Like the hare in the fable, workaholics make a big splash, crash, and then burn. If you're an optimal performer, however, you're like the tortoise. You plod along, showing consistent, high-level performance over time. Optimal performing doesn't contain the adrenaline highs, the ups and downs, or the stress of work addiction. The attention comes more slowly to optimal performers, but the delayed gratification pays off in the end.

The following tips can help you as the clinician assist workaholics to learn the benefits of replacing temporary highs now with greater, longer-lasting rewards over their career trajectory:

❖ *Don't let work dominate your life.* When you feel overloaded, don't cancel dinner with a loved one or your afternoon aerobics class. These are the very activities you need to help you maintain balance. Typically, workaholics think that staying at the office for two more hours is the answer to achieving results. But that usually makes them more tired and less clear-headed and often leads to more work overall. Maintaining outside interests and exercising daily brings a clearer perspective to your work and gives you more vitality to get out from under the pile of work. Plan for spare time just as you would an important business meeting. Schedule time for doing things you like to do best.

❖ *Delegate and negotiate.* If you're someone who has trouble turning a project over to someone else, learn to delegate in order to perform optimally. Review your workload and determine what part you can turn over to an assistant or coworker. If deadlines are too tight, negotiate them with your supervisor. Deadlines can almost always be modified, although the worka-holic mind-set won't let you readily admit that. Develop a plan explaining the need for the extension, and suggest a revised time frame. Or come up with a creative alternative. Tina, a production manager for a New York symphony orchestra, found herself working fifteen hours more a week without a pay increase. Instead of spending several hours watching sym-phony rehearsals, she put a college intern in charge with a cell phone so she could be reached in a pinch. A Merrill Lynch senior biotechnology analyst who was swamped with sixty-hour workweeks found a way around a hir-ing freeze to get his projects started. He recruited a graduate student from Harvard who helped him two days a week for free.[27]

❖ *Learn the art of prioritizing your work.* Have clear and practical priorities. Don't overplan. The clearer you are about what you want to accomplish and how you plan to accomplish it, the more focused and efficient and the less stressed you will be. Identify the key aspects of your job. Pay attention to the essentials first and put the nonessentials on the back burner for now, or farm them out to another employee.

❖ *Take charge of your technology.* More people are working in cafes and coffee houses, on airplanes, and at home, making the corporate work space dead zones of empty cubicles—a ghost town.[28] Don't fall into the trap of using the extra time that your technology provides to do more work instead of taking a leisurely break. Make sure you're in charge of your cell phone or laptop, rather than letting your technology be in charge of you. You can have time-saving technology without becoming a slave to it. You can check your e-mail twice a day, for example, instead of every time the computer beeps. You can turn off your smart phone at a reasonable hour and put lim-its on when and where you choose to carry a laptop—declaring off limits your Caribbean cruise or your trek through the Amazon jungle. I suggest that clients leave their laptops in the trunk of the car when they arrive home. Or at the very least, I urge them to put their technological tools away in a drawer after a reasonable day's work—just as you would put away ingredients and utensils after baking or carpentry tools after building shelves in your den.

COPING WITH A WORKAHOLIC BOSS

You might have a client who works under the boss from hell. Your clients can't fire the boss, but they can take some action that will benefit them in the long run. Here are some ways to deal with a workaholic boss:

❖ *Avoid anger and impatience.* These are the traits of workaholics who are socially isolated and task focused. Remain tactful and diplomatic, even when you're frustrated. Talk with your boss and try to see his or her human side. Try to find an idea, pastime, or point of view that gives you common ground to connect with your boss so that you can stay objective and see the problem as bigger than just the two of you.

❖ *Schedule a meeting with your boss to find out what his or her expectations of you are, and the expectations of your boss's boss.* Ask exactly what type of performance is expected of you in order for you to receive an excellent review rating. According to some experts, 99 percent of the time work hours are not among the factors.[29] This practice ensures that you won't be downgraded for not putting in extra hours. Make sure your boss understands your point of view, the importance of your personal life, and your expectations concerning job demands. Make priorities, set goals, and schedule your time accordingly.

❖ *Reach out to coworkers who are experiencing similar problems with the boss.* Start support-group meetings before or after work, or during lunch in designated places at the work site. By meeting together and talking about your problems constructively, you can develop a rich support system to draw on in the job setting. When appropriate, schedule a group meeting with the boss and explain your concerns in a constructive way. Ask for feedback or ground rules so that all of you can be productive and avoid future problems.

Part II

Recovery from
Work Addiction

9

Your Workaholic Brain

*The longest journey one must take is
the eighteen inches from the head to
the heart.*
                        —Ramprasad Padhi

George

Like many workaholics, my battle began in childhood. I was born in the rural
South, the youngest of four children. My father, who was twenty years older
than my mother, became severely handicapped from a stroke when I was five
years old. My strong-willed mother had to take care of my father, her three
teenage children, and me, insisting that we rise above our rural environment
and become successful in a more sophisticated world.

My siblings were victims of my mother's tenacity, insistence on perfectionism, and relentless criticism when the highest results were not achieved. But
I was more defiant and strong-willed like my mother. As I grew into adolescence, Mother and I constantly fought, but she instilled in me a strong sense
of survival, achievement, perfectionism, and ego. Her psychological demands
of perfection and accomplishment, along with my need to demonstrate to the
world that I was worthy, ultimately spawned my workaholism.

My drive for achievement, success, and hard work became evident in high
school. I became president of the student body, was voted most popular, was
inducted into the national honor society, was selected "king teen," and accomplished records in track. In college, the pattern continued when I was elected
president of my class each year, achieved the dean's list, made captain of the
track team, and managed several money-making endeavors.

After college, I attended officer candidate school, where I graduated as Dis-
tinguished Military Graduate. In my three-year tour of duty in Germany, I

met and married a wonderful German woman who was graduating from the university. After my tour of duty, we moved back to the United States. Perhaps I had an instinctive sense of what I needed to maintain my work addiction because my wife was kind, bright, nurturing, and supportive—traits that fed my workaholic control and drive for perfection.

After returning stateside, I enrolled in a prestigious MBA program, where I was informed that the student with the highest grade point average in the first year would be granted a full scholarship in the second year. This challenge was just the spark to ignite my workaholism, my need to demonstrate that I was worthy. My incessant studying—ten-to-twelve-hour days, seven days a week—landed me the scholarship while simultaneously enabling my workaholic behaviors.

Despite the fact that we were newlyweds and my wife was adjusting to a new country, I increased my workload. I became an officer in the National Guard and a student consultant with a local real estate firm. After completing my MBA, I saw that with a "little extra effort" (three weeks of studying nonstop for sixteen to eighteen hours a day), I could get my CPA as a "tag on" to my MBA, before starting my employment with a national accounting firm shortly after graduation. As the world applauded, little did I see the toll it was taking on my marriage and my own mental well-being.

Once I started my career, my workaholism flourished. I was promoted to manager in three years, which normally took five; in three additional years to senior manager, which usually took five; and then to partner in three more years, which took five for most people. I had to prove to the world and to the insecurity inside me that I was worthy and measured up. It was essential to be the best. I didn't understand that "even in the fast lane there is a speed limit."

Early in my career we had two children, a daughter, then a son two years later. My wife didn't work outside the house and basically raised the children. One could argue that parenthood is a partnership with each partner assuming an appropriate role. In our case, the scales tipped too far in the direction of me doing too much of the wage earning and too little parenting. I rationalized that I was providing my family with material riches that would make them happy. What they wanted, however, was more of a father and husband.

My wife complained that every Friday the fathers in the neighborhood were home in the early afternoons, while I worked until seven and eight o'clock at night and returned to work on Saturday. My children wondered why Dad would take work with him on vacation and silently slip off to work while Mom did fun vacation things with them. Later in life, my daughter vowed to never be like her father; to her credit, she learned early the importance of balancing work and family.

Although there was constant stress among the four of us, my wife struggled to keep the peace among the kids so I could work more, unwittingly enabling my addiction. Often I would displace my stress on her, becoming verbally abusive, condescending, and manipulative. With my children, I was controlling and didn't give them the strong emotional guidance they needed from a father. Even though my career soared as top producer, it didn't satisfy me or make me truly happy. I continued to raise the bar without stopping to "smell the roses."

At its peak, my workaholism manifested itself in many ways:

- ❖ I worked incessantly at work and at home.
- ❖ I multitasked to support my workaholism (simultaneously eating, talking on the phone, dressing, and grooming).
- ❖ I ignored the emotional needs of my family.
- ❖ I had few meaningful friendships.
- ❖ I carried on social conversations with people, looking them straight in the eyes, my mind back at work.
- ❖ I was competitive and measured in everything I did. When I exercised, I had to exhaust myself; when reading "for pleasure," I timed myself to see how many pages per hour I could read; when I played games with others, I had to win.
- ❖ I was impatient in grocery lines, in traffic, or jockeying for a position getting into sports events.
- ❖ I attempted to control and manipulate everything in my work and social environment.
- ❖ I drove my subordinates at work to stretch toward unrealistic goals.
- ❖ I set high standards for my children to achieve.
- ❖ I limited my sleep, many times having to use sleep aids to rest.
- ❖ I deprived myself of personal time to relax.

In summary, I was a ticking time bomb, headed toward a classic workaholic disaster. Only my strong constitution kept me from being totally burned out. Still, the work place and society applauded, adding fuel to my workaholism.

Recovery sometimes comes in strange ways. At sixteen, my son started on a journey that ended up with him becoming a heroin addict. Little did I know that his addiction would become my salvation. My wife and I tried to "fix" his addiction, and the more we tried to help, the more we enabled him, and the more our lives spun out of control. We put him in numerous treatments, but nothing worked. As he continued his drug addiction, dismissed by society as a "loser," I continued my work addiction, applauded by the world as a "winner."

To deal with our son's problem, my wife and I found Al-Anon, where people search for serenity after dealing unsuccessfully with addicts in their lives. Al-Anon saved my marriage, my sanity, and my career. I quickly learned that recovery must be focused on me, not on controlling things outside my control, including my son. Al-Anon's serenity prayer taught me to ask God to "grant me the serenity to accept the things I cannot change, the courage to change the things I can, and the wisdom to know the difference."

Even though I attended church regularly, the Twelve-Step program brought me more in touch with my Higher Power. I admitted that my life was out of control, that my work was consuming me, and that I had to turn my life over to a power greater than me. I examined my character defects as well as my asset traits that hindered or facilitated serenity. I came face to face with such shortcomings as impatience, control, rage, ego, enabling, fear, and out-of-control drive for more and more achievements. The epiphany came when I realized that most of these character defects fueled my work addiction, and that to achieve serenity, I had to become aware of these defects and then take action to address them.

With movement toward serenity, gratitude has flowed. No longer do I dwell in the past or become obsessed with the future. I attempt to live in the present and am happy to report that I have more balance in my life. As an active workaholic, my "asset allocation" was 90 percent work and 10 percent life. Through my recovery program, I am balancing work, play, family, and self. I am better at setting boundaries of what I'm willing and not willing to do. If I relapse into old behavior, I'm able to recognize what's happening and employ remedial action.

I'm quick to point out that I'm a work in progress. I know I'll relapse in the future. But when I do, I'll forgive myself and continue to work through progress, not perfection. I understand that once a workaholic, always a workaholic, and I need to go periodically to my Higher Power as I seek self-help. Plus, I've come to understand that achieving balance and serenity is not a destination; it's an ongoing journey that needs ongoing maintenance. And the good news is: I can now sit in a chair and read a great book, spend an afternoon in the park with my grandkids, or have a nice dinner with my wife without keeping my ear on the phone or my eye on my e-mail!

Knowing Your Gray Matters

As you can see from his story, George was able to recover from workaholism because he shifted his mental outlook. As he commented, he realized that even the fast lane has a speed limit, and he took a different course of action. Here's another way of putting it: as a result of taking charge of his workaholism and changing his old unhealthy work habits, George actually changed the neural pathways in his brain. I realize this sounds far-fetched, but I'm not on crack! I'll get to how you can change your brain in a minute. But first let's get to know your brain. If you're like most people, you might not even know about your own brain, and yet your brain is who you are. It's the boss of your mind and body. So it's important for you to know what it's up to, especially when workaholism has you in its clutches.

Your brain is about the size of your fist and weighs about as much as a cantaloupe—around three pounds. Although it's made up mostly of water, the human brain contains as many as 100 billion neurons. These neurons connect through long, spidery arms and communicate with each other through electrochemical signals. Your brain never shuts down; it's active even when you're asleep.

With modern imaging techniques, science has advanced our understanding of this amazing organ and, in particular, of the aftermath of prolonged stress as it relates to addictions such as work addiction. Studies conducted on process addictions such as compulsive gambling show that brain scans of compulsive gamblers are associated with blunted mesolimbic-prefrontal cortex activation.[1] Although brain imaging studies haven't been performed with workaholics, I am convinced that significant brain differences exist between workaholics and nonworkaholics.

Working from Your "Reptilian" Brain

If you're a workaholic, you probably work from your "reptilian" or survival brain. When you're besieged by work stress, studies in neuroscience explain what happens on a cellular level to spark your inner workaholic firestorm. The brain is prewired to kick into red alert to keep you safe. It constantly scans your inner and outer worlds for danger, reacting automatically to perceived threats, even though you're not fully aware of it.

At one time in our species' history, the primitive fight-or-flight response (also known as the stress response), would have switched on at breakneck speed to help you survive attacks from other tribes and wild animals. Our laid-back ancestors who didn't worry about danger were killed off by unsuspected attackers, but our vigilant ancestors survived. As a result, our DNA carries an evolutionary heritage that leaves us with ruminations and worries about what could have been in the past and about what is yet to come.[2]

Even though you don't have to worry about attacks from lions or tigers (unless you work in a zoo), your brain and body carry the heritage of these old fears. Emotional reactions come from the limbic system, sometimes called the "reptilian brain" or "emotional brain." When this part of your brain registers situations as threatening, your stress response fires up. The limbic system is a complex set of brain structures (including the amygdala, hypothalamus, and hippocampus) buried beneath the prefrontal cortex on top of the brain stem. It's responsible for the formation of memories and emotions related to survival, such as anxiety, fear, and anger.

When you're in workaholic mode, threatening situations like tight deadlines, having to make a complicated presentation at work, relentless pressure from a difficult boss, racing against the clock, threat of job loss or unemployment, and intrusive electronic devices—all activate your fight-or-flight response. Your hypothalamus acts as a thermostat for your limbic system, controlling balance in such bodily functions as hunger, thirst, sex, and response to pain.

This primitive mechanism sends emergency instructions to the rest of your body through one arm of your autonomic nervous system—the sympathetic nervous system (SNS)—squirting out a neurophysiological cocktail of adrenaline and cortisol. These messages cause your SNS to amp up sweating, heart rate, blood pressure, and breathing; it tenses muscles and slows digestion, priming your body for action against the threat. Under the workaholic gun for prolonged periods of time, your inner alarm system stays on alert mode, raising your risk of heart disease, type 2 diabetes, chronic pain, and a compromised immune system. Even if you're not a workaholic, you might be working like one. Studies show that 40 percent of all workers today feel overworked, pressured, and squeezed to the point of anxiety, depression, and disease.[3]

THE AMYGDALA: GETTING IN TOUCH WITH YOUR INNER REPTILE

Whether you're a workaholic or not, work stress can cause you to rant and rave, freeze in fear, or try to escape. Your brain's reaction in the present is often driven by past events that are no longer deadly or unsafe. In other words, your workaholic brain and body overreact to small things that create unnecessary and unpleasant stress in the present moment—all in an effort to keep you safe.

Here's how that works. Imagine peeking inside your own brain from a side view (see figure 9.1). The limbic system, or "reptilian brain," houses old hurts from the past. Current events that echo ancient hurts can trigger reactions from the past, activating memories of earlier situations buried deep within your reptilian brain that angered, hurt, or scared you.

In the center of your limbic system resides a tiny, almond-shaped gland called the amygdala. This gland contains a library of old feelings linked with past events that protects you from harm. Your amygdala senses present threats

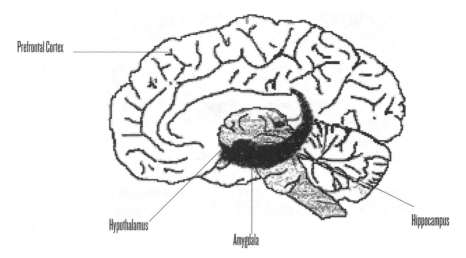

Figure 9.1. Drawing of a side view of the human brain

similar to those already recorded by the reptilian brain, and it kicks into survival mode to defend you. When your buttons get pushed, you can feel the moment when your amygdala dumps a tonic of enzymes into your bloodstream that makes your heart pound. Like a tidal wave, the surge of adrenaline and cortisol hijacks your thoughts and leaves your emotions in control. How stressed out are you? To find out your "stress age," you can take the quiz called "How Stressed Are You?" on my website (www.bryanrobinsononline.com), click "show results," and view your score in seconds.

Dousing Your Inner Firestorm

See if you can recall an unpleasant or traumatic situation that you experienced early in life. Then make two columns labeled "present" and "past." In the "present" column, jot down what situations make you sizzle today because of your past. Then jot down the past experience in the second column. What does your blueprint from the past tell you about what is written in the library housed in your amygdala? And what role, if any, do you think your amygdala might have played in these episodes? George's amygdala blueprint said he wasn't good enough, that he had to exceed the standards of others. So he constantly tried to prove himself in the present at school, at work, and even at play, outpacing others in grocery lines or jockeying for seats at sporting events —while simultaneously sacrificing his mental well-being and relationships with loved ones.

The Big Chill: Rewiring Your Brain to Stay Cool under Pressure

Over time, your brain's perceptions of threats in your self-imposed workaholic demands and deadlines can result in chronic mental and physical problems. Whether you're a harried parent, driven business person, or worried retiree coping with an uncertain future, eventually these stressors catch up with you. They force your brain to adapt negatively to them as only it can. But there's good news. This same process of negative adaption can be used to heal as well as harm. Did you know that you can reengineer your brain to calm your knee-jerk reactions? Sound like frontier science fiction? Hold on. I can see you rolling your eyes, but don't defriend me yet. Your brain is prewired to be pliable, just like a cut on your hand prompts your body to produce new, healthy skin.

Neuroplasticity

An innate ability called *neuroplasticity* allows you to use your mind to rewire the structure and functioning of your brain, no matter how old you are. Your brain has the ability to change its own structure as a result of your taking different actions in response to changing circumstances, as I explained with George at the beginning of this chapter.

Scientists at the National Institutes of Mental Health report that your brain has the ability to change its wiring and grow new neural connections through regular practice and repetition of tasks.[4] In other words, you can create a healthier brain by bringing balance to old workaholic habits. The new practices reshape nerve cells and change the way your brain works.[5] For workaholics, a rewiring could happen by intentionally activating your parasympathetic nervous system (PNS)—the second branch of your autonomic nervous system—with relaxing and calming activities. Examples are meditation, yoga, relaxation responses, tai chi, Qi-gong, deep breathing, and various mindfulness techniques that I discuss in the next chapter. Some experts go so far as to say it would take less than two months for you to alter your neural functioning.[6] Other examples of rewiring your workaholic brain include intentionally slowing down your work pace, rearranging your life's priorities, paying more attention to loved ones whom you've ignored, or spending time doing fun things you've never done before.

Remember that old saying, "whatever fires together, wires together"? By taking a different tack from your old workaholic patterns (such as getting home for dinner at six o'clock as promised, instead of working until nine), you can wire more positive work habits with healthier actions and get calmer as a result. With some dedication to intentionally changing your old habits, you can change the way your brain is firing in the moment. So when you do something different, the firing of neural pathways wires the different approach and its outcome. After practicing them regularly, you'll find that relaxation, spontaneity, and balance start to feel as comfortable as an old pair of faded jeans.

Activating Your Parasympathetic Nervous System

As I mentioned earlier, your autonomic nervous system (ANS) plays a starring role in your mental work life when it is engaged by your hypothalamus (see figure 9.1). Usually, you're not aware of your ANS except when your workaholic mode stresses you out and your ANS revs up your body functions. Your ANS is composed of two parts (see figure 9.2): (1) The *sympathetic nervous*

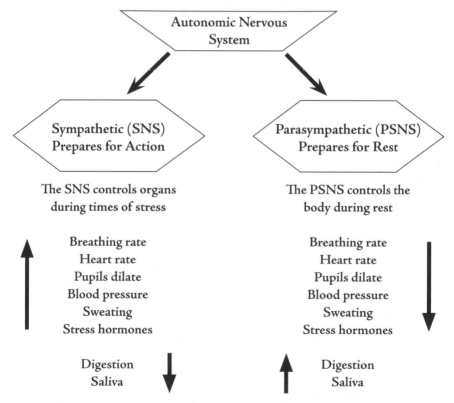

Figure 9.2. Two branches of your autonomic nervous system. Reprinted from Elaine Miller-Karas and Laurie Leitch, *Trauma Resiliency Model Level 2 Training Manual* (Claremont, CA: Trauma Resource Institute, 2012). Used with the permission of the authors.

Your Decision-Fatigued Brain

When you make decisions after working days on end, chances are they'll be different from the ones you'd make after your brain has had a rest period. Why? Scientists have discovered a phenomenon known as DECISION FATIGUE—which is what happens when your brain is worn out, depleted of mental energy.[7] Decision fatigue is why many workaholics have no mental energy left over for activities outside of work.

After hours of nonstop working, you have a problem: your brain gets fatigued. The longer you work and the more choices you make in those extended work hours, the more difficult it is for your strained mind to make decisions. It becomes hard to make even ordinary decisions, such as what to wear, where to eat, how much to spend, or how to prioritize work projects. So you start to take short cuts, permitting your newly licensed teenager to drive the car on an icy night or opting out of responsibilities and decision making at home. You're short with coworkers and loved ones; you eat junk food instead of healthy meals; you tell your spouse to pick what restaurant to go to.

The solution is to activate your rest and digest response. Your brain needs restorative rest just like your body does when you're tired. Ask yourself how much time you devote to your PNS to keep your mind and body in harmony. If you're like most workaholics, your answer would be "not enough." You can switch on your PNS instead of your SNS by engaging in certain activities such as brisk exercise, yawning, relaxing in nature, and power napping, and in practices such as deep breathing, progressive muscle relaxation, prayer, meditation, laughing, yoga, massage, and tai chi.[8]

system (SNS) is the gas—that part of your autonomic nervous system that functions in opposition to the parasympathetic nervous system by mobilizing your body's defense systems to induce your stress response for survival. (2) The *parasympathetic nervous system* (PNS) is the brakes—that part of your autonomic nervous system that functions in opposition to the sympathetic nervous system by calming your body's defense systems to induce your "rest and digest" response.

When you're under siege by hard-driving workaholic impulses, the SNS activates your body functions to help you deal with your "urgent tasks." Your parasympathetic nervous system (PNS) dampens down your body functions in nonemergencies, allowing you to relax. Although you need both systems, your SNS and PNS work in opposition to each other. Your SNS acts as the gas to help you meet deadlines, stand before your coworkers and make a challenging presentation, or compete with your peers for higher positions. To help you become productive and successful when facing stressful conditions, your SNS dilates your pupils, increases your heart rate, opens bronchial tubes in your lungs, and inhibits secretions in your digestive system. In contrast, your PNS acts as the brakes so that you can slow down, relax, and give your inner alarm system a break. It constricts your pupils, decreases your heart rate, constricts your bronchial tubes, and stimulates activity in your stomach and intestines.

SELF-REGULATION AND RECOVERY FROM WORKAHOLISM

Both systems are vital for life, and bringing a balance between the two is the holy grail of workaholic recovery. When workaholic behaviors cause your SNS to trump your PNS to the point where your mental and physical health are at stake, you can activate your "rest and digest" response. In recovery, workaholics learn balance and self-regulation, are more attuned to themselves, and see work as simply a necessary and sometimes fulfilling obligation. Self-attunement activates your PNS, creating a soothing, calmer approach to work tasks and giving you greater satisfaction and joy on the job.

Brain scans demonstrate that contemplation of nature, meditating, and praying activate your brain's frontal lobes (behind your forehead) and reduce activity in the parietal lobes (at the top rear of your head). These changes heighten your body's production of dopamine (a neurotransmitter released in the brain that creates euphoria and a sense of well-being) and dampen the production of epinephrine (a hormone associated with stress). Neuroscientists say these neurological changes create a feeling of calm, unity, and transcendence—a feeling of unification with God or heightened consciousness.[9]

THE PENDULUM

The pendulum here refers to the natural swing of your nervous system between sensations of well-being and stress or tension. The following exercise brings attention to the presence of natural relaxation that can get eclipsed by workaholism.

With your eyes closed, notice a place in your body where you feel stress. It can show up as pain, tension, an ache, or a sense of constriction. Then swing your attention to a place inside where you feel less stress or no stress. Focus there on the absence of stress, noticing your bodily sensations: steady heartbeat, slowed breathing, warm skin, softened jaw, relaxed muscles. Remain focused there and note the sensation. Then imagine that sensation spreading to other parts of your body.

Now shift back to the place where you originally felt stress. If the tension has decreased, focus on the reduction of tension for a minute or so. Continue moving your attention back and forth between what is left of the tension and the places in your body where you feel comfortable or relaxed. As you shift from one to the other, note where the tension is lessening and spend some time paying attention to the lessening so that it can spread to other parts of your body. If you notice that you feel calmer and more peaceful, you have just activated your parasympathetic nervous system.

BUILDING AN INNER RESOURCE

When you're under pressure, it helps to have a resource that you can use to lower stress from the urge to work. A resource is anything that helps you feel better by activating your parasympathetic nervous system. It can be something you like about yourself, a positive memory or experience, person, place, pet, spiritual guide, or anything that gives you comfort, joy, or serenity. You simply bring that resource to mind, along with all the details that make that resource sustain or nurture you. One of my resources is the memory of sipping morning coffee on the screened porch of a rented beach house, watching a shrimp boat—with sea gulls swooping over the bow—putter across the backdrop of a huge red-ball sunrise.

Now as you describe the details of your resource to yourself, direct your attention to your internal sensory experiences and notice what's happening within you. Note where in your body you feel the sensations that are pleasing to you. Pay attention to what is happening inside you. Notice your breathing, heart rate, and muscle tension. Bring your awareness to the changes and notice, for example, that your breathing might be slowing down or your muscles relaxing. Spend some time underscoring whatever is changing. As you end the exercise, bring your attention to your whole body and notice all the changes that have occurred since you focused on your safe harbor. Stay with that change for a few moments.

Beef Up Your Prefrontal Cortex and Your State of Mind

Your prefrontal cortex is the part of the brain located behind your forehead in the frontal lobes. It is responsible for executive functions that allow you to reason logically, predict outcomes, judge right from wrong, and think rationally and abstractly.

Neuroimaging techniques show that stress diminishes activity in your prefrontal cortex and that long-term work stress can damage neurons, shrink areas of your brain, and impair thinking.[10] But if you want to be more alert, kinder, and more productive at work, you're in luck. Brain scans at Harvard University and the University of California at Los Angeles show that through the regular practice of meditation, you can minimize brain shrinkage and cognitive decline and build thicker neural tissues in the prefrontal cortex.[11] Once beefed up, your gray matter sharpens your attention, amps up your immune system, neutralizes the amygdala's hot-headed reactions, heightens your compassion, and shifts you into a calmer, kinder state of mind.

REWIND THE MINI-MOVIES PLAYING IN YOUR HEAD

The authors of the book *Buddha's Brain*, describe what they call "mini-movies" that play in your head.[12] Think of your brain as a simulator that is constantly running mini-movies—brief clips that are the building blocks of conscious mental activity. These mini-movies of past or future events at one time wired you for survival because through repeated neural firing patterns your brain strengthened your learning of successful behaviors.

Today, because of your genetic heritage, your brain continues to produce short movie clips that have nothing to do with survival or with what's happening in the present. But even if you know that, it's easy to get caught up in the movie's story line and stress yourself out in the heat of the moment. During work, the movie clips can pull you out of the present and create stressful thoughts and feelings. The movie might take you a thousand miles away, where you fret about a lost account, agonize about an unreachable work goal, or rehearse for a challenging presentation at work. Your mini-movies can become bars on an invisible cage that trap you in a life smaller than the one you could actually have—much like a tiger released into a large zoo park that continues to crouch as if it's still confined in its old pen. You have the power to create a horror movie or a musical comedy in your head. The choice is yours!

Overriding Your Old Brain's Threats

When you're frazzled from overworking, you can avoid urgent, impatient action and cool down your amygdala by using your executive function to challenge perceived threats. Here are some examples of how to do that:

❖ Try to see the upside of downside situations—to see the roses instead of the thorns: "I have to pay more taxes this year than ever before" becomes "I made more money this year than I've ever made."

✧ Be adventurous and take small risks in new situations instead of predicting negative outcomes without sticking your neck out: "I won't go to the office party, because I'm afraid I won't know anyone" becomes "If I go to the office party, I might have a chance to meet new coworkers."

✧ Make an effort to focus on the good news wrapped around bad news: "The flu made me miss the chance to shine in the presentation at work" becomes "I missed the presentation but I've recovered now, and the colleague to whom I delegated the task landed the account for the firm."

✧ Avoid blowing things out of proportion and letting one negative experience rule your whole life pattern: "I didn't get the promotion, so now I'll never reach my career goals" becomes "I didn't get the promotion, but there are many more steps I can take to reach my career goals."

TAKING A BIRD'S-EYE VIEW

Another way to change your brain's wiring is to get in the habit of engaging your prefrontal cortex when workaholism blindsides you. Your prefrontal cortex gives you the capacity to take a breath, step back, and regain the perspective of an outsider in the midst of threats.

Next time you're pressed, go inside yourself and focus on your inner experience. Acknowledge and listen to your feelings. Then ask, "What am I feeling in my body right now? What are the feelings telling me? If my heart wasn't slamming against my chest, what would I do right now?" When in response to pressure you engage the executive function of your prefrontal cortex, it's easier to separate from automatic limbic reactions, stay cool, and make smart decisions.

When I realize that my limbic system is activated, I check in with myself and ask if I'm angry, upset, or worried. I acknowledge those feelings as parts of myself. Then I have a dialogue with those feelings: "I know you're upset. How can I help?" This gives me immediate separation from the reactions, throws the switch in the executive function of my brain, and enables me to act instead of react.

THE PRINCIPLE OF CHOICE

The psychologist Viktor Frankl once said: "Between stimulus and response there is a space. In that space is our power to choose our response. In our response lies our growth and our freedom."[13] Frankl made these wise remarks years before we knew anything about neuroplasticity. But he was describing a strategy to activate the prefrontal cortex to keep you from going into orbit. I often use this strategy as a means to trump the amygdala, using the acronym WAIT:

Watch for activated parts of you that are triggered by workaholic thoughts or situations. Once you notice the activation, you're in that awareness space.

Avoid your usual reaction and imagine stepping back and taking a breath on the inside.

Invite your activated response to relax so that you can choose your response by acting instead of reacting.

Turn each workaholic stimulus into an opportunity to act until you create new neural pathways that undo old workaholic habits. You'll feel calmer and more empowered in your work and personal life.

Tips for Clinicians

By now you might be dehydrated, because the brain can be a pretty dry subject. But there are many clinical approaches you can take to help workaholics understand the neuroscientific risks of what's happening to their nervous systems and what they can do to reduce those risks.

PSYCHOEDUCATION

I recommend that you encourage workaholic clients to read about neuroplastic transformation and how they can reregulate their own nervous systems. Bibliotherapy helps workaholics gain an understanding of what happens when they overload themselves with work projects, multitask, shackle themselves to electronic devices, or bite off more work tasks than they can complete. You can help them understand the consequences when their limbic system reacts to workaholic stress as if they are in physical danger. After a while, the sympathetic nervous system stays on for an inordinate amount of time and the body becomes unable to tolerate down times. So it's very difficult for workaholics to relax and have a normal life. Consequently, they are drenched in the adrenaline and cortisol cocktail that I discussed earlier, which causes multiple health problems and truncates the trajectory of their work careers. Check out the appendix for resources you can use to demonstrate to workaholics how they can self-regulate, calm their nervous systems, and find their work resilient zone (see chapter 11).

SELF-REGULATION ACTIVITIES

You can share activities with workaholic clients that activate the parasympathetic nervous system, many of which I described earlier in this chapter. Over time, these practices have an automatic effect of regulating the stress response. You can remind your clients of the importance of calming the mind and body so as to put the brakes on the sympathetic nervous sytem. You can also cite the latest findings in neuroscience and how they demonstrate that the basics (exercise, sleep, and good nutrition) never go out of style. For example, new research shows that under prolonged stress such as a workaholic lifestyle, the brain loses its self-regulating capacity. Overloaded with work stress, the human brain becomes dysregulated, and brain cells shrivel up and die. But because of the brain's plasticity, exercise can switch on certain genes that pump up the brain's level of galanin—a peptide neurotransmitter that tones down the body's stress response by regulating the brain chemical norepinephrine (or adrenaline). In other words, exercise, in effect, protects brain cells from being destroyed by stressful overwork.[14]

ENCOURAGE CLIENTS TO "WATCH" THEIR INNER WORKINGS

Most workaholics approach work as if they're under threat, as if something bad might happen when they're not chained to the desk, even when there's no reason to be. Remind clients that the limbic system is designed to exaggerate their fears and worries for their protection. Encourage them to get curious and see if they can gain more clarity about why they're on red alert for no good reason. To help them get underneath the red alert, suggest that they ask themselves questions like, "What am I afraid of?" (they probably fear not being good enough or being ineffective), "What are the chances of that really happening?," and "What is the worst thing that could happen?"

Then have them call on their brain's curiosity, instead of their self-judgment, as the gateway to clarity and calm. This approach keeps them from attacking themselves and makes it easier for them to see what's really going on. In addition, it kicks in the executive function, creating an impartial and bird's-eye view of their out-of-control work patterns and self-created, stressful work situations. Once they heighten their awareness, you can suggest the acronym, WAIT, as a maintenance tool.

10

Mindful Working

When we pause, allow a gap and breathe deeply, we can experience instant refreshment. Suddenly we slow down, look out, and there's the world. It can feel like briefly standing in the eye of the tornado or the still point of a turning wheel.

—Pema Chodrin

Cooper

In March of 2011, just after my forty-seventh birthday, I was driving to the office as early as I could get on the road. I'd made it my habit to get to the office before anyone else so I could "get ahead of the game" and organize my next accomplishment. During the drive there wasn't anything specific causing stress in my mind—no major project looming or big meeting I was preparing. Halfway through my short twenty-two-minute drive I began experiencing a rapid heart rate, extreme chest pain, and a panicky feeling—*something* was wrong. While driving I used my cell phone to call my primary care physician and made an appointment for that afternoon. I kept going and arrived in my office drenched in perspiration and shaken.

By the time I arrived at my doctor's office that afternoon, my pulse, heart rate, and blood pressure were spiking off the charts, and my head felt like it was ready to explode. I could tell by the look on the doctor's face that he was concerned for my safety. After checking my vital signs he quickly asked his nurse to call 911. I was taken in an ambulance to a hospital emergency room and monitored for signs of a heart attack.

This health crisis was a surreal experience, but it didn't end that afternoon.

After nothing clinically significant was found during my brief hospital stay, a few days later I drove myself to a local emergency room at the urging of my cardiologist during another bout of racing heart rate and high blood pressure. An angiogram was scheduled to assess the health of my heart and cardiac vessels. Three days later testing showed no blockage. This time I left the hospital with a renewed appreciation for my mortality and my responsibility to my three children and wife, Tiffany. Something had to change.

The expense of several days of hospitalization, disruption for my family, and the worry I caused everyone was a wake-up call. The realization that I had lost a week's worth of productivity was equally devastating to me at that time. My compulsive work habits, feverish attention to details, and nonstop thinking about how to get the most out of my work day was not serving me, my family, or the firm.

I began slowly altering how I spent my time. I forced myself to leave the office at six o'clock. I planned a few more activities with the kids and started to adjust my outlook. But about ten to twelve months into this renewed focus on a more family-friendly schedule, I began to experience low- grade melancholy. I became indifferent to my work projects. I had trouble concentrating, plus getting out of bed in the morning was sometimes difficult. The reality of my lifestyle and the chemical nature of it was becoming a factor in my daily routines. For the first time in my life I woke up to the fact that I had no hobbies, few leisure- time pursuits, only one or two good friends, and limited memory of anything beyond the last work conquest. I had known this deep sense of foreboding only one other time, when I had back surgery early in my twenties, just having graduated college and landed my first real career job. But this time there was no physical injury; my body was fine, but my spirit was broken. And I was confused.

Reading *Chained to the Desk* opened my eyes to the addictive power of the adrenaline I experienced from working too much. Now as I altered my routine, I started coming off the constant happy hits of adrenaline. My psychological addiction to that chemical fix of overwork was finally unmasked. I had another turning point at 30,000 feet aboard an airplane reading through the Twelve Steps. I began to consider that I was facing something that required more than a quick fix or a simple change of heart. This was life altering and needed my full attention. As I wept in my seat, alone and emotionally and mentally exhausted, I made a commitment to do something I never had done in my adult life: give up control.

In the middle of it all I recognized that previous managers, colleagues, work teams, and whole organizations were coconspirators in creating my overworked mind and addicted body. In all candor, the earliest drivers of my "disease" came to me as I began recognizing that while my dad had done what he thought best, the lack of validation, restricted range of emotion, and the role modeling that one's capacity to work was the most critical definition of self was at the heart of my behaviors. I'm certain his father had operated in the same fashion, without ever realizing that it produced a reliable workhorse who was shut down emotionally and largely unavailable to others or himself.

I have a carefully crafted career, strong earning power, the respect of colleagues, and a legacy of accomplishments and contributions to the organizations I've served. But in stepping back I recognize that throughout my adult life I consistently neglected nurturing my own needs, that I frequently worked to obtain the acknowledgment of others when what I needed was time spent with my dad in my formative years. My faith in God, the recognition that I am enough without having to prove it through work, and the opportunity to love my children in the most wholesome way are what motivate me today. There is a knife-edge boundary between healthy work and workaholism. And I fight to stay on the right side each day.

As I work to express my emotions more fully I feel an enormous influx of energy and youthfulness. While I have one year before I turn fifty, releasing myself from this shame and disconnection has unleashed an ocean of confidence and exuberance—not aimed at more work but rather at experiencing the many blessings of those little moments with my young kids that will make a lifetime of memories. I caught this vision of what can be just in time, and I plan to enjoy every minute of my new lease on life.

Are You Out of Your Present Mind?

Cooper's story of rushing to the office to "get ahead of the game" is a typical example of what I call "mindless working." Workaholics are in fast-forward speed much of the time, trying to get to the good stuff—heading for the nirvana of pleasure and skipping over what's happening now. You know what I mean. You have to get through the traffic jam to your appointment instead of *being* in the traffic jam. You have to hop in and out of the shower to get to work instead of *being* in the shower. You have to rush through lunch so you can complete the project on your desk instead of *being* present with each bite. The workaholic habit of mindless working often leads to heart or other physical problems.

Is your mind like Grand Central Station, with so many thoughts coming and going that you don't have a chance to pause and catch your breath? Do you frantically work on projects, focused on the next item on the agenda without regard to what it's doing to you mentally and physically? Are you worried about whether the boss will like the finished product or thinking about what you'll be doing this weekend? These out-of-the-moment episodes create loads of stress and disconnect you from yourself and your surroundings. Before you know it, you're mired in your own stress juices.

Your mind could be wandering right now. You could be thinking about what you ate for lunch and what you "should" have eaten. You could be worried about unpaid bills or about an unfinished project, wondering how you'll meet the deadline. Or you might be replaying in your head an argument you had with your spouse. When your mind wanders too much, it could be stressing you out or at the very least preventing you from actualizing your full potential at work.

WHEN YOU STRAY, YOU PAY

Harvard University researchers have found that the human mind wanders 47 percent of the time, and that when you stray, you pay. When your mind wanders, you're more stressed out and unhappy than when you stay in the here and now. The Harvard researchers found that people were happier—no matter what they were doing, even working overtime, vacuuming the house, or sitting in traffic—if they were focused on the activity instead of thinking about something else.[1]

I have referred to these out-of-the moment episodes as brownouts—tuning out the here and now, memory lapses during conversations, or momentary forgetfulness because you're out of your present mind.[2] But you don't have to let a mental fog eclipse your self-attunement, submerging you in your own stress juices. Your presence of mind gives you the power to flip the pattern around, landing you in the driver's seat, putting you back in charge. When you pay attention and fully engage in each moment, you discover your daily world in a completely different way. And your life takes on a fresh glow. That's what this chapter is about: how to work mindfully and productively in an alert, active, calm manner.

HOW YOU USE YOUR MIND AT WORK MAKES A DIFFERENCE

Scientists say that the way you use your mind can determine how much work stress or work productivity you have. Keeping your focus on the present instead of ruminating about what already happened (which you can't change anyway) or about what might happen (which you can't control anyway) keeps your stress level down, makes you more effective at work, and makes for a happier life. When you get swallowed up by job pressures or career disillusionments, you end up paying the price at some point. If you're like most people, you have to work—whether you're caught in the drudgery of a dead-end job, worrying about losing your job, trying to turn a passion into a career, or supporting a family by whatever means necessary. Given that reality, it's common that workaholics don't do more to improve their working lives.

Although you've probably heard the adage "work smarter, not longer," it's not easy to translate that philosophy into everyday work schedules. But that's what mindful working can help you do: bridge that gap. Burgeoning evidence-based studies from the medical, psychotherapeutic, and scientific communities have demonstrated that a mindful approach to work has dramatic pay-offs for employees, the workplace, and corporate America. As a result, companies such as Google, Yahoo, Time Warner, and Apple, as well as the US military, have begun to integrate mindfulness principles into the training of their workers. For example, a Google engineer designed a mindfulness course called "Search inside Yourself" to enrich and maximize the work productivity and personal fulfillment of Google's employees, giving them a better way of coping with work stress.[3]

What Is Mindfulness?

Mindfulness, once considered an occult Eastern spiritual practice, has achieved respectability in the United States as a viable clinical technique. Jon Kabat-Zinn's evidence-based research program called mindfulness-based stress reduction at the University of Massachusetts Medical Center has brought mindfulness into mainstream treatment, and it has special significance for treating workaholism.[4]

Mindfulness is not a religion; it's an ancient practice that modern science has revived to bring about change in our lives from the inside out. It's the ability to pay compassionate, nonjudgmental attention to what you're thinking and feeling and to what's happening inside your body and around you in the present moment. As you practice this technique, you train your mind to do what it doesn't do instinctively: to come back to the present, to enjoy the moment, and to appreciate your life instead of focusing on survival worries ("What if I get laid off?" or "Can I measure up?"). With practice, mindfulness gets you to a state where your mind is relaxed and alert at the same time.[5] A growing body of scientific evidence attests to the link between mindfulness and well-being.[6]

Practicing Mindfulness Exercises

Mindfulness practices aren't as easy as I make them sound, but they're not all that difficult either. Even though you're not aware of it, you're judging yourself

Sidestepping Your Mental Fogs

Mindfulness techniques are powerful antidotes for dodging mental fogs. In four simple steps, you can harness the social circuitry of your brain, enabling you to be attuned to your own mind:

1. Keep your focus in the present moment.

2. Move at a steady, calm pace.

3. Be attuned to yourself and your surroundings.

4. Accept without judgment whatever you're aware of that arises in each moment.

Kayakers say the best way to escape when you're trapped in a hydraulic—a turbulent, funnel-shaped current—is to relax, and it will spit you out. But the natural tendency is to fight against the current. And that can keep you stuck, even drown you. Similarly, the way to get unstuck from a torrent of survival thoughts streaming through your mind is to welcome them and watch them with curiosity. Let them come and go without personalizing, judging, resisting, or identifying with them. And eventually they will float away.

and your experience of others much of the time. And your mind might be miles away from your body, caught up in streams of survival thoughts about future or past judgments.

Take time right now to notice your thoughts. In a relaxed position, put yourself fully into the present moment. Try watching the thoughts streaming through your mind with a nonjudgmental attitude. You don't have to do anything but pay attention to them. Don't try to change or fix them. Just be aware of them. Are the thoughts centered on the future or the past, or are they focused in the present? Are they calm and serene, or worried and anxious? You'll probably notice that they're preparing you to react to situations with more stress than necessary. Or they might be replaying a negative situation that you could have handled differently. This type of paying attention to your mind is an example of mindful awareness.

Now let's do another exercise that takes your attention to your body:

❖ Turn your attention to your fingers and focus there for a minute.

❖ Wiggle your fingers and notice how this sensory experience feels. Focus on how the wiggling looks and sounds. Do you hear any crackling in your joints or sounds of skin against skin? What else are you aware of?

❖ Notice if you judge yourself or the exercise, or if you have trouble staying focused.

❖ Now ask youself if this exercise gave you an immediate connection to the present moment. Or did your judgment interfere with your being fully engaged? If you were fully engaged during the exercise, you might have noticed that previous worries or stressful thoughts were absent.

Mindful Working: Rx for Workaholism

Most solutions to job stress, workaholism, and workplace problems impose change from the outside in. Sometimes this works, but more often it doesn't. When applied to work addiction, the practice of mindfulness brings about change from the inside out, regardless of workplace circumstances or the nature of job problems. I call this simple solution to an epidemic problem facing the American workforce *mindful working*—the intentional, moment-to-moment awareness of what's happening inside you and immediately around you accompanied by self-attuned, compassionate interest during your daily work schedules and routines.[7]

When you're working mindfully, you keep your attention on the stream of the process, instead of just focusing on completion of the task. You're able to bring curious, nonjudgmental attention to your work and notice moment-to-moment body sensations, mental processes, and feelings that arise while you're working or thinking about your job during the best of times and the worst of times. In addition, you master schedules, difficult work relationships, and new technologies instead of becoming slaves to them. Instead of beating yourself up when things fall apart, you can use self-compassionate attunement to ease yourself through work stress, business failures, job loss, or worry and anxiety about career goals.

MINDLESS WORKING AND SURVIVAL SUFFERING

In a given day, how many people do you notice (yourself included) who drive while texting, stroll in the park on a beautiful day with a cell phone glued to their ear, or simultaneously eat lunch, type a memo, and talk on the phone? We have become a nation of multitaskers, blind to the present moment. As long as the workday continues to invade personal time, life becomes an endless series of intrusions that can swallow you up, disconnecting you from yourself and others. If you don't take time for self-reflection, it's easy to get caught in a race that leaves you hurried and harried.

If you're like most workaholics, you're engaged in mindless working—toiling around the clock at a survival level. Your mind creates stress even when none is really present for one reason: survival. When your body perceives a threat, worry causes you to respond as though the threat is real even when it's just imaginary.

Stress or depression over a downturn in the economy, loss of a promotion, a faltering relationship with a boss or colleague, or fear of an upcoming job challenge creates survival suffering (or high arousal in your nervous system). When you're in survival suffering, you're working mindlessly. You lose your attunement, and your mind begins to use you. Your worry and stress feed dread and uncertainty. Then your mind imagines the worst (for example, "I'll probably fall flat on my face"), and the worry and dread become the real problem, eclipsing the original situation. You become hijacked by the internal suffering—a magnification of the original problem. When you practice mindful working, you use present-moment awareness to flip the survival suffering around. Then you calmly navigate workplace woes with clarity, self-compassion, courage, and creativity. And you're more efficient and productive at work.

SELF-REGULATION AND MINDFUL RECOVERY

If you're an active workaholic, chances are that you're disconnected from yourself, and you view working as a place safe from life's threats and challenges. Faced with such "reptilian threats" as tight deadlines, a challenging presentation at work, relentless pressures from a difficult boss, threat of job loss or unemployment—all activate your fight-or-flight response. You'll remember in Cooper's story that this primitive mechanism pumped out a flood of adrenaline and cortisol, priming his body for action. These stress hormones raise your heart and respiration rates, tense your muscles, and slow your digestion. As I mentioned in the previous chapter, constant workaholic pressures cause your inner alarm system to stay on alert mode, raising the risk of high blood pressure, heart attack, type 2 diabetes, chronic pain, and a lowered immune system. In Cooper's case, his body was experiencing panic even though he wasn't consciously aware of any stress, an example of mindless working.

In mindful recovery, you learn balance and self-regulation. You keep close watch on your personal life, moving at a reasonable pace and staying attuned to your inner world and your interactions with others in an alert, compassionate way. Your self-attunement activates the parasympathetic nervous system, creating a soothing, calmer approach to work tasks. Chances are that if you're a workaholic, you're usually on autopilot, allowing work tasks to dominate every aspect of your life.

Mindful working gives you present-moment awareness of your thoughts, emotions, and what you're feeling in your body as you navigate the workday. You know when to close your laptop, mentally switch gears, and be fully present in the moment—when your teenager agonizes over her first crush or your partner or spouse reflects on the details of the day.

When you work mindfully, you can turn off your work appetite and pay attention to your surroundings. But your insatiable workaholic appetite occludes your awareness of yourself, others, and your physical surroundings. You're preoccupied with work no matter where you are—walking hand in hand at the seashore or hiking with a friend. Family and friends, or any kind of inner awareness, are little more than a vague, if pleasant, backdrop. But when you work mindfully, you're as emotionally present in off-work times as you are during work hours. In contrast, the relationship with work is the central connection of the workaholic's life, the place where life really takes place, the secret repository of drama and emotion, as compelling as the place other addicts experience with booze or cocaine.

In mindful recovery, you appreciate the wonderful mystery of being alive without the need for work highs or numbing yourself with multitasking and busyness. Jon Kabat-Zinn describes the advantages of that inner mindful connection: "Mindfulness provides a simple but powerful route for getting ourselves unstuck, back in touch with our own wisdom and vitality. It is a way to take charge of the direction and quality of our own lives, including our relationships within the family, our relationship to work and to the larger world and planet, and most fundamentally, our relationship with ourself as a person."[8]

The Pause That Refreshes

Scientists have discovered that the way to reclaim your work life and personal life is through mindfulness. People who meditate have less stress, fewer health problems, improved relationships, and longer lives.[9]

Some people get so used to living with stress and chaos that it becomes a habit, and they add stress to their lives even when they don't mean to. Does that sound like you? Ask yourself how often you race through the day without pausing to consider who you really want to be. Mindful investment of your energy, not time management, is the key to work happiness and success. Experts argue that you can manage your energy by taking breaks, getting ample sleep, paying attention to who you are, what you're doing, and where you're going from moment to moment. These actions create optimal work conditions, high performance, health, work success, and personal renewal.[10]

HITTING YOUR PAUSE BUTTON

If performance energy or lack of it begins on the inside, doesn't it make sense that to harness it you would start there, too? To begin this process, look inside where your performance energy resides—inside your skin, where you live, think, and feel. Start by considering the ways you can slow down the pace and rhythm of your life, bringing gentle awareness to your thoughts and feelings. Treat yourself with kindness on the inside instead of cracking the whip. Think about whether you're master or slave to your crammed schedules and electronic devices. Set aside times to eat slower instead of what one mindfulness expert called "the three G's": "gobble, gulp, and go."[11] And avoid eating while standing, walking, driving, working, or otherwise being on the run.

To create mindful conditions at work, say no to new projects when you're already overcommitted. Or you might give yourself time cushions when setting important deadlines and do just one activity at a time, devoting your conscious attention to it. You might delegate work tasks (if you are in a position to do so) or prioritize them, eliminating or setting aside for now those that are the least important or unnecessary. Or you might give yourself extra driving time to arrive at your destination and extra time between appointments so you can have a conversation with a colleague. The examples are endless, and you'll have to tailor your strategies to the unique rhythm and style of your job and personal life.

KEEP A MINDFUL WORK DIARY

A mindful work diary can help you document progress in using your mind instead of letting it use you. You can record your success in avoiding the workaholic highs and lows and become more mindful of your unwitting work habits and the perspective you have on your job. A work diary can help you pinpoint situations that detour you from a mindful approach to work. It can trigger changes you'd like to make in dealing with work challenges and become more efficient and satisfied in your job. The diary becomes a road map of your journey from mindless to mindful working as you apply the practices in this chapter and describe the outcomes.

According to Thich Nhat Hanh, the mindfulness with which we walk the line between a turbulent work world and our inner steadiness determines our happiness: "When we are able to take one step peacefully and happily, we are working for the cause of peace and happiness for the whole of humankind. . . . We can do it only if we do not think of the future or the past, if we know that life can only be found in the present moment."[12]

Types of Mindfulness Practices

You can practice mindfulness in several different ways and to varying degrees. If you have the time, dedication, and interest, you can practice *focused attention mindfulness meditation*. You set aside time in the day to sit down in a quiet place and focus your attention on your breathing, a mantra, or another object of concentration. The equivalent in building an exercise regimen would be working out on a StairMaster for twenty minutes a day or going to the gym for an aerobics class three times a week. The appendix has extensive resources for you to learn how to practice focused attention meditation.

If you want to go hog wild, you can attend an intensive event at a mindfulness workshop or retreat center. Mindfulness intensives are held in a specific place with a group of people, often in silence, for an extended period of time. The exercise equivalent would be biking in the Tuscan countryside for a week or going to a weight-loss spa for several days. There are many excellent retreat centers across the United States. The major ones are listed in the appendix.

But if meditation is new territory for you, a good entry into mindfulness is *open awareness meditation*. You can practice it with a minimum of time and dedication by simply being mindful during activities such as eating, cooking, walking, and working that are already built into your day.

OPEN AWARENESS DURING YOUR WORKDAY

You could even practice open awareness right now. As you read on, you might find your mind wandering from time to time. Just be aware of your wandering mind, accept that wandering, and gently bring your mind back to the words on the printed page. An open awareness exercise can be any brief activity that makes you aware of what's happening as it's happening in the flow of your daily routines. Earlier in this chapter, I gave you an open awareness exercise that asked you to be mindful of your thoughts. Then I gave you a second one that asked you to be aware of your hands. A third type of open awareness exercise takes you beyond yourself with moments of mindful awareness that pertain to any activity you're deliberately paying attention to in the present.

You intentionally walk with present-moment awareness by bringing your attention to the sensations of your feet against the ground, or by noting the feel of the air, sights, and sounds around you as you walk. When you weed the garden, you can pay attention to the plants' resistance against your hands as you tug on them, and the sound of stubborn roots and smells of fresh soil as you unearth the weeds from their home.

When you clean the toilet bowl, brush your teeth, drive your car, or cook a pot of soup, you can step out of your thought stream and make yourself fully present in the activity. While waiting in the doctor's office, you can practice mindful listening. In line at the grocery store, you might tune in to your body sensations. Stuck in traffic, you can practice mindful deep breathing.

You can do the following brief mindfulness exercises during your workday:

❖ Take off your socks and shoes and feel your toes in the carpet. Pay close attention to how the carpet feels against your feet. If you have an open window, focus on the sounds of chirping birds or inhale the fragrance of a flower.

❖ During lunch, sit down and give food your full attention, being present with each bite. Pause before starting a meal, noticing the colors and textures while inhaling the smells of the food. Eat your lunch slowly and deliberately. Chew food two or three more times than you usually do to taste it fully, paying attention to each ingredient and savoring each morsel. You will taste your food in a completely different way; for example, instead of tasting tuna salad, discover the flavor of celery as it crushes against your teeth, the bursting tartness of pickles, and the blending of the tuna and green lettuce. Take a sip of a beverage and be with the sensation against your tongue and stay with the felt sense as it slides down the back of your throat.

❖ After eating, stand and stretch your body. Let yourself fully feel the stretch, noticing where tension is held and released. Shake the part of your body where you sense tension. As you continue to stretch, bring your attention to each part of your body that has remained tightened. Bend over and touch your toes and feel that stretch, visualizing the tension in your body evaporating.

A MINDFUL WORKING EXERCISE

The following open awareness exercise can help you slow down and pay closer attention to your body, mind, and spirit during your workday:

The next time you go to your work site, imagine you have entered your workplace for the first time. Notice the entranceway, the architecture of the outside and inside of the building, and the people at their work stations. Look at your coworkers as if you've never seen them before, seeing and appreciating them with renewed interest. Notice what hangs on the walls and the textures and colors of the walls, ceiling, and floor. Smell the flowers on someone's desk. Be aware of how your colleagues are dressed and the colors of a blouse or jacket a colleague is wearing. Pay attention to who conforms to rules and who marches to the beat of their own drum. What sounds do you hear, and what smells (such as cologne or freshly brewed coffee from the break room) permeate the air?

Be mindful of your coworkers' faces. Look into the eyes of a business associate, subordinate, or boss. Then look beyond their facial expressions and into their hearts, where their true selves reside, noticing what's imprinted there. Do they look happy or sad? Ready to embrace the day or wishing they were back home in bed? Are they smiling or frowning? Who has wrinkles and worry lines, and whose face is stress-free? Do people in this work environment touch each other or keep their distance? Do they affirm one another or put each other down with sarcasm and cutting remarks? Are they pulling together as a team or working against one another, coming apart at the seams?

Notice what you're thinking and feeling as you mindfully examine your workplace. If you notice yourself making judgments, try not to judge yourself for judging. Instead, see if you can substitute curiosity and compassion for the people or situations you're judging. (I'll talk more about compassion in the next chapter).

Tips for Clinicians

If we clinicians were to read early Buddhist texts, we would be convinced that the Buddha was essentially a psychologist. So it's possible to practice Buddhist-derived meditation and ascribe its aspects to the psychological view of the mind while maintaining your own beliefs in other religious traditions.

The combination of brain science, mindfulness, and therapeutic techniques has become enormously popular and highly effective in twenty-first-century psychotherapy. This unique blend has been applied to many diverse problems, such as anxiety, depression, addictions, and bad eating and spending habits. Mindfulness techniques have relevance for workaholics, who seem especially vulnerable to the evolutionary pressures of working from the "reptilian brain." By using mindfulness techniques, you can help workaholics develop an internal locus of control that helps them feel more empowered over their internal and external work demands. Michael Yapko described the value of using mindfulness in psychotherapy: "It [mindfulness] teaches people that they can find resources inside themselves they didn't know they had and change their self-definition as a result."[13]

THE TURTLE WON THE RACE

By slowing down, workaholics can accomplish more and do a better job. In the process, they gain self-respect and admiration from coworkers. You can help clients make a conscious effort to slow down the pace of their daily lives by intentionally eating, talking, walking, and driving slower. You can help clients explore ways to prevent rushing by building time cushions between appointments and scheduling extra time to get to destinations.

As I discussed above, meditation is a highly effective way to slow down and feel calm. The purpose of meditation is to quiet the mind so that the individual can hear what is already there. Scientific research has shown that meditation slows down heart rates and changes brain-wave patterns. It has a positive effect on the immune system, increasing the production of certain life-sustaining hormones. You can suggest many types of meditation that help workaholics unwind from work highs and manage stress, including progressive relaxation exercises, yoga, quiet reflection, daily inspirational readings, prayer, and mindfulness meditation.[14]

LIVING IN THE PRESENT

Mindful working offers simple ways to avoid future-focused "survival working," in which workaholics are hurrying, rushing, and juggling too many projects with jangled nerves. For example, you might suggest that clients steer clear of "grabbing, gulping, and going"—eating while standing, driving, being on the run, or while watching TV. They could consider treating mealtime as a singular activity with value in its own right. Sitting down, eating slowly, and chewing a few extra times before swallowing, as well as appreciating the food's textures, aromas, and tastes, will help them relax and enjoy the meal as well as aid in digestion.

In clinical settings, we observe that when clients intentionally slow down certain body movements related to stress, the process brings up emotions, giving the nervous system time to reregulate itself, time to develop new habits so the parasympathetic nervous system can put the brakes on the sympathetic nervous system. This allows recovering workaholics to approach work demands in a calmer, more balanced, and relaxed way.

Another approach with workaholic clients is to help them become more aware of their preoccupation with the future to the exclusion of the present. In one exercise, clients come up with ways they can begin living in the now and resisting the mind's attempts to preoccupy them with tomorrow or next week. You might suggest that clients rediscover things in their world that they take for granted or ignore, and that they look at the people and things around them as if they are seeing and enjoying them for the first time. Here are examples of mindfulness exercises that you can use with clients to help them slow down instead of getting caught up in the work tornado:

❖ Try a mindful exercise during your morning shower. Pay attention to the sounds and feel of thousands of beads of splashing water popping against your skin. Hear the rushing sounds against your shower curtain and smacks of water against the tub. As you lather your body, be aware of the smell and feel of the slippery soap gliding over your naked skin, and the soap bubbles swelling and popping on your neck, arms, and chest. Notice how the water feels rolling down your body, the fresh fragrance of shampoo and its cleansing sensation against your scalp. As you dry off, feel the fabric of the towel against your naked skin. Continue your present-moment awareness while brushing your teeth and going through the rest of your morning routine.

❖ Prepare a meal mindfully—as if you're cooking it for the first time. Pay close attention as you assemble the ingredients. Notice the unique character of each vegetable, fruit, or piece of meat—the myriad colors, diverse smells, and varied textures of foods. Even the sounds vary as you chop, slice, cut, grind, and pound. You might pop an ingredient into your mouth, noting its texture against your tongue and its unique taste before you blend it into a final dish. As you combine the different ingredients, notice the visual transformation as they become one. As you're cooking, observe the chemical changes when the separate items morph into a collected whole. Inhale the aroma, seeing if you can still identify the unique individual smells or simply one succulent blend. When you sit down to eat, take in the smells and colors of the meal before you dig in.

After clients complete a few of these exercises, ask them to consider the following questions to deepen their mindfulness experience:

1. As you looked at your usual routines in a new way, what did you notice?
2. Were you aware that there's more happening around you and inside you than you realized?
3. Did your thoughts kick into gear and try to rush you through the activity?
4. Were your old stressors along for the ride, or did they stay behind?
5. As you notice where your mind is from moment to moment, do you feel more connected to yourself? Does your life seem more vivid?

11

Your Work Resilient Zone
Finding Your Positive, Compassionate Self

The way to do is to be.

—Lao-tzu

Art

From the time I was eighteen, I stuffed into my hip pocket each day a worn week-at-a-glance. It became my bible and scorecard, dictating every hour of devotion to my disease, ensuring I wouldn't forget an appointment in my daily frenzied pace. Its margins were crammed with lists of tasks to accomplish between meetings and before going to bed. As long as I was working, thinking about work, or lining up work in my notebook, I felt in control, important, powerful. When I recall it, the fearful, shameful, guilty self of my childhood seems like someone from another planet.

At forty-eight, I was in my ninth year of recovery from work addiction. My childhood was the meat of a dysfunctional family sandwich. I was pressed on one side by a tyrannical, workaholic father whom I rarely could please. Around him I was always fearful that I would be (and often was) scolded or punished for some awkward, selfish, or mean-spirited thing I hadn't intended to do. On the other side was an apprehensive and distant mother, always within arm's reach of potent prescription drugs. Around her I experienced constant anxiety and rejection, feeling I wasn't worthy enough for kisses, hugs, or other expressions of love. Confusion and conflict dominated my family communication. Exuberance was criticized. Sadness was ridiculed. Tenderness was wrapped in mock gestures, delivered with sarcasm.

Around spontaneous, self-assured kids, I felt puny, ugly, and unpopular. I felt safest and most in control when playing alone. I could then pretend I was one of my favorite heroes: a powerful, cherished champion of justice, battling alone (or with some animal companion) against incredible odds on behalf of the unloved and powerless. Thus, my childhood nurtured the lethal seeds that later blossomed into work addiction: self-denial, self-control, poor self-image.

When I hit puberty, pouring myself wholeheartedly into school and extra-curricular projects enabled me to control my emotions at the same time I was creating a socially acceptable self-image. The only price I had to pay was to spend every waking hour working hard at something. By the time I was eighteen, I had become a professional musician, seeded tennis player, boxing champion, state-champion track athlete, straight-A student, and National Merit Scholar. I was president of a statewide youth fellowship and a high-school selection for Boys' State. For two years I went steady with the school's most popular cheer-leader, and a month before graduation I received a scholarship to Harvard.

Despite the accolades, my parents' attitudes toward me didn't change: my accomplishments were still never enough to impress my father or to win my mother's warmth. My response? Already deep in my disease, I dug a little deeper, tried a little harder, won more honors. By now I was learning to get strokes elsewhere: from teachers, coaches, and friends. Awards and publicity became replacements for acceptance and affection. Most of all, the constant pace of work numbed my mind to unpleasant, unresolved feelings of shame, powerlessness, and lack of love.

College devastated me. My entire sense of self-worth had been robed in the grandiosity of high-school self-images. My view of life was of perpetual conflict, in which only superior people survived and were worthy. At Har-vard, however, it seemed every student was better than me! What's more, they all seemed to know exactly who they were and what they wanted to do with their lives—whereas I hadn't a clue. Teenage work addiction had been so all-consuming for me that I'd been too busy—and afraid—to discover who I really was or what career might actualize my true self. For three undergraduate years, I battled suicidal depression.

At the end of my junior year, I decided to pursue a career in law. As a crimi-nal defense attorney, I could actually wield the power I had fantasized about all my life, fighting real battles in courtrooms for the sake of justice, the power-less, and the oppressed.

I finished law school and for the next five years litigated criminal cases. I was proud of not taking a vacation during that entire time. My relentless activity pitched me day and night into preparing and conducting trials, which contin-ued to anesthetize my feelings of self-doubt, while the stakes involved provided me with the adrenalized, grandiose illusion that my work was a matter of life or death. This was years before I realized that the powerless, oppressed per-son I'd been defending in court was really the quaking little child buried deep within me; the causes I'd been championing stood for all the battles I'd never won as a boy; and each law student I'd mentored with such loving parental care was really myself.

Nearing burnout in the courtroom, I jumped at an offer to write a law book and teach in law school. Evenings and weekends allowed me to sweep up my infant son and trudge off on mountain hikes; paternal bonding could take place—and fatherhood justified through my strenuous activity. Thanks to work addiction's blend of anesthesia and adrenaline, ten years of fatherhood flashed by.

One day my wife nearly killed herself and our second son while driving the car under the influence of marijuana. The next day she checked herself into a drug rehabilitation center, where she was diagnosed as an alcoholic and addict. Her courageous action not only rescued her life and our marriage but saved my life as well. While participating in her recovery program, it dawned on me that descriptions of the addict's life, thoughts, and feelings fit me perfectly. All I had to do was substitute "compulsive working" for "compulsive drinking/ using," and I saw that I was as much an addict as anyone.

At one point, I drafted a long letter to the rehabilitation clinic, describing my symptoms, and asking if there were any treatment programs for work addicts. But this cutting-edge clinic for recovering addicts knew of none. So I attended meetings of Alcoholics Anonymous. On the gut level of shame, fear, desperation, and self-esteem, the stories I heard at AA were my story, too.

I finally realized I couldn't recover alone and started a Workaholics Anonymous group in my city. In its first two years over a hundred people attended. I volunteered for WA's first World Service Organization. Getting to know scores of other recovering workaholics apprised me of the immensity of this insidious disease: its deep roots, its subtle forms, its range of rationalizations, and its enormous cultural encouragement.

Nearly every day of recovery I unearth some new facet of my work addiction: how its fear of true feelings goads me toward activity and away from contemplation or uncensored feeling of emotions; how its dread of powerlessness tempts me to control everything inside and outside my life; how its anxiety over the worth of my true self urges me to hide behind false self-images. I'm fully resigned to the fact that this cunning and baffling disease will never leave me.

But at every WA meeting I encounter love, strength, and renewed hope; I hear some new wisdom I can apply to my life; I discover another useful tool of recovery. I am discovering, accepting, and nurturing my true self by myself. For the first time in my life I'm in touch with the awesome range of my genuine feelings—and gradually learning not to hide, channel, change, or flee from them. On good days I experience incredible wonder and joy from just being alive. My sick, fictional life is finally over. Though its arrival was a long time coming, my real story's just begun.

Performance-Enhancing Drugs for Work Resiliency

In recovery circles it's often said that the process of recovering from addiction is "an inside job." As you can see in Art's touching story, nowhere is that more true than with workaholism. Work addiction is exemplified in attitude and unhealthy work habits. Changing your mental outlook along with your work habits are performance-enhancing drugs that can arm you with work resiliency.

Listed below are ten common workaholic habits that create stress and prevent balance in your life. You probably saw many of them in Art's story. Which ones apply to you? Jot down the habits that describe your personal outlook or work pattern. Then in the blank space devise a work plan with healthy changes that can help you find your resilient zone.

1. Emphasizing the external world of *doing* with little attention to your internal world of *being*

2. Quantifying what you do (seeing it and measuring it) in order to feel good about yourself

3. Putting your self-care needs last, until all the work is done

4. Having difficulty being in the present moment

5. Focusing too much on the final product instead of on the progress you're making

6. Scheduling yourself to the hilt, allowing little or no flexibility or spontaneity

7. Defining yourself and others by accomplishments instead of human qualities

8. Feeling incomplete and unfinished without something to keep you busy

9. Engaging in self-judgment instead of self-compassion when you make mistakes or can't accomplish enough

10. Taking work too seriously instead of lightening up

MY HEALTHY WORK HABITS CHECKLIST

1.

2.

3.

4.

5.

The other performance-enhancing drugs that can help you work healthier, smarter, and more productively are positivity, optimism, and self-compassion. Let's start with negativity's counterpart, positivity. I'll show you ways to build on positive thoughts, emotions, and experiences. Then we'll move into optimism and self-compassion and explore ways for you to expand your work resiliency.

The Lowdown on Positivity and Work Resilience

To say that you're not going to worry, that you're just going to be happy, doesn't do justice to the scientific underpinnings of positivity's depth and power as an antidote to work addiction. Scientists have discovered that positivity stretches your mind open to take in as much as you can, widening your span of possibilities. In one study, researchers assigned 104 people to one of three groups: group 1 experienced positive feelings (amusement or serenity); group 2 experienced negative feelings (anger or fear); and group 3 experienced no special feelings (neutrality). Then the researchers said, "Given how you're feeling, make a list of what you want to do right now." The positive group had the longest list.[1]

Why was that? A positive outlook leads you toward more possibilities than negativity or neutrality does. When you're dealing with a stressful situation, positivity showcases the range of possibilities. It helps you focus on a positive outcome that negativity hides from view. Simply put, negativity keeps you focused on the problem, whereas positivity helps you find solutions to it.

Positivity acts as a stress buffer when you're mired in workaholism, broadening your mind and range of vision. When you're under the gun with looming deadlines or overloaded with work tasks, your mind is designed to constrict and target the negative threat. If you're searching for a solution to a work crisis, your negative emotions keep you focused on the problem. Without knowing it, you focus on the stressful event and block out the big picture. But positive feelings like lightheartedness, joy, curiosity, gratitude, love, and hope expand your range of vision.

Quiz: How Wide is Your Work Resilient Scope?

Is your work resilient scope narrow or broad? The wider it is, the more work resilient you are. To find out, read the following statements. Write next to each one the number that fits: 1 (strongly disagree), 2 (disagree), 3 (agree), or 4 (strongly agree).

____   1. Life is full of problems.

____   2. I usually assume people will take advantage of me.

____   3. Things never turn out the way I want.

____   4. Nothing I do is good enough.

____   5. Whatever can go wrong will go wrong.

____   6. I'm a born loser.

____   7. Trouble follows me wherever I go.

____   8. I'm not a worthy person.

____   9. I can't change the way things are.

____   10. I don't have what it takes to meet most challenges.

____   Total Score

SCORING: Add up the numbers and put your total score in the blank at the bottom. The lower your score, the more work resilient you are. Use the following key to interpret your score: 10–20 means you have a wide scope that makes you work resilient; 21–29 means you have a medium-width scope that you can expand; 30–40 means you have a narrow scope that needs broadening in order for you to become more work resilient.

WIDENING YOUR MINDSCAPE

As a result of many experiments, scientists know that when you intentionally broaden your scope, your work stress automatically lifts. A positive scope widens your attention, shifts your outlook, expands your world view, and allows you to take more in and see many ways to face work challenges. The more you take in, the more ideas and actions you add to your toolbox.

There's a lot of wisdom behind the old adage, "Look on the bright side." Think about it this way: when work stress hangs over you like a cloud, you can't see the sun. But when you can create positive feelings, it helps you part the cloudy thinking and let the sun shine through. As your scope widens, you see the big picture of possible solutions instead of getting mired in the challenging situation.

BROADENING YOUR POSITIVITY

Look over the list of ten negative statements in the quiz. As you read down the list, notice the constrictive tone of the statements and how they cloud out possibilities. Notice how you feel as you complete the list. Not so hot, huh?

Now go back and broaden each statement to include possible solutions. For example, you might reword the first statement as, "Life does contain problems, but there are also solutions to problems; I can focus on the possibilities." After you've broadened the statements, notice the difference in tone. Do you notice a difference in how you feel? I'll bet you feel more uplifted.

Now it's your turn. Make a list of three or four negative statements you've had recently. Write them exactly as you hear them in your mind's echo chamber. Then go back and decrease the negativity by adding possibilities. Try to rewrite the statements genuinely in ways that are truthful for you. Pay attention to how you feel as you add more positivity.

STACKING YOUR POSITIVITY DECK

It's simple science. When you have positive emotions on a regular basis, they have cumulative benefits that trump your negative emotions. Scientists call this strategy the "broaden and build" effect.[2] Here are some broaden-and-build strategies you can use to stack your positivity deck and blunt workaholic habits:

1. Step back from work situations and come up with a wide range of possible solutions.

2. Tell yourself work problems are not personal failures and that nothing is permanent. Every event has a beginning and an ending.

3. Broaden your scope beyond work demands and think of the full range of things that make your life meaningful.

4. Practice positive self-reinforcement instead of making negative self-judgments.

5. Dwell on positive subjects and focus on positive aspects of your life where you can make a difference. Avoid high-stress media reports, violent movies, or squabbles in the office.

6. Hang out with positive coworkers. Like negativity, positivity is contagious. When you surround yourself with positive colleagues, positivity rubs off on you.

7. Give yourself a pat on the back when you reach a milestone or important accomplishment. Tell yourself how awesome you are: "I knew I could do it!"

8. Focus on the solution, not the problem. If there's a problem in the office, encourage coworkers to brainstorm and come up with possible ways to fix it instead of getting stuck in the complaints.

9. Reframe gloomy prospects in a positive way. Few situations are 100 percent bad. Tom was upset that he had to pay a half- million dollars in taxes; he had lost sight of the fact that he'd earned five million that same year. He was so caught up in his loss that it eclipsed his gain. Tom was a rich man living an impoverished life—all because of his narrow scope.

UNDERSCORE THE UPSIDE

Negativity can be a knee-jerk reaction that you might not be aware of. A friend of mine loved the warm, long days of summer. One day in June, on the longest day of the year, I said to her, "You must be on cloud nine." She replied, "No, I'm sad because tomorrow the days start getting shorter again." When I pointed out how she was shrinking her joy, she was surprised that her narrow scope had hijacked her. She was able to broaden her outlook, remembering how she'd looked forward to this time of year, and savor the warm weather instead of focusing on the cold days to come.

If you're like many workaholics, your mind automatically constricts situations without your realizing it. Perhaps you focus on times where you failed, things that make you hot under the collar, or goals that you still haven't accomplished: "Same lousy job, the usual inconsiderate coworkers, the office party was nothing to write home about."

You build up your negativity deck without realizing it. And that becomes the lens you look through. You can reverse your negative mind-set with practice in finding the upside. Don't let pleasantness slip by without underscoring it. Start taking the pleasant aspects of the world into your mind: "I enjoy conversations with my coworker"; "I love the smell of freshly brewed coffee from the break room"; or "The smell of those flowers at my work station is wonderful." When you underscore the small things around you that you appreciate, it cheers you up and grows positive feelings.

THE UNDO EFFECT OF POSITIVITY

Studies show that a positive outlook can undo the damage that workaholic stress and negativity do to your mind and body, making you more work resilient. Positive events in your life help repair cardiovascular wear and tear caused by the stress response to negative events. Positive emotions send your body a different message than negative emotions, putting the brakes on the stress juices, activating your parasympathetic nervous system, and calming you down.

Positive feelings contain the active ingredients that enable you to escape from debilitating stress and grow stronger. Positive thinkers are able to cope better with adversity because they can see solutions to stressful problems. Positivity helps you think in terms of "we" instead of "me," to look past imagined threats from people of different races, genders, or ages. In addition, it gives you an appreciation for the common ground you share with others. This broadening automatically draws you closer to friends and family. And you're more likely to feel oneness with strangers, people of different lifestyles and ethnic groups, and cultures around the world.[3]

AN ATTITUDE OF GRATITUDE

The gratitude exercise helps you see the flip side of the narrow scoping that builds without your knowledge. When you count your blessings, you broaden your outlook and get an emotional lift. Write down as many things as you can think of that you're grateful for, that make your life worth living. Then make a list of the people, places, and things that bring you comfort and joy. Your list can include material items, such as cars, electronic devices, clothes, jewelry, houses, trips, and so on. It can include loving relationships, children, pets, and coworkers. And it can include your health and the health of your loved ones.

After you've made your list, reflect on your appreciation for each item. Practice this exercise regularly until you begin to see more positive aspects of your life. And you'll be more aware of how full it is than of whatever may be lacking.

Finding Your Work Resilient Zone with Optimism

Scientists say that we focus on a flawed spot rather than an overall shiny surface, which can make success look and feel like failure. In graduate school, Lyn got upset when she got an A- in a course and asked to take the final exam over in hopes of making an A+. To Olympic athletes, a gold medal is great, but a silver or bronze one can be a disappointment.

Organizational research shows that an optimistic disposition pays off in job hunting and promotions, that optimists achieve more career success than pessimists, and that optimism has beneficial effects on physical and psychological well-being.[4] Compared to their sunnier coworkers, disgruntled workers have trouble looking on the bright side, working as team players, thinking outside the box, and finding solutions in problems. Coworkers and managers lack confidence in pessimists, and they don't trust them to lead. Pessimists are shut out of top assignments and their careers are derailed because they get mired in work tasks instead of surmounting them.

No wonder studies show that optimists have lower stress levels and more stable cardiovascular systems. You can also see why blood samples reveal that optimists have stronger immune systems and fewer stress hormones than pessimists.[5] Optimists know and believe in their capabilities and adopt healthier habits. Statistics show that optimists have fewer health complaints, healthier relationships, and live longer than pessimists.[6]

Optimists don't possess some magical joy juice. They're not smiley-faced romantics looking at life through rose-colored glasses. They are realists who take positive steps to cope with stress rather than succumbing to it. Think about it. Being able to see the positive side of a negative situation can arm you with weapons to overcome the obstacles you face.

Practice looking for the silver lining in situations you perceive as negative. Even if your life is stressful, find one or two positive things that you enjoy and look forward to. Surround yourself with optimists instead of pessimists who pull you down. Pay attention to the attitude you bring to work or home and try to keep negativity in check.

In a pinch, your mind-set tends to be negative. But you can ask, "Is the glass half empty or half full?" See the gains in your losses, the beginnings contained in your endings. When you hit forty, you can think of the milestone as half a life left or half a life lost. When you enter a rose garden, you can savor the beauty and fragrance of the flowers or feel repelled by the thorns. You can usually find at least a granule of good in anything bad when you look for it.

FIND OPPORTUNITY IN STRESSFUL EVENTS

Once you understand that positivity is always present when you're grumpy or negative, you can start to focus your mind more on the positive side and build it up. Try using these steps to shine a different light on your workaholism:

1. Pinpoint the challenge or opportunity contained in work problems.

2. Empower yourself. Remember the personal resources you have at your disposal to overcome work challenges and how they provide opportunities for you to learn more about yourself.

3. Take the viewpoint that mistakes and shortcomings at work are lessons for you to learn (focus on open-ended curiosity), not failures for you to endure

(avoid close-ended judgments). Ask yourself what you can learn from the challenge so that you'll be more resilient next time.

4. Turn the stressor around by focusing on the opportunity it contains. Ask yourself: "How can I make this situation work to my advantage?," "Can I find something positive in this negative situation?," or "What can I manage or overcome in this instance?"

PUT ON YOUR WIDE-ANGLE LENS

Like the zoom lens of a camera, the mind tends to zero in on challenging situations, magnifying problems and hardships and obscuring the big picture. What about you? Do you look at life through a zoom lens or a wide-angle lens?

One way to find out is to identify a problem you have. Perhaps your mutual fund isn't worth as much as it used to be, or you worry that you will have to pull several all-nighters to get caught up at work. Once you recognize a complaint, put on your wide-angle lens by pulling up the big picture, seeing the complaint in the scheme of your whole life. As you broaden your outlook, how important is the unfavorable judgment you've made about your life or yourself? If you're like most people, the complaint loses its sting when you put it in a wider context. The philosophical question, "If you're on your deathbed, what do you wish you'd done differently?" automatically activates your wide-angle lens.

LOOK FOR THE GIFT IN A COSMIC SLAP

In an interview with Barbara Walters, the actress Elizabeth Taylor said she laughed when doctors told her she had a brain tumor. Walters gasped. But Taylor wisely continued, "What else are you going to do?" Actually Taylor's attitude proves you can do a lot when adversity strikes. The actor and comedian Richard Belzer once said, "Cancer is a cosmic slap in the face. You either get discouraged or ennobled by it." But if you're not a natural-born optimist, you can learn coping skills to face the seismic events in your life.

The main skill is to discover the gift in adversity. Then focus on how that gift changes your life for the better. In referring to the motorcycle accident that paralyzed him, Sean said, "It was probably the greatest thing that ever happened to me." The accident changed Sean in ways that otherwise would not have been possible. Recovering workaholics and alcoholics often say hitting bottom is their greatest blessing because it wakes them up to a brand-new way of living. After going through the heartache of a broken relationship, for example, many people say they find healthier, more meaningful relationships.

Studies show that the meaning in your cosmic slaps can enrich your life if you're willing to look for that meaning.[7] Research on trauma survivors shows that adversity can have the following benefits:

* Help you see you're stronger than you thought
* Bring new meaning to your life
* Take you deeper into your spirituality
* Deepen the closeness you feel to yourself and others

An amputee from the Iraq War counsels other disabled soldiers. A person with HIV donates time to help raise money for AIDS research. Adversity's biggest gift is helping you see your inner fortitude and your ability to find richer meaning that you might not have known was there.

Self-Compassion and Your Overworked Mind

In the previous chapter, I described mindful working as a way to be present in the moment, paying attention to your thoughts and emotions without passing judgment. Don't get me wrong: you need your judgment. That's how you make sense of the world around you. But when your overworked mind overestimates threats, your judgment pumps up the volume, raising your stress level. And there comes your judgment—that kick-butt voice inside your head —telling you how worthless, selfish, dumb, or bad you are. The bad feelings sabotage your success.

If you're like many workaholics who kick themselves around for their shortcomings, you probably have a deep belief that this treatment can help you do better. Or you might worry that giving yourself too much leeway would turn you into a total slacker. Truth be told, negative self-judgments actually increase workaholism and decrease productivity. In contrast, self-compassion—the kind, supportive treatment you give yourself each step of the way during personal shortcomings, challenges, and setbacks—is a powerfully resilient recovery tool. Studies show that when you substitute self-compassion for self-judgment, you foster positive change as you face just about any work challenge.[8]

PUT DOWN YOUR GAVEL

Kristin Neff at the University of Texas reports that when you're hard on yourself, it's difficult to bounce back after a setback. And you're more prone to anxiety and depression, which can sabotoge your work performance. But when you replace negative self-judgment with self-compassion, you recover quicker. And if you don't have self-compassion, don't worry: you can develop it. After an eight-week program of mindfulness-based stress reduction (composed of yoga, meditation, and relaxation exercises), Neff says that 90 percent of the participants had increased their self-compassion.[9]

FIRST AND SECOND ZINGERS

Have you ever found that the more you scratch a spot that itches, the more it itches? And the scratching just makes it worse? Maybe you can't do anything about the itch, but you can do something about the scratch. Workaholism is a lot like that. When work stress zings you, your reaction can add insult to injury, making you suffer worse. Your reactions to your work pressures are "second zingers"—the ones you sting yourself with. The first zinger is unpleasant

Standing Up to Your Inner Bully

If you're like most workaholics, you have an inner bully that runs your life. It kicks you around and keeps you focused on your flaws so that you constantly feel as if you're struggling internally. The workaholic's solution? Work longer and harder. Of course, that's not the real solution. Immersing yourself in work mires you deeper in the problem because it'll never be enough. That's why we call it work addiction.

The real solution is to develop more self-kindness to balance your self-judgment. And research suggests that encouragement and self-support can be a game changer. The more self-compassion you have, the greater your emotional well-being.[10]

Research shows that self-compassion can limit the distress that leads to emotional binges (the what-the-hell effect). People high in self-compassion can admit their mistakes without self-condemnation. They can pick themselves up, brush themselves off, and maintain healthier emotional habits with less risk of falling back into addictive or extreme behaviors.[11] It follows that workaholics seeking balance in their lives have a greater chance of success when they employ self-compassion instead of self-judgment.

So amp up your kind, compassionate side when you stumble. Let it replace your inner bully, who kicks you every time you're down. Then notice how much more supportive and encouraged you feel from one workday to the next. And notice the difference it makes in your outlook, job performance, and ability to maintain your work-life balance.

for sure, but sometimes the real distress comes from your second-zinger reaction instead of the event itself. If you can avoid reacting when uncontrollable events zing you, you can reduce your stress and workaholic behavior.

When you fail at something, make a mistake, or have a setback, judging yourself creates a second layer of stress, making you more likely to give up. Facing an upsetting situation with impartiality reduces the intensity of your stress. Self-judgment throws you into a cycle of setbacks: "I ate a piece of carrot cake" spirals into, "I've already blown my diet now, so I might as well eat a second piece" which turns into, "I'm such a loser; I'll never get this weight off." The second zinger (the stress you put yourself through) makes you feel bad, not eating the cake. The bad feelings throw you into a cycle of seeking comfort in the very behavior you're trying to conquer. When you remove the second layer of condemnation, you feel an ease in dealing with the real stressor.

Suppose you hit your head on a kitchen cabinet. After the first zinger of pain, comes the second zinger of judgment: "Ouch! I'm such a klutz!" Sometimes second zingers trigger more second zingers through association. Maybe a friend is late for dinner (first zinger), and you feel your blood boil (second zinger). Your judgment of the situation brings up memories of abandonment as a child (another second zinger).

Sometimes you might have a second-zinger reaction where there's no first zinger to begin with. In these situations, your inner judgment creates stress by imagining there's a first zinger. Suppose even before you begin a presentation to colleagues you have a sinking feeling that it will go south. If you stop to think about it, the tension (second zinger) comes from an inner judgment (another second zinger) predicting that you'll mess up. It's the self-judgment that distresses you; there is no first zinger.

PRACTICING EQUANIMITY

Equanimity is a meditation term that refers to the ability to stay calm in the middle of a distressing situation. When stress zings you, meditation helps you see the difference between the first and second zinger. As you develop the skill to see them as separate, you realize you don't have to react every time you get zinged. Known as equanimity, this distinction is good medicine for producing work resiliency because it softens your reactions. In other words, you are able to be present with your mental reactions without reacting to them.

Achieving equanimity is not as easy as it sounds. Pulling it off is as difficult as resisting the urge to scratch an itch. And it takes practice. Like most people, you've identified with your stream of thoughts that make you think the second zinger is your only choice. After you pay attention to your first and second zingers for a while, though, equanimity can give you an inner feeling of separation from the urge to react. It lets you feel disappointment without suffering or frustration without acting out. It keeps you from adding more suffering on top of suffering.

How many times, for instance, have you been in the middle of an activity that required your full attention when someone interrupts you? Maybe you're irritated. The interruption is the first zinger and your irritation is the second zinger. Equanimity helps you recognize that you're irritated, but it cushions you from the irritation so that you don't zing yourself again (in this case, you don't blow up).

Stressful first zingers can hijack your emotions and carry you away. But the second zingers add another layer of distress. As you start to notice and bring self-compassion to bear when you face second zingers, you can greatly increase your work resiliency.

STOPPING SECOND ZINGERS IN THEIR TRACKS

Comforting talk to yourself can help in such stressful situations as job interviews, the aftermath of a job loss, racing against a deadline, or falling flat on your face in a presentation. Give this mindfulness exercise a shot: Next time work stress zings you, pay attention to your second zinger without judgment. A first zinger can be a stress-related body pain, an upsetting thought about your job, or a high-pressured work situation. Note how many times you have a strong reaction such as smouldering resentment, lashing out, or both. If you are able to practice equanimity, note those times, too. See if you are able to observe yourself without judgment. If you discover that you did judge, see if you can refrain from judging yourself for judging.

Self-compassion can soothe the stressors associated with work addiction, not because you replace negative feelings with positive affirmations, but because as you embrace your negative feelings, new positive emotions rise up within you.[12] When you're kinder to yourself and accept your shortcomings and limitations with compassion, you are better able to deal with the stressful situation, not the added negative feelings from self-judgment.

Next time you're under the workaholic gun, talk to yourself in soothing terms that help you cope instead of using harsh words that make you feel worse and undermine your coping ability. If you'd like to know how self-compassionate you are (as if you didn't already know), you can go to Kristin Neff's official website (www.self-compassion.org/test-your-self-compassion-level) and take her self-compassion test. A program will then calculate your score for you.

Tips for Clinicians

Positivity, optimism, and self-compassion are effective tools for you to use in helping clients find their work resilient zone and recover from workaholism.

CONSIDER TEACHING RESILIENT TOOLS

The good news is that these resilient tools can be taught to people who lack them. Researchers at Stanford University have developed a training strategy to help give people the skills to open up to others' suffering. Called Compassion Cultivation Training, the nine-week program has shown promise in teaching participants how to nourish their own compassionate instincts and how to feel another's pain without being engulfed by it.[13] Emory University has a similar program that teaches compassionate meditation and studies its influence on participants. Experts say that self-compassion is not natural for everyone, and in fact taking an eight-week course in it has been found to be highly effective.[14]

You can use the following factors to assess your workaholic clients' resilient zone and their ability to maintain it:

✣ The strain of having others dependent on you

✣ The number and frequency of traumatic events you've faced

✣ Outside pressures and self-imposed pressures

✣ The degree of your responsibilities and commitments

✣ Strong supportive relationships

✣ Your ability to take care of yourself

✣ Your overall physical health

✣ A positive outlook

Workaholics can control only some of these factors. But you can help them focus on their resources instead of their losses. Explore how they can find their resilient zone by assessing where they are with these practices: staying healthy, getting ample sleep, exercising, eating well, drawing on their optimism, broadening their narrow work scope, establishing strong social contacts, noticing and shifting their internal reactions, and limiting outside and self-imposed pressures.

RESILIENCY AND TAKING RISKS

On the flip side, the route to the resilient zone is through stepping into unfamiliar territory and the unexpected. I realize this sounds contradictory, but it's one of life's paradoxes: you build resilience by having a degree of control while embracing novelty. Workaholics are more likely to find their resilient zone if they stick their necks out than if they settle into "safe" ruts and routines.

You can encourage them to broaden themselves by facing new challenges, meeting different people, developing a new skill or hobby, spending more time being instead of doing, learning a new game, or traveling to new places.

12

Work-Life Balance and Workaholics Anonymous

I fear the day that technology will surpass our human interaction. The world will have a generation of idiots.

— Albert Einstein

Bernadette

I was the only daughter born to first-generation southern European immigrants. I grew up in a family that subscribed to the American dream of hard work, toil, and sacrifice. Both my parents were workaholics. I don't remember my family relaxing in the living room and talking among ourselves except when guests came over. And that experience was hardly soothing because "La Bella Figura" (Italian for a way of living that projects good image, proper behavior, beauty, and aesthetics) kicked into high gear.

As a child, I was recognized only when I excelled academically or musically or had some kind of social accomplishment. After launching my career as a mental health and international public health expert, my childhood template of workaholism took charge. I traveled to many foreign lands, working for humanitarian organizations, and worked as a university lecturer and international agency director. I stayed hours at the office long after my colleagues had gone. My around-the-clock working and my inability to transition from office to home caused problems in my marriage and in responding to my son's needs.

I began to investigate Twelve-Step recovery programs and eventually located a Workaholics Anonymous (WA) meeting in someone's home in my area. The connection with others who had struggled with work addiction and had found tools to apply, share, and support was a comforting and anxiety-reducing experience. I was inspired by members who shared their own stories of hope, strength, and faith. The Twelve-Step spiritual component launched me into a search to reexamine my own spirituality, since I had moved away from my childhood religion years before. My search took me on a journey of many years into Western and Eastern faiths and philosophies, which provided communities of people to share. Plus, it helped shape my reliance on a Higher Power and see the connections among all living beings and accept the unpredictability of life and the importance of a daily spiritual practice, including meditation.

My relationships with my son and husband began to change, too. I continued to work the WA Twelve Steps, which gave me insights into the underlying problems of work addiction and the importance of putting supports in place. WA helped me set boundaries with work and make amends to my husband and son. I began to act more responsibly to meet their needs and demonstrate the importance of integrity and honesty. The job changes I made after beginning my WA recovery considered my child- care and relationship needs, and I reduced my full-time job to a half-day one.

Nowadays when I leave the office, I realize there will be work to do the next day, and I set priorities. I don't take on additional projects until critical aspects of current ones are completed. I am grateful for my life and the blessings of family, friends, and neighbors. And I seek to share those gifts with others and to keep a healthy balance in all that I do.

Invasion of the Balance Snatchers

Bernadette's story illustrates how a childhood template of hard work and accomplishments can dictate your priorities in adulthood. This chapter is about identifying your balance snatchers—those external forces that insinuate themselves into your life, throwing it into turmoil. I will show you how you can work hard, be kind to and compassionate with yourself, keep a positive attitude, and maintain balance with the three Rs: relaxation, recreation, and relationships.

In our technologically driven culture, there are more things to do as life moves faster. And as the line that once protected private hours gets erased, you might feel that your work-life balance is off. Although information technology and the workplace enable work addiction, they are no more to blame for it than the ABC store is to blame for alcoholism, or the grocery store for food addiction. Workaholics are often lonely wage earners who arrive at their desks before anyone else and are the last to leave. They prefer not to take time

Don't Be a Desk Potato

Your brain needs a bird's-eye view to help you see the workaholic waters you've been swimming in, reflect on your life, and gain insights on what you want to change. Research shows that stepping back from your familiar environment gives you a new perspective on your everyday life.[1] These studies support the importance of breaks, lunch hours, and vacations to get outside of your workaholic mind-set. A bird's-eye view gives you an objective perspective on how workaholism has dominated your life and what you can do to achieve more balance.

Don't be a desk potato. Your body wasn't designed to be deskbound for long periods of time. Prolonged sitting reduces blood and oxygen flow, causes weight gain, and leads to heart disease and type 2 diabetes. Take frequent work breaks and go on short, five-minute strolls outside the office, or up and down a flight of stairs in inclement weather. Exercise at your desk. Stand up, breathe deeply, shake, twist, and stretch high to release the built-up tension.

Take time out to get away from your work routines and work tools. Step back and examine what work habits snatch your balance and what you need to change to recover. If getting away from your everyday work surroundings isn't possible, spend one day going through your work routines, imagining that you're viewing them through the eyes of an outsider. As you move through your day, note what you see with curiosity, as if it's a first-time experience. Is it the rush of another pressure- cooker day or exciting challenges that lie ahead? Do you crack the whip or treat yourself with kindness? Are you enslaved by your cell phone, iPad, or laptop? Or do you master your electronic devices by taking time to see what's going on around you with renewed interest? Do you sneer at other people who don't move as fast as you? Or are you more tolerant of their slower pace? After going through this exercise, notice if you have any aha moments or a renewed appreciation for what you've been missing.

off, or if they do, they take their work along with them. Fun and laughter are frivolous wastes of time, and workaholics feel contempt for people who are humorous, carefree, and underproductive or who keep an even pace in their work lives.

Even if you're not a workaholic, chances are that you're having trouble finding work-life balance. A team of Canadian and American researchers found that nearly half of US workers take work home with them and that many of them say work interferes with family, social, and leisure aspects of their lives.[2] People who work more than fifty hours a week have the most interference in their personal lives. Forty percent of people under forty-five say they check their work e-mail after hours or on vacation; one in seven say electronic devices cut into time spent with spouses, and one in ten say these devices cut into time spent with their children.[3]

Watch out. They're everywhere: the balance snatchers that invade your life, creating work addiction, debilitating you, and making you less efficient in your job. Are you stretching your days into the wee hours to juggle more tasks, taking work home, leashing yourself to electronic devices, making yourself available 24/7, giving up much-needed vacation time? Living this way keeps your natural defenses on high alert, marinating you in your stress juices (cortisol and adrenaline), and clobbering you with mental and physical fatigue.

Research shows that work stress turns you into a more disgruntled, less effective worker.[4] Compared to managers putting in fewer hours, those who work longer hours suffer greater anxiety, depression, and burnout and have twice the number of health-related problems. And British researchers observed that long workweeks in high-pressured jobs contribute to the risk of burnout and heart attack. Workers who put in more than eleven hours a day were 67 percent more likely to have a heart attack than those who had a more balanced work schedule.[5] "Recharging Your Batteries: Don't Be a Desk Potato" gives you some steps to take to prevent the balance snatchers from taking over your life.

Draw a Line in the Sand

In the space below, name some balance snatchers that have invaded your life:

1.

2.

3.

4.

5.

Then go down the following list of some tried and true ways to set boundaries and check the ones you can apply so that work doesn't invade every corner of your personal life:

❖ Arrange to power down and clock out at a certain time.

❖ Take work home with you only when it's absolutely necessary and an exceptional case.

❖ Master your electronic devices instead of becoming a slave to them. Turn them off on breaks, at lunch, and after hours. Put away your laptop, iPhone, or pager just as you would a hammer or saw after working on a cabinet in the den. Make it a rule: no work tools in bed, at the table, or in the den while watching TV.

❖ Learn to say no when someone asks you to do something you don't have time for.

❖ If you have to add a new task, take another one off your to-do list.

❖ Tell yourself there's a limit to what you can do, put the rest out of the picture, and see this as a strength, not a weakness.

❖ Dial back on overtime to reduce your health risks and follow the adage, "Work smarter, not longer."

❖ Stay fit outside the office and think of your work site as the Olympics, where your physical and mental endurance hinges on being in good shape. Then prime yourself with good nutrition and vigorous exercise, avoid nicotine, and if you drink, use alcohol only in moderation.

❖ Make an appointment with yourself and schedule something fun in your time off. Indulge yourself with a hobby, hot bath, manicure, yoga, facial, reading, or meditation. Just fifteen or twenty minutes of personal time a day can lower your stress and raise your energy level.

Leisure Sickness or Work Withdrawal?

The talk show host Joy Behar said, "I don't like to relax; it stresses me out." And she's not alone. Many people have trouble sitting still, especially workaholics. You may be among the ranks of those who can't seem to quiet their minds. Studies show that calming your mind can be one of the best antidotes to work stress.[6]

The problem is some workaholics start to feel sick as soon as they stop working. If you're like most workaholics, chances are that you've used this as an excuse not to slow down. Dutch scientists use the term "leisure sickness" to label the 3 percent of hard-driving workers who fall ill during weekends and vacations.[7] But hold on—not so fast. Don't let this flawed diagnosis keep you from hitting your pause button.

"Leisure sickness" is a misnomer. The conditions for physical illness are already set up before you start to unwind. So when you get headaches, muscle soreness, a cold, or flu-like symptoms on weekends or time off, it's not because you stopped working and are relaxing. It's because you've been under chronic workaholic stress without realizing it. The real stress bubbles up when you slow down, not because you're relaxing but because you're withdrawing from your nose-to-the grindstone work habits. Stress withdrawal has been compared to withdrawing from steroids.

Research shows that, because overwork acts as an anesthetic, workaholics ignore or minimize physical aches and pains while working. An abrupt slowdown is a shock to your system. You feel a sudden loss of control when there's no structure and things are open- ended. It's like driving a car at ninety miles per hour and then slamming on the brakes. Once you slow down, the cortisol-adrenaline drench that once energized you now compromises your immune system, giving a free pass to opportunistic viruses. You have fatigue, a sore throat, or muscle pain that you hadn't noticed before as your body goes through work withdrawal.

By easing away from your workaholic tendencies before taking time off, you're less likely to get sick. If you're a workaholic, your fatigued mind isn't used to time cushions, short breaks, or delegating work projects that take your system off red alert. But standing, stretching, moving around, or walking around the block or up and down stairs increases blood flow and oxygen throughout your body, lowering blood pressure and boosting overall mental alertness.

Here are some tips to create a seamless transition to relaxation during your time out of the office so that you can return renewed and refreshed:

❖ Buffer your work exits and reentries. Don't work right up until the moment you leave and head back to work as soon as you get off the plane. Schedule an extra day off before you depart and another when you return, to ease back into work slowly.

❖ Have a plan. When you're away, limit your connection to the office and don't check your electronic devices more than once or twice a day.

❖ Choose a point person. In your absence, have someone you trust manage day-to-day tasks and make sure your coworkers know you'll be away. In your out-of-office voicemail and e-mail messages, designate a single person to be contacted on matters you consider important.

❖ Breathe deeply. Meditating and paced breathing stimulate your parasympathetic nervous system, which works to balance the surges of adrenaline and cortisol from work stress. When your lungs are full of air, your body can't produce adrenaline, so it's your body's way of getting you to relax.

❖ Balance activities. Alternate your time between staying active and resting. A run on the beach and ten minutes of meditation together give you two different kinds of biochemical boosts.

Work-Life Balance with the Twelve Steps

Twelve-Step programs have worked for millions of people with a variety of addictions, including those addicted to alcohol and other drugs, food, gambling, shopping, and certain types of relationships. The Twelve Steps also help those who are committed to a program of spiritual recovery from a life of compulsive, uncontrollable, and harmful work habits. The Steps of Workaholics Anonymous[8] are vehicles for healing work compulsions and establishing a more meaningful and fulfilling lifestyle:

1. We admitted that we were powerless over work—that our lives had become unmanageable.

2. We came to believe that a Power greater than ourselves could restore us to sanity.

3. We made a decision to turn our will and our lives over to the care of God as we understood God.

4. We made a searching and fearless moral inventory of ourselves.

5. We admitted to God, to ourselves, and to another human being the exact nature of our wrongs.

6. We became entirely ready to have God remove all these defects of character.

7. We humbly asked God to remove our shortcomings.

8. We made a list of all persons we had harmed and became willing to make amends to them all.

9. We made direct amends to such people wherever possible, except when to do so would injure them or others.

10. We continued to take personal inventory and when we were wrong promptly admitted it.

11. We sought through prayer and meditation to improve our conscious contact with God as we understood God, praying only for knowledge of God's will for us and the power to carry that out.

12. Having had a spiritual awakening as the result of these steps, we tried to

carry this message to workaholics and to practice these principles in all our affairs.

The only requirement for membership in Workaholics Anonymous is a desire to stop working compulsively. There are no dues or other fees for WA membership; the organization is supported by member contributions. WA is not allied with any sect, denomination, political group, organization, or other institution; does not wish to engage in any controversy; and neither endorses nor opposes any causes. The organization's primary purpose is to help members stop working compulsively and to carry the message of recovery to workaholics who are still suffering.

The History of Workaholics Anonymous

The first chapter of Workaholics Anonymous was started on the East Coast in April 1983 by a New York corporate financial planner and a schoolteacher who had been "hopeless" workaholics, as they described themselves. They founded WA in an effort to help others who suffered from the disease of workaholism and to stop working compulsively themselves. They were joined in their first meeting by the spouse of the planner who started WorkAnon, a program of recovery for those in relationships with workaholics. At about the same time, a nurse who was suffering from burnout in her high-stress job began one of the first chapters on the West Coast. Other chapters sprang up spontaneously and autonomously throughout the United States and in other countries. In March 1990 representatives from various chapters in four US states got together for the first time and officially formed the World Service Organization for Workaholics Anonymous.

The Signposts of Workaholism

1. We find it hard to love and accept ourselves. Work has become our means of gaining approval, finding our identity, and justifying our existence.

2. We have used work to escape our feelings. Thus, we have deprived ourselves of knowing what we truly need and want.

3. By overworking, we have neglected our health, relationships, recreation, and spirituality. Even when we are not working, we are thinking of our next task. Most of our activities are work related. We have denied ourselves the enjoyment of a balanced and varied life.

4. We have used work as a way to deal with the uncertainties of life. We lie awake worrying; we overplan and overorganize. By being unwilling to surrender control, we have lost our spontaneity, creativity, and flexibility.

5. Many of us grew up in chaotic homes. Stress and intensity feel normal to us. We seek out these conditions in the workplace. We create crises and get adrenaline highs by overworking to solve them. Then we suffer withdrawals and become anxious and depressed. Such mood swings destroy our peace of mind.

6. Work has become addictive. We lie to ourselves and others about the amount we do. We hoard work to ensure that we will always be busy and never bored. We fear free time and vacations and find them painful instead of refreshing.

7. Instead of being a haven, our home has become an extension of our workplace. Our family and friends are often our enablers.

8. We have made unreasonable demands on ourselves. We don't know the difference between job and self-imposed pressure. By overscheduling our lives, we become driven, racing to beat the clock, fearful that we will get behind, and binge-work in order to catch up. Our attention is fragmented by trying to do several things at once. Our inability to pace ourselves leads to breakdown and burnout. We have robbed ourselves of the enjoyment of working.

9. Many of us are perfectionistic. We have not learned to accept mistakes as part of being human and find it hard to ask for help. Because we believe no one can meet our standards, we have difficulty delegating and so do more than our share of work. Thinking ourselves indispensable often prevents our progress. Unrealistic expectations cheat us of contentment.

10. We tend to be overly serious and responsible. All activity must be purposeful. We find it hard to relax and just be; we feel guilty and restless when not working. Because we often make play into work, we rarely experience recreation and renewal. We have neglected developing our sense of humor and rarely enjoyed the healing power of laughter.

11. Waiting is hard for us. We are more interested in results than process, in quantity than quality. Our impatience often distorts our work by not allowing it proper timing.

12. Many of us are concerned with image. We think looking busy makes people think we are important and gains their admiration. By surrendering our self-approval, we are alienated from ourselves.

The Tools of Workaholics Anonymous

WA has developed tools of recovery that supplement the Twelve Steps (listed above). The tools are guidelines for living happily, joyously, and free from work addiction one day at a time. They include:

* *Listening.* We set aside time each day for prayer and meditation. Before accepting any commitments, we ask our Higher Power and friends for guidance.

* *Prioritizing.* We decide which are the most important things to do first. Sometimes that may mean doing nothing. We strive to stay flexible to events, reorganizing our priorities as needed. We view interruptions and accidents as opportunities for growth.

* *Substituting.* We do not add a new activity without eliminating from our schedule one that demands equivalent time and energy.

* *Underscheduling.* We allow more time than we think we need for a task or trip, allowing a comfortable margin to accommodate the unexpected.

* *Playing.* We schedule times for play, refusing to let ourselves work nonstop. We do not make our play into a work project.

* *Concentrating.* We try to do one thing at a time.

* *Pacing.* We work at a comfortable pace and rest before we get tired. To remind ourselves, we check our level of energy before proceeding to our next activity. We do not get "wound up" in our work, so we do not have to unwind.

* *Relaxing.* We do not yield to pressure or attempt to pressure others. We remain alert to the people and situations that trigger pressure in us. We become aware of our own actions, words, body sensations, and feelings that tell us we're responding with pressure. When we feel tension, we stop to reconnect to our Higher Power and others around us.

* *Accepting.* We accept the outcomes of our endeavors, whatever the results, whatever the timing. We know that impatience, rushing, and insisting on perfect results only slow down our recovery. We are gentle with our efforts, knowing that our new way of living requires much practice.

* *Asking.* We admit our weaknesses and mistakes and ask our Higher Power and others for help.

* *Meetings.* We attend WA meetings to learn how the fellowship works and to share our experience, strength, and hope with each other.

❖ *Telephoning.* We use the phone to stay in contact with other members of the fellowship between meetings. We communicate with our WA friends before and after a critical task.

❖ *Balancing.* We balance our work involvement with efforts to develop personal relationships, spiritual growth, creativity, and playful attitudes.

❖ *Serving.* We readily extend help to other workaholics, knowing that assistance to others adds to the quality of our own recovery.

❖ *Living in the Now.* We realize we are where our Higher Power wants us to be in the here and now. We try to live each moment with serenity, joy, and gratitude.

The Problem

Workaholism takes many forms, among them deriving our identity and self-esteem from what we do; keeping overly busy; neglecting our health, relationships, and spirituality; seeing everything as work related; having no desire to do anything (work avoidance or burnout); procrastinating; postponing vacations and rest; doing unnecessary work; worrying; demanding perfection; avoiding intimacy; and being controlling.

All these are ways we cope with the pain of having lost our sense of being and of not feeling good enough. Overscheduling our lives with activities is how we run from ourselves. We keep busy to blot out our feelings. We enjoy the adrenaline highs that come from intensity and rushing to meet deadlines. Maybe we are praised and promoted at work for being responsible and hard working. We may even be employed by a workaholic company that uses praise and promotion to encourage our addiction. Yet we have paid an enormous price for these "rewards." We have traded self-awareness for burying our pain in work. We have endangered our health and destroyed our relationships. We may have often wondered, "Is this all there is?"

Because there are many misconceptions about workaholism, recognizing it may take a long time. It is both a substance (adrenaline) and a process (overdoing) addiction and is not limited to our paid work life. We can also be workaholic in hobbies, keeping fit, housework, volunteering, or trying to save the world. All of these activities may appear admirable, but if they mean self-abandonment because of incessant doing, they represent work addiction.

Since workaholism is a progressive disease, we become increasingly driven until we hit bottom. The bottom may come in the form of a serious health problem or an ultimatum from a partner, employer, or friend. At some point, *workaholic* is no longer a label we prize. We realize that we have to change.

To help us in our recovery, there are the Twelve Steps of Workaholics Anonymous. Because our work addiction is so entrenched in our lives, the process seems overwhelming. How much time will recovery take? We are already too busy! What do we do with our commitments and responsibilities?

The Solution

As our pain intensifies, we begin to gain willingness—willingness to admit that we are addicted to work, that our lives are unmanageable, and that our way hasn't worked; willingness not to have all our questions answered immediately or to expect a quick fix; willingness to say, "I'm sick. I want to recover and I need help." In Workaholics Anonymous, this admission of powerlessness is Step 1. We have found it helpful to take this step and those that follow with others in WA.

From this initial willingness comes more willingness. Step 2 tells us that a power greater than ourselves can restore us to sanity. This power can be God, another Higher Power, the universe, the WA group—whatever is our source of strength.

Step 3 involves making a commitment to turn our will and our lives over to God as we understand God. Letting our Higher Power guide us requires giving up control, not being irresponsible. Our will now becomes a tool to turn self-will into willingness. For those of us who pride ourselves on being self-sufficient and strong-willed, taking this step involves a new way of thinking.

In Step 4 we make a written inventory of ourselves in relation to our workaholism. We include both our shortcomings and our assets. We ask a WA member for help on how to do Step 4. By taking a close look at ourselves, we become acquainted with the lovable person we truly are, the person we have lost in busyness.

Because many of us feel shame about how our work addiction has hurt ourselves and others, it is healing to do Step 5 and talk to an understanding person. This person can be anyone we choose. When we share our secrets, we often find that others have had similar experiences.

Steps 6 and 7 ask us to prepare ourselves inwardly to make amends to those we have harmed. In Step 8 we list those people, and in Step 9 we make amends, prudently. After these Steps are completed, many of us discover that a great burden has been lifted, that we have a sense of freedom and peace.

Recovery from workaholism is not a cure but a lifelong process. We are granted only a daily reprieve that is contingent on our maintaining our abstinence and growing spiritually. In Step 10, we continue the process begun in Step 4—gaining awareness of our feelings and taking responsibility for our words and actions. Taking Step 11 strengthens our conscious contact with our Higher Power, begun in Step 2, by having us stay in touch through prayer and meditation.

Step 12 tells us we can maintain and expand the spiritual awakening we experienced in doing all the preceding steps. We can do this by carrying the WA message of recovery to other workaholics and by practicing these principles at work, at home, on vacations—everywhere.

The best way for us to keep from sliding back into old habits is to share the news of our WA recovery with others: "We can't keep it unless we give it away." We carry the message by being an example of a recovering workaholic in our daily activities, as well as by giving service in WA.

Following the Steps brings us in touch with our inner wisdom and our spirituality. As we learn to accept ourselves as we are, we experience a new attitude toward work and activity. We enjoy our work more and find ways to work more effectively. When work has its proper place, you can find time to have fun and to nurture your health, relationships, and creativity.

We welcome you to our program and wish for you the recovery, serenity, and self-enjoyment we have found.

Tips for Clinicians

If you're keeping your work and life fairly well balanced, you'll have a lot to say to clients about how to find and hold that balance. Achieving balance when you're a workaholic requires more than cutting back on hours. It involves getting through the denial of your work addiction, deep personal introspection and insights, and attention to the parts of life that you have been neglecting.

DENIAL

Work addiction is a disorder that tells you that you don't have it. Many workaholics disassociate themselves from the traits of work addiction. Comments such as "I don't work that much," "I spend lots of time with my family," and "I have lots of friends and hobbies" are part of the process of denial.

A closer look shows that workaholics' family lives, vacations, friendships, and hobbies often resemble their jobs in being overly scheduled, rapid-fire, and focused on money making. You can help clients with denial by having them describe the balance in their lives and probe them about the comments that family members or colleagues make in regard to their work style. Outsider feedback is often in direct contradiction to the workaholic's assertion. You can use these contradictory reports and comments as evidence with which to confront the denial. Also, spouses, partners, or other loved ones can be invited to attend sessions to give firsthand accounts that might contradict and break through the workaholic's denial. In most cases, someone has penetrated the workaholic's denial before he or she first shows up for counseling.

One of the first comments many workaholics make when they come to therapy is, "Don't tell me I have to quit my job," punctuated by rationalizations such as "I have two kids to support. Are you going to pay my mortgage while I quit work?" or "I love my job." The workaholic's biggest fear is that the only way to recover is to slash work hours or change jobs. The implied belief is: "Either I work or I don't. There is no in between." These statements reflect the rigid all-or-nothing thinking discussed in chapter 4. It reflects their inability to envision a flexible balance between work and leisure or between work and family. It also reflects the driving fear that if they give up their compulsive working, there will be nothing left of their lives and their world will fall apart. This fear comes from having their identity wrapped up solely in work. These beliefs cause workaholics to avoid therapy and, in many cases, to cling more tenaciously to their work for security.

I've found that it's important to be prepared to deal with clients' resistance and to reassure them that the number of working hours has little to do with the kinds of changes necessary, and that they are the architect of any and all changes in their lives. This can relieve clients, give them a sense of control, and help them focus on the pertinent issues in therapy. Typical clients blame their jobs or their families for their work addiction. Here's where you can explain the enabling process and help them identify their enablers. You can also help them to separate the enablers in their lives from their work addiction, so that they can assume more responsibility for overworking.

Clients often need you to redirect their attention to the source of their pain, which is inside rather than outside. It's not unusual for workaholics to blame their problems on today's lifestyles and pressures. But blaming the company, the recession, or the need for two paychecks only rewards self-destructive behaviors and distracts everyone from the real source of the problem. Blaming fast-paced society and modern technology lets workaholics off the hook. Although they have choices about the way they live, they may be unwittingly choosing to continue their addiction while claiming they have no choices. Having workaholics become aware of their responsibilities, instead of blaming the enablers, helps them become more accountable and empowers them instead of victimizing them. You can consider asking workaholics to do a cost-benefit analysis on paper of the pluses and minuses of their compulsive working. This exercise can help them see their losses more concretely and weigh the advantages against the disadvantages.

MANAGING WORK AND PERSONAL TIME

I have found it helpful to have clients evaluate their time-management effectiveness. I suggest that you discuss the art of prioritizing and delegating and have clients bring in specific examples of ways they practice these skills. You can also help them focus on what requires immediate attention and refrain from imposing unrealistic deadlines; evaluate their ability to ask for help when they need it; explore reasons why they find asking for help difficult; and propose how they might be better served by delegating work.

Consider suggesting that clients set aside daily personal time to destress their lives and create clear-minded thinking. You can recommend ample rest, regular exercise, and getting three nutritionally balanced meals a day rather one or two, as well as advising clients to avoid eating on the run, while working, between meals, or while watching television. It's important to investigate the underlying reasons why workaholic clients inevitably fail at following the sort of balanced regimen that many other people find simple and easy. Thus, the underlying reasons for the difficulty and failure become the focus for the therapeutic session, and you can acknowledge and reward even the smallest gains that build into larger ones over time.

THE SWEETNESS OF DOING NOTHING

Many clients find, when they examine the balance in their current lives, that there's no room for leisure, play, or idle moments. So I often assign them "homework" that involves doing something fun that produces no end product and that requires spontaneity and flexibility. These activities are usually process oriented, like free-form painting, digging in the garden, soaking in a hot bath, or walking barefoot in a rain shower.[9] The Italians call it *il dolce far niente*, "the sweetness of doing nothing." It doesn't translate in the United States, where tasks and schedules define us. The closest equivalent we have is *killing time*. But *il dolce far niente* demands far more from you: that you intentionally let go and make being a priority. You can introduce this "foreign" concept to clients as a lead-in to help them find the sweetness of being alive—spending time in the present moment without a goal by doing something for just the sheer pleasure of it.

Another way to help your clients draw a line between work and time off is to have them compose a "to-be list" alongside their "to-do list." For each do item on their list, ask them to put a be item in the column beside it. Examples might include sitting outdoors, listening to nature sounds; and taking a walk, noticing the feel of your feet against the ground and the smells in the air.

You might also consider recommending hobbies, sports, and pastimes that can be done "imperfectly" and that immerse clients in process rather than outcome. Richard, a sixty-two-year-old bank president, took up golf but committed himself not to keep score, not to hurry from hole to hole, and to stay focused on having a good time instead of on winning—the opposite of his behavior at the office. He told me that business associates marveled when, for the first time, they saw his fun, lighthearted, and playful side. Golf, originally a therapy task, became a joy.

Appendix

*More men are killed by overwork
than the importance of the work
justifies.*
                    —Rudyard Kipling

Further Readings

BOOKS RELATED TO RECOVERY FROM WORKAHOLISM

Amen, Daniel. *Change Your Brain, Change Your Body*. New York: Three Rivers, 2010.
   How to use your brain to get and keep the body you want.
Benson, Herbert, and William Proctor. *Relaxation Revolution*. New York: Scribner, 2010.
   The latest scientific proof that your mind can heal your body, with descriptions of
   how to apply mind-body techniques to treat a variety of health conditions.
Brock, Tara. *Radical Acceptance: Embracing Your Life with the Heart of a Buddha*. New
   York: Bantam, 2003. Helps you realize your true nature and gain self-acceptance.
Burns, David. *Feeling Good: The New Mood Therapy*. New York: HarperCollins, 1999.
   An outline of scientifically tested cognitive techniques on how to change your per-
   spective, lift your spirits, and develop a positive outlook on life.
Cameron, Julia. *The Artist's Way: A Spiritual Path to Higher Creativity*. New York: Tar-
   cher, 2002. Discusses your enemy within—core negative beliefs—and shows the
   power of affirmations as your biggest ally in achieving inner peace.
Crowley, Katherine. *Working with You Is Killing Me: Freeing Yourself from Emotional
   Traps at Work*. New York: Warner, 2006. Tips on extreme bosses, corporate culture,
   and how to protect yourself in the workplace.
Davidson, Richard, and Sharon Begley. *The Emotional Life of Your Brain*. New York:
   Hudson Street, 2012. How your brain patterns affect the way you think, feel, and live,
   and how to change them.
De Graaf, John, ed. *Take Back Your Time: Fighting Overwork and Time Poverty in
   America*. San Francisco: Berrett-Kochler, 2003. How to avoid overscheduling and

overworking and live a fuller, more well-rounded life. Includes chapters by Vicki Robin, Juliet Schor, and Bill Doherty.

Doidge, Norman. *The Brain That Changes Itself*. New York: Penguin, 2007. Stories of personal triumph, showing how you can change and stressproof your pliable brain.

Edlund, Matthew. *The Power of Rest: Why Sleep Alone Is Not Enough*. New York: HarperCollins, 2010. Strategies for relaxed concentration to help you become more alert and fully engaged with your body, your work, and the people you love.

Fredrickson, Barbara. *Positivity*. New York: Three Rivers Press, 2009. Top-notch research on how positive emotions can stressproof you and help you see new possibilities, bounce back from setbacks, connect with others, and become the best version of yourself.

Germer, Christopher. *The Mindful Path to Self-Compassion*. New York: Guilford, 2009. Shows you how through self-compassion you can free yourself from destructive thoughts and emotions.

Gilbert, Paul. *The Compassionate Mind: A New Approach to Life's Challenges*. Oakland, CA: New Harbinger, 2009. Reveals the evolutionary and social reasons why the brain reacts so readily to threats and shows that we are also wired for kindness and compassion.

Hanson, Richard, and Richard Mendius. *Buddha's Brain: The Practical Neuroscience of Happiness, Love and Wisdom*. Oakland, CA: New Harbinger, 2009. Draws on the latest neuroscience research on how you can stimulate and strengthen your brain for a less stressful, more fulfilling life.

Hendrix, Harville. *Getting the Love You Want: A Guide for Couples*. New York: St. Martin's, 2008. A look at how the template from your upbringing (called the Imago) frames the kinds of relationships you form at home, work, and play.

Hobfoll, Steven, and Ivonne Hobfoll. *Work Won't Love You Back: The Dual-Career Couples' Survival Guide*. New York: W. H. Freeman, 1996. How to keep your marriage intact when both partners work.

Kornfield, Jack. *Meditation for Beginners*. Boulder, CO: Sounds True, 2008. The benefits of meditation and how to get started, go deeper, and maintain a daily practice.

LeClaire, Anne. *Listening below the Noise: A Meditation on the Practice of Silence*. San Francisco: HarperCollins, 2009. By detaching yourself from the hustle of your hectic lifestyle, you can listen to your deepest self and find a center for your life.

Lipsenthal, Lee. *Enjoy Every Sandwich*. New York: Crown, 2011. An inspirational book on living a fearless, full life as if each day were your last.

Loehr, Jim, and Tony Schwartz. *The Power of Full Engagement: Managing Energy, Not Time, Is the Key to High Performance and Personal Renewal*. New York: Free Press, 2003. Provides a fundamental insight—that the number of hours in a day is fixed, but the quantity and quality of energy available to us is not—that has the power to revolutionize the way we live.

Neff, Kristin. *Self-Compassion*. New York: HarperCollins, 2011. A scientific and personal look at how self-compassion reduces stress and promotes stress resilience and happiness.

Newberg, Andrew, and Mark Waldman. *How GOD Changes Your Brain*. New York: Ballantine, 2010. Breakthrough findings in neuroscience showing the link between brain chemistry, spirituality, and stress reduction.

Robinson, Bryan. *The Art of Confident Living*. Deerfield Beach, FL: HCI, 2009. A guide to a better and happier life for people on the fast track who've lost touch with themselves, and for anyone looking to develop more confidence at work, at home, at play.

———. *The Smart Guide to Managing Stress*. New York: Smart Guide, 2012. A practical guide for managing stress to improve your life, career, relationships, and mental state and to increase your joy, calm, and productivity.

Robinson, Bryan, and Nancy Chase, eds. *High-Performing Families: Causes, Consequences, and Clinical Solutions*. Washington: American Counseling Association, 2001. A look at families on the fast track and at what causes that lifestyle and its consequences and solutions.

Robinson, Bryan, and Claudia Flowers. "Symptoms of Workaholism: Pop Psychology or Private Pain?" In *Handbook of Addictive Disorders*, edited by Richard H. Coombs. New York: John Wiley and Sons, 2004. Examines the symptoms and problems of workaholism, going beneath the pop-psychology allegations and exposing the intense private pain this addiction can cause for workaholics as well as their friends and families.

Robinson, Joe. *The Guide to Getting a Life*. Berkeley, CA: Berkeley Publications, 2003. An impassioned manifesto about the need to take vacations to restore your body and soul.

Rossman, Martin. *The Worry Solution: Using Breakthrough Brain Science to Turn Stress and Anxiety into Confidence and Happiness*. New York: Crown, 2010. An easy-to-follow plan to relieve stress and anxiety by training your brain's imagination.

Salzberg, Sharon, and Joseph Goldstein. *Insight Meditation*. Boulder, CO: Sounds True, 2001. A workbook, a set of informational cards, and two CDs that take you step by step through a comprehensive training course in basic meditation.

Schwartz, Tony. *The Way We're Working Isn't Working*. New York: Simon and Schuster, 2010. A blueprint for a new way of working and a more satisfying way of life, providing a road map for how to develop a fully engaged workforce.

Siegel, Daniel. 2010. *The New Science of Personal Transformation*. New York: Bantam. Shows how to make positive changes in your brain and your life and heal from stressful events.

Siegel, Ronald. *The Mindful Solution: Everday Practices for Everyday Problems*. New York: Guilford, 2010. Offers a path to well-being and comprehensive mindfulness practices for coping with life's inevitable hurdles.

Tan, Chade-Meng. *Search inside Yourself: The Unexpected Path to Achieving Success, Happiness (and World Peace)*. New York: HarperOne, 2012. Shows what one major corporation has done to help employees find an unexpected path to achieving success, happiness, and world peace.

Thich Nhat Hanh. *Peace in Every Step: The Path of Mindfulness in Everyday Life*. New York: Bantam, 1991. Brings ancient Buddhist teachings to modern problems.

Tolle, Eckhart. *The Power of Now: A Guide to Spiritual Enlightenment*. Novato, CA: New World Library, 2004. A spiritual approach to inner peace that brings tranquility by leaving the analytical mind and its false created self, the ego, behind.

Workaholics Anonymous. *The Book of Recovery*. Menlo Park, CA: Workaholics Anonymous World Recovery, 2005. A comprehensive overview of workaholism, from individual stories to a step-by-step guide to successful recovery and practical information
on how to get meetings started.

DAILY READINGS

Beattie, Melody. *Gratitude*. Center City, MN: Hazelden, 2007. Features stirring affirmations that inspire readers to appreciate the really important things in life.

Hanson, Rick. *Just One Thing: Developing a Buddha Brain One Simple Practice at a Time*.
Oakland, CA: New Harbinger, 2011. Offers simple brain- training practices you can
do every day to protect against stress on the job.

Kundtz, David. *Awakened Mind*. San Francisco: Conari, 2009. One-minute wake-up
calls to a bold and mindful life.

———. *Quiet Mind: One-Minute Retreats from a Busy World*. San Francisco: Conari,
2000. Meditations and reflections to restore calm and clarity that hectic schedules
and lifestyles steal from you.

Nepo, Mark. *The Book of Awakening*. San Francisco: Conari, 2000. Reflections on having
the life you want by being present in the life you have.

Thich Nhat Hanh. *Walking Meditation*. Boulder, CO: Sounds True, 2006. Details various kinds of walking meditations and demonstrates how to do them with an accompanying DVD and CD.

Tolle, Eckhart. *Stillness Speaks*. Novato, CA: New World Library, 2003. How to connect
to the stillness that brings you inner peace.

Audiovisual Material

VIDEOS

Are You a Workaholic?

This video was produced by CBS Miami and features three famous South Florida workaholics: Dr. Karent Sierra, television star on *The Real Housewives of Miami*; Miami-Dade
Mayor Carlos Gimenez; and the Miami Heat's DJ, Irie. Each of them took my WART
test, and they discuss how their scores reflect their busy lives. Go to http://miami.cbslo-
cal.com/video/7943501-are-you-a-workaholic/#UJ4-6Y47tow.email.

Interview with a Workaholics Anonymous Member

This thirty-minute video shows an interview with a member of WA and the wife of a
workaholic. Order from Workaholics Anonymous, PO Box 289, Menlo Park, CA 94026.

Married to the Job

Taped by the Canadian Public Broadcasting Company, this thirty-minute video shows
people dealing with work addiction. It includes portions of a Workaholics Anonymous

meeting in Los Angeles. Order from Workaholics Anonymous, PO Box 289, Menlo Park, CA 94026.

Mindful Solutions for Success and Stress Reduction at Work

This video shows mindful techniques that can be used in the workplace to reduce job stress. Order from Mindful Solutions, Los Angeles, CA, www.elishagoldstein.com.

Overdoing It: When Work Becomes Your Life

In this thirty-minute documentary, which I hosted, seven people present deeply personal stories that portray the consequences of work addiction—inner misery, neglected families, broken marriages and relationships, physical problems, and even death. The video shows why people become workaholics, how the addiction has affected their lives, and where they sought help. Available on VHS only. Order from 1-800-582-9522 or WTVI Video, 3242 Commonwealth Avenue, Charlotte, NC 28205.

Working while on Vacation

NBC Nightly News/NBC Universal produced this interview with me about how Americans are either taking work on vacations or not taking vacations at all. Go to www.bryanrobinsononline.com. On the home page under "Recent Media Appearances," click on "Working while on Vacation" to view the video.

Working with Stress

This educational video on workplace stress describes factors that create or worsen job stress and practical measures to reduce them. Order from National Institute for Occupational Safety and Health, 1600 Clifton Road, Atlanta, GA 30333.

AUDIOTAPES

Being and Living with a Recovering Workaholic

This audiotape describes what it's like living with someone with work addiction. Order from Northern California Workaholics Anonymous Intergroup, c/o Mandana House, 541 Mandana Boulevard, Oakland, CA 94610.

Workaholics Anonymous Interview

This is an audiotape of an interview with the founder of WA, Dan G. Order from Northern California Workaholics Anonymous Intergroup, c/o Mandana House, 541 Mandana Boulevard, Oakland, CA 94610.

SAMPLE CDS FOR RELAXING

Jarre, Maurice. *Music for Relaxation, Meditation.*
Kern, Kevin. *Bathed in Dawn's Light.*
——. *iRelax during a Busy Day.*

McLaughlin, Billy. *Guitar Meditations.*
Stagg, Hilary. *Leaving the Workday Behind.*

Support Organizations and Websites

American Institute of Stress

www.stress.org
124 Park Avenue
Yonkers, NY 10703
A clearinghouse for information on all stress-related subjects, the institute produces a newsletter on the latest advances in stress research and relevant health issues.

Beck Institute for Cognitive Therapy and Research

www.beckinstitute.org
GSB Building
City Line and Belmont Avenues, Suite 700
Bala Cynwyd, PA 19004
The Beck Institute was founded in 1994 as an outgrowth of the psychotherapy developed by Dr. Aaron Beck, known as cognitive therapy. The institute provides state-of-the-art psychotherapy and research opportunities and serves as an international training ground for cognitive therapists at all levels. Cognitive therapy lends itself to the treatment of work addiction, because workaholics tend to be more in touch with their thinking than with their feelings. Many opportunities are available at this institute for clinicians who would like beginning or advanced training in cognitive therapy.

Benson-Henry Institute for Mind/Body Medicine

www.massgeneral.org
Massachusetts General Hospital
55 Fruit Street
Boston, MA 02114
This website offers help if you're experiencing the negative effects of work-related stress, including steps for how to elicit the relaxation response and a line of CDs for relaxation.

Center for Mindfulness in Medicine, Health Care, and Society

www.umassmed.edu
55 Lake Avenue North
Worcester, MA 01655
A global leader in mind/body medicine, the center hosts Jon Kabat-Zinn's eight-week mindfulness-based stress reduction program, intensive training that asks participants to draw on their inner resources and natural capacity to actively engage in caring for themselves and finding greater balance, ease, and peace of mind.

Esalen Institute

www.esalen.org
55000 Highway 1
Big Sur, CA 93920
An education center located on the California coast, Esalen hosts a convergence of mountains and sea, mind and body, East and West, and meditation and action through workshops on meditation, yoga, movement, work-study programs, and personal retreats to nourish your body, mind, and heart.

Imago Relationships International

www.imagotherapy.com
160 Broadway, East Building, Suite 1001
New York, NY 10038
Institute for Imago Relationship Therapy was founded in 1984 by Harville Hendrix. It offers face-to-face learning opportunities, including national and international workshops for couples and singles, and products that teach the dynamics of the love relationship in achieving personal growth. The institute's mission is to transform marriages and relationships and to improve parenting. The Imago Relationship Therapy approach is one of the best approaches I know for couples struggling with work addiction. Write or call to locate a certified Imago therapist in your area or for dates and locations of workshops for couples across the United States.

Insight Meditation Society

www.dharma.org/ims
1230 Pleasant Street
Barre, MA 01005
This is one of the Western world's most respected retreat centers for learning and deepening your meditation practices.

Institute for Meditation and Psychotherapy

www.meditationandpsychotherapy.org
35 Pleasant Street
Newton, MA 02459
The institute is dedicated to the training of mental health professionals interested in the integration of mindfulness, meditation, and psychotherapy.

Kripalu Center for Yoga and Health

www.kripalu.org
PO Box 309
Stockbridge, MA 01262
Offers workshops and retreats, a professional school, and online newsletter—all designed to teach the art and science of yoga and to produce thriving and healthy individuals and society.

Mind and Life Institute

www.mindandlife.org
7007 Winchester Circle, Suite 100
Boulder, CO 80301
Seeks to understand the human mind and build a scientific understanding of how to cultivate compassion and wisdom. Website contains an interactive mind and life blog.

National Institute for Occupational Safety and Health (NIOSH)

www.cdc.gov/niosh
Center for Disease Control and Prevention
1600 Clifton Road
Atlanta, GA 30333
Provides national and world leadership to prevent workplace illnesses and injuries and conducts research into occupational safety and health matters.

Omega Institute

www.eomega.org
150 Lake Drive
Rhinebeck, NY 12572
Omega retreats are designed to help you unplug from life's demands and deal with the daily pressures through the de-stressing, relaxing, and renewing your soul. The center offers workshops, trainings, retreats, and vacations where you can create your own schedule of meditation, massage, bodywork, acupuncture, tai chi, qigong, and physical activities.

Positive Emotions and Psychophysiology Laboratory

www.positiveemotions.org
Studies how your positive emotions affect thinking patterns, social behavior, and physiological reactions. The ultimate goal is to understand how positive emotions can combat stress, create well being, and transform lives for the better.

Robinson, Bryan E.

www.bryanrobinsononline.com
My website includes a monthly blog with resources and tips on how to recover from workaholism, outsmart stress, achieve work-life balance, and maintain stress resilience.

Self-Compassion: A Healthier Way of Relating to Yourself

www.self-compassion.org
Kristin Neff provides information about self-compassion, intended for students, researchers, and the general public. The site contains exercises to increase self-compassion, self-compassion meditations, and a test to gauge how self-compassionate you are.

Trauma Resource Institute

www.traumaresourceinstitute.com
PO Box 1891

Claremont, CA 91711

Holds the mission of restoring resiliency after trauma by expanding bottom up capacity, taking people from despair to hope.

Workaholics Anonymous

www.workaholics-anonymous.org

World Service Organization

PO Box 289

Menlo Park, CA 94026

This Twelve-Step support group has chapters nationwide. The purpose of WA is to help people stop working compulsively. Packets for starting new chapters of WA can be obtained from the address above.

The Psychometric Properties of the Work Addiction Risk Test

The Work Addiction Risk Test (WART) has been used clinically and in research. It has been tested for reliability and validity and is currently used around the world by researchers, graduate students, clinicians, and the general public to assess the prevalence of work addiction. Scientists in the Netherlands and Spain tested and borrowed items from the WART for their research.[1]

RELIABILITY OF THE WART

The test-retest reliability of the instrument is 0.83, and the coefficient alpha for the individual items is 0.85.[2] An internal consistency estimate of reliability (Cronbach's alpha) of 0.88 was obtained for the twenty-five WART items,[3] and the split-half reliability of the inventory with 442 respondents was 0.85.[4]

VALIDITY OF THE WART

Face validity and content validity were established for the instrument with five major subscales emerging: overdoing, self-worth, control-perfectionism, intimacy, and mental preoccupations/future reference.[5] Twenty psychotherapists, randomly selected from a state list, critically examined the twenty-five items on the WART for content validity. They were asked to identify twenty-five items from a list of thirty-five that most accurately measured work addiction. Selected test items had generally high content validity, with an average score of 89 out of a possible 100, and 90 percent of the psychotherapists scored 72 or higher.[6]

Concurrent validity was established on the WART in a study with 363 respondents.[7] Scores on the WART were correlated at 0.40 with generalized anxiety on the State-Trait

Anxiety Inventory[8] and 0.37 with the Type A Self-Report Inventory.[9] Correlations with moderate to low significance were obtained on the four scales of the Jenkins Activity Survey, the most commonly used measure of Type A behavior: 0.50 on the Type A scale, 0.50 on the speed and impatience scale, 0.39 on the hard-driving and competitive scale, and 0.20 on the job involvement scale.[10]

Concurrent validity also was demonstrated between the WART and the thinking/feeling scale on the Myers-Briggs Indicator in a study with ninety participants.[11] A regression analysis revealed that WART scores correlated more with the T end of the Myers-Briggs scale than with the F end. In addition, WART scores were significantly higher for respondents who worked more than forty hours a week than for those who worked fewer than forty-one hours per week.

AROUND THE WORLD WITH THE WART

A Dutch version of a work addiction scale (called the DUWAS) was constructed, taking nine of its seventeen items from the WART, and a short version of the DUWAS used six of the original items from the WART.[12] The results of the study showed internal validity of the tests using items from the WART. In addition, negative correlations in the study confirmed that workaholism is a negative construct, as my studies have suggested over the years.

A study at Central Queensland University in Australia reported that scores on the WART were correlated with scores on the Smartphone Problematic Use Questionnaire, which measures the negative impact of smart-phone use such as euphoria (as in addictive highs), withdrawal symptoms, interpersonal conflict, and problems in the workplace.[13]

Research studies using the WART are currently being conducted in the following countries: Belgium, Hungary, India, the Phillippines, Poland, Slovenia, and Turkey.

The WART has been translated into Spanish, Dutch, Polish, and Slovenian.

Notes

Notes to the Introduction

1. Wayne Oates, *Confessions of a Workaholic* (New York: World, 1971).
2. Chris Wright, "The Truth about Workaholism," *The Fix: Addiction and Recovery, Straight Up*, 24 September 2012, www.thefix.com/content/reckless-pursuit-being-busy, accessed 10 October 2012.
3. Samantha Rush, "Problematic Use of Smartphones in the Workplace: An Introductory Study," PhD diss., Central Queensland University, 2011.
4. International Center for Media and the Public Agenda, "The World Unplugged: Going 24 Hours without Media" (University Park: University of Maryland, 2011).
5. Bryan Robinson, "Chained to the Desk: Work May Be the Great Unexamined Therapy Issue of Our Time," *Family Therapy Networker*, July–August 2000, 26–37.
6. Steve Yoder, "Is America Overworked?" *Fiscal Times*, 16 February 2012.
7. Heather Berrigan, "Is the Workplace the Real American Idol?" *Living Church Foundation*, 30 November 2003, 1.
8. Wright, "The Truth about Workaholism."
9. Bryan Robinson, *The Smart Guide to Managing Stress* (New York: Smart Guide, 2012).
10. Neil Chesanow, "Vacation for the Health of it," *Endless Vacation*, January–February 2005, 31–32.
11. CareerBuilder, "One-in-Four Workers Can't Afford to Take a Vacation." *CareerBuilder Survey*, 25 May 2011.
12. Hugo Martin, "Survey Finds Lots of Unused Vacation Time," *Los Angeles Times*, 25 November 2012.
13. Stephanie Rosenbloom, "Please Don't Make Me Go on Vacation," *New York Times*, 10 August 2006.
14. Marilyn Machlowitz, *Workaholics: Living with Them, Working with Them* (Reading, MA: Addison-Wesley, 1985).
15. Daniel Seligman, "The Curse of Work," *Fortune*, 7 March 1994, 133.
16. Quoted in Wright, "The Truth about Workaholism."
17. Quoted in Loren Stein, "Workaholism: It's No Longer Seen as a Respectable Vice," *A Healthy Me*, 25 March 2006, 2.
18. Quoted in Emilie Filou, "Death in the Office," *World Business*, July–August 2006, 19–22.

19. American Psychiatric Association, "Current Procedural Terminology (CPT) Code Changes for 2013," http://www.psychiatry.org/practice/managing-a-practice/cpt-changes-2013, accessed 14 June 2013.

Notes to Chapter 1

1. See, for example, Sandra Haymon, "The Relationship of Work Addiction and Depression, Anxiety, and Anger in College Males," PhD diss., Florida State University, 1992; Bryan Robinson, Claudia Flowers, and Chris Burris, "An Empirical Study of the Relationship between Self-Leadership and Workaholism 'Firefighter' Behaviors," *Journal of Self-Leadership* 2 (2005): 22–36; Janet Spence and Ann Robbins, "Workaholics: Definitions, Measurement, and Preliminary Results," *Journal of Personality Assessment* 58 (1992): 160–78.
2. Ishu Ishiyama and Akio Kitayama, "Overwork and Career-Centered Self-Validation among the Japanese: Psychosocial Issues and Counselling Implications." *International Journal for the Advancement of Counselling* 17 (1994): 167–82.
3. Parul Sharma and Jyoti Sharma, "Work Addiction: A Poison by Slow Motion," *Journal of Economics and Behavioral Studies* 2 (2011): 86–91.
4. Consult the appendix for a more detailed explanation of the psychometric properties of the WART, or refer to the following research studies: Claudia Flowers and Bryan Robinson, "A Structural and Discriminant Analysis of the Work Addiction Risk Test," *Educational and Psychological Measurement* 62 (2002): 517–26; Bryan Robinson, "Concurrent Validity of the Work Addiction Risk Test as a Measure of Workaholism," *Psychological Reports* 79 (1996): 1313–14; Bryan Robinson and Bruce Phillips, "Measuring Workaholism: Content Validity of the Work Addiction Risk Test," *Psychological Reports* 77 (1995): 657–58; Bryan Robinson and Phyllis Post, "Validity of the Work Addiction Risk Test," *Perceptual and Motor Skills* 78 (1994): 337–38; Bryan Robinson and Phyllis Post, "Split-Half Reliability of the Work Addiction Risk Test: Development of a Measure of Workaholism," *Psychological Reports* 76 (1995): 1226; Bryan Robinson, Phyllis Post, and Judith Khakee, "Test-Retest Reliability of the Work Addiction Risk Test," *Perceptual and Motor Skills* 74 (1992): 926; Sandra Swary, "Myers-Briggs Type and Workaholism," honors thesis, Georgia State University, 1996.

Notes to Chapter 2

1. Bryan Robinson, Claudia Flowers, and Chris Burris, "An Empirical Study of the Relationship between Self-Leadership and Workaholism 'Firefighter' Behavior," *Journal of Self-Leadership* 2 (2005): 22–36.
2. Bryan Robinson, *Work Addiction* (Deerfield Beach, FL: HCI, 1989).
3. Wayne Oates, *Confessions of a Workaholic* (New York: World, 1971).
4. Diane Fassel describes work anorexics in *Working Ourselves to Death* (San Francisco: Harper and Row, 2000).
5. Gayle Porter, "Organizational Impact of Workaholism: Suggestions for Researching

the Negative Outcomes of Excessive Work," *Journal of Occupational Health Psychology* 1 (1996): 70–84.

6. Fassel, *Working Ourselves to Death*, 82.

7. For a more detailed explanation of the psychometric properties of the WART, see the appendix or the research studies listed in note 4 of chapter 1.

8. Wayne Sotile and Mary Sotile, *The Medical Marriage: A Couple's Survival Guide* (New York: Birch Lane, 1995).

9. Edward Hallowell and John Ratey, *Driven to Distraction: Recognizing and Coping with Attention Deficit Disorder* (New York: Simon and Schuster, 1994), 182.

Notes to Chapter 3

1. See, for example, Bryan Robinson, "Adult Children of Workaholics: Clinical and Empirical Research with Implications for Family Therapists," *Journal of Family Psychotherapy* 11 (2000): 15–26; Bryan Robinson, "Workaholism and Family Functioning: A Profile of Familial Relationships, Psychological Outcomes, and Research Considerations," *Contemporary Family Research* 23 (2001): 123–35; Jane Carroll and Bryan Robinson, "Depression and Parentification among Adults as Related to Parental Workaholism and Alcoholism," *Family Journal* 8 (2000): 360–67.

2. Quoted in Marilyn Machlowitz, "Workaholics Enjoy Themselves, an Expert Says: It's Their Family and Friends Who Pay," *Psychology Today*, June 1980, 79.

3. Bryan Robinson, "The Workaholic Family: A Clinical Perspective," *American Journal of Family Therapy* 26 (1998): 63–73.

4. Anthony Pietropinto, "The Workaholic Spouse," *Medical Aspects of Human Sexuality* 20 (1986): 89–96.

5. Barbara Killinger, *Workaholics: The Respectable Addicts* (New York: Fireside, 1992).

6. Robert Klaft and Brian Kleiner, "Understanding Workaholics," *Business* 38 (1988): 37.

7. Quoted in Terri Finch Hamilton, "Women Susceptible to Working Whirl," *Grand Rapids Press*, 27 June 1991.

8. See, for example, Nancy Chase, *The Parentified Child: Theory, Research, and Treatment* (Thousand Oaks, CA: Sage, 1998); Gregory Jurkovic, *Lost Childhoods: The Plight of the Parentified Child* (New York: Brunner-Mazel, 1997).

9. Ishu Ishiyama and Akio Kitayama, "Overwork and Career-Centered Self-Validation among the Japanese: Psychosocial Issues and Counselling Implications," *International Journal for the Advancement of Counselling* 17 (1994): 168.

10. Reports of the first research study can be found in these two sources: Bryan Robinson and Phyllis Post, "Work Addiction as a Function of Family of Origin and Its Influence on Current Family Functioning," *Family Journal* 3 (1995): 200–206; Bryan Robinson and Phyllis Post, "Risk of Addiction to Work and Family Functioning," *Psychological Reports* 81 (1997): 91–95.

11. Bryan Robinson and Lisa Kelley, "Adult Children of Workaholics: Self-Concept, Anxiety, Depression, and Locus of Control," *American Journal of Family Therapy* 26 (1998): 223–38.

12. Robinson, "Workaholism and Family Functioning."

Notes to Chapter 4

1. Diane Fassel and Anne Wilson Schaef, "A Feminist Perspective on Work Addiction," in *Feminist Perspectives on Addictions*, ed. Nan Van Den Bergh (New York: Springer, 1991), 199–211.
2. Ibid., 208.
3. Gayle Porter, "Organizational Impact of Workaholism: Suggestions for Researching the Negative Outcomes of Excessive Work," *Journal of Occupational Health Psychology* 1 (1996): 74.
4. For more information on how to build your confidence in everyday life, see Bryan Robinson, *The Art of Confident Living* (Deerfield Beach, FL: HCI, 2009).
5. Quoted in Annmarie L. Geddes, "The Pitfalls of Being Addicted to Work," *Cleveland's Small Business News*, June 1995, 57.
6. Porter, "Organizational Impact of Workaholism," 75.
7. Bryan Robinson, *Don't Let Your Mind Stunt Your Growth* (Oakland, CA: New Harbinger, 2000).
8. See, for example, Judith Beck, *Cognitive Behavior Therapy: Basics and Beyond* (New York: Guilford, 2011); David Burns, *Feeling Good: The New Mood Therapy* (New York: HarperCollins, 1999); Albert Ellis and Windy Dryden, *The Practice of Rational Emotive Behavior Therapy*, 2nd ed. (New York: Springer, 2007).
9. Ishu Ishiyama and Akio Kitayama, "Overwork and Career-Centered Self-Validation among the Japanese: Psychosocial Issues and Counselling Implications." *International Journal for the Advancement of Counselling* 17 (1994): 167–82.
10. I will discuss the importance of self-compassion in later chapters. For two excellent evidenced-based books on the subject, see Christopher Germer, *The Mindful Path to Self-Compassion* (New York: Guilford, 2009); Kristin Neff, *Self-Compassion* (New York: HarperCollins, 2011).

Notes to Chapter 5

1. Gloria Steinem, foreword to Bryan Robinson, *Overdoing It: How to Slow Down and Take Care of Yourself* (Deerfield Beach, FL: HCI, 1992), ix–xii. Used with permission.
2. See, for example, Diane Fassel, *Working Ourselves to Death* (San Francisco: Harper and Row, 2000); Bryan Robinson, "The Workaholic Family: A Clinical Perspective," *American Journal of Family Therapy* 26 (1998): 63–73; Bryan Robinson and Phyllis Post, "Work Addiction as a Function of Family of Origin and Its Influence on Current Family Functioning," *Family Journal* 3 (1995): 200–206; Bryan Robinson and Phyllis Post, "Risk of Addiction to Work and Family Functioning," *Psychological Reports* 81 (1997): 91–95.
3. Elaine Miller-Karas and Laurie Leitch, *Trauma Resiliency Model Level 2 Training Manual* (Claremont, CA: Trauma Resource Institute, 2012).
4. J. M. MacDougall, T. M. Dembroski, J. E. Dimsdale, and T. P. Hackett, "Components of Type A, Hostility, and Anger-In: Further Relationships to Angiographic Findings," *Health Psychology* 4 (1985): 137–52.

5. Gloria Steinem, *Revolution from Within: A Book on Self-Esteem* (New York: Little, Brown, 1992).

6. For an excellent discussion of emotional incest, see Patricia Love, *The Emotional Incest Syndrome: What to Do When a Parents' Love Rules Your Life* (New York: Dutton, 1990).

7. Rebecca Jones and Marolyn Wells, "An Empirical Study of Parentification and Personality," *American Journal of Family Therapy* 24 (1996): 150.

8. Ibid.

9. Malcolm West and Adrienne Keller, "Parentification of the Child: A Case Study of Bowlby's Compulsive Care-Giving Attachment Pattern," *American Journal of Psychotherapy* 155 (1991): 425–31.

10. Ibid., 426.

11. John Bowlby, "The Making and Breaking of Affectional Bonds," *British Journal of Psychiatry* 130 (1977): 201–10.

12. In her book *On Death and Dying* (New York: Macmillan, 1969), Dr. Elisabeth Kübler-Ross identified five stages of grief that the dying and their loved ones typically go through: shock, denial, bargaining, anger, and acceptance.

13. For a comprehensive examination of family-of-origin roles, see Sharon Wegscheider, *The Family Trap* (Palo Alto, CA: Science and Behavior, 1979). For how these roles apply to children of alcoholics, see also Bryan Robinson and Lyn Rhoden, *Working with Children of Alcoholics: The Practitioner's Handbook* (Thousand Oaks, CA: Sage, 1998).

Notes to Chapter 6

1. Bryan Robinson, Jane Carroll, and Claudia Flowers, "Marital Estrangement, Positive Affect, and Locus of Control among Spouses of Workaholics and Spouses of Nonworkaholics: A National Study," *American Journal of Family Therapy* 29 (2001): 397–410.

2. Bryan Robinson, Claudia Flowers, and Kok-Mun Ng, "The Relationship between Workaholism and Marital Disaffection: Husbands' Perspective," *Family Journal* 14 (2006): 213–20.

3. Edward Walsh, "Workaholism: No Life for the Leisurelorn?" *Parks and Recreation*, January 1987, 82.

4. Anthony Pietropinto, "The Workaholic Spouse," *Medical Aspects of Human Sexuality* 20 (1986): 89–96.

5. Daniel Weeks, "Cooling Off Your Office Affair," *North West Airlines World Traveler Magazine*, June 1995, 59–62.

6. Ann Herbst, "Married to the Job," *McCall's*, November 1996, 130–34.

7. Harville Hendrix, *Getting the Love You Want: A Guide for Couples* (New York: St. Martin's, 2008).

8. Paul Deluca, *The Solo Partner: Repairing Your Relationship on Your Own* (Point Roberts, WA: Hartley and Marks, 1996).

9. Ishu Ishiyama and Akio Kitayama, "Overwork and Career-Centered Self-Validation

among the Japanese: Psychosocial Issues and Counselling Implications," *International Journal for the Advancement of Counselling* 17 (1994): 178.

10. Bryan Robinson, *Work Addiction* (Deerfield Beach, FL: HCI, 1989).

11. Studs Terkel, *Working* (New York: Pantheon, 1974).

12. Ann Bailey," He Puts Work ahead of the Family," *First for Women*, August 2003, 91.

13. Stephen Betchen, "Parentified Pursuers and Childlike Distancers in Marital Therapy," *Family Journal* 4 (1996): 100–108.

14. Ibid., 103.

15. Thomas Fogarty, "The Distancer and the Pursuer," *Family* 7 (1979): 11–16; Thomas Fogarty, "Marital Crisis," in *Family Therapy: Theory and Practice*, ed. Paul Guerin (New York: Gardner, 1976), 325–34.

16. Bryan Robinson and Phyllis Post, "Work Addiction as a Function of Family of Origin and Its Influence on Current Family Functioning," *Family Journal* 3 (1995): 200–206.

17. Hendrix, *Getting the Love You Want: A Guide for Couples*; Harville Hendrix, *Getting the Love You Want: A Couples Workshop Manual* (New York: Institute for Relationship Therapy, 1994).

Notes to Chapter 7

1. See, for example, Virginia Kelly and Jane Myers, "Parental Alcoholism and Coping: A Comparison of Female Children of Alcoholics with Female Children of Nonalcoholics," *Journal of Counseling and Development* 74 (1996): 501–4; Phyllis Post and Bryan Robinson, "A Comparison of School-Age Children of Alcoholic and Nonalcoholic Parents on Anxiety, Self-Esteem, and Locus of Control," *Professional School Counselor* 1 (1998): 36–42; Phyllis Post, Wanda Webb, and Bryan Robinson, "Relationship between Self-Concept, Anxiety, and Knowledge of Alcoholism by Gender and Age among Adult Children of Alcoholics," *Alcoholism Treatment Quarterly* 8 (1991): 91–95; Bryan Robinson and Lyn Rhoden, *Working with Children of Alcoholics* (Thousand Oaks, CA: Sage, 1998); Sandra Tweed and Cynthia Ryff, "Adult Children of Alcoholics: Profiles of Wellness amid Distress," *Journal of Studies on Alcohol* 52 (1991): 133–41; Wanda Webb, Phyllis Post, Bryan Robinson, and Lynn Moreland, "Self-Concept, Anxiety, and Knowledge Exhibited by Adult Children of Alcoholics and Adult Children of Nonalcoholics," *Journal of Drug Education* 20 (1992): 106–14.

2. Anthony Pietropinto, "The Workaholic Spouse," *Medical Aspects of Human Sexuality* 20 (1986): 89–96; Bryan Robinson, *Work Addiction* (Deerfield Beach, FL: HCI, 1989); Gerald Spruell, "Work Fever," *Training and Development Journal* 41 (1987): 41–45.

3. See, for example, Bryan Robinson, "Children of Workaholics: What Practitioners Need to Know," *Journal of Child and Youth Care* 12 (1998): 3–10; Bryan Robinson and Jane Carroll, "Assessing the Offspring of Workaholics: The Children of Workaholics Screening Test," *Perceptual and Motor Skills* 88 (1999): 1127–34; Bryan Robinson, "Adult Children of Workaholics: Clinical and Empirical Research with

Implications for Family Therapists," *Journal of Family Psychotherapy* 11 (2000): 15–26; Bryan Robinson, "Workaholism and Family Functioning: A Profile of Familial Relationships, Psychological Outcomes, and Research Considerations," *Contemporary Family Research* 23 (2001): 123–35.

4. Bryan Robinson and Lisa Kelley, "Adult Children of Workaholics: Self-Concept, Anxiety, Depression, and Locus of Control," *American Journal of Family Therapy* 26 (1998): 223–38.

5. See, for example, Kelly and Myers, "Parental Alcoholism and Coping"; Robinson and Rhoden, *Working with Children of Alcoholics*; Webb, Post, Robinson, and Moreland, "Self-Concept, Anxiety, and Knowledge Exhibited by Adult Children of Alcoholics and Adult Children of Nonalcoholics."

6. Sheri Navarrete, "An Empirical Study of Adult Children of Workaholics: Psychological Functioning and Intergenerational Transmission," PhD diss., California Graduate Institute, 1998.

7. Elaine Searcy, "Adult Children of Workaholics: Anxiety, Depression, Family Relationships and Risk for Work Addiction," master's thesis, University of South Australia, 2000.

8. Jane Carroll and Bryan Robinson, "Depression and Parentification among Adults as Related to Parental Workaholism and Alcoholism," *Family Journal* 8 (2000): 360–67.

9. Barbara Killinger, *Workaholics: The Respectable Addicts* (New York: Firefly, 1991).

10. Wayne Oates, *Confessions of a Workaholic* (New York: World, 1971); Bryan Robinson, *Overdoing It: How to Slow Down and Take Care of Yourself* (Deerfield Beach, FL: HCI, 1992); Bryan Robinson, "Relationship between Work Addiction and Family Functioning: Clinical Implications for Marriage and Family Therapists," *Journal of Family Psychotherapy* 7 (1996): 13–29.

11. Quoted in Marilyn Machlowitz, "Workaholics Enjoy Themselves, an Expert Says: It's Their Family and Friends Who Pay," *Psychology Today*, June 1980, 79.

12. Oates, *Confessions of a Workaholic*.

13. Tina Harralson and Kathleen Lawler, "The Relationship of Parenting Styles and Social Competency to Type A Behavior in Children," *Journal of Psychosomatic Research* 36 (1992): 625–34; Patti Watkins, Clay Ward, Douglas Southard, and Edwin Fisher, "The Type A Belief System: Relationships to Hostility, Social Support, and Life Stress," *Behavioral Medicine* 18 (1992): 27–32.

14. Karen Woodall and Karen Matthews, "Familial Environment Associated with Type A Behaviors and Psychophysiological Responses to Stress in Children," *Health Psychology* 8 (1989): 403–26.

15. Pietropinto, "The Workaholic Spouse."

16. Bryan Robinson, *The Art of Confident Living* (Deerfield Beach, FL: HCI, 2009).

17. Quoted in Daniel Weeks, "Cooling Off Your Office Affair," *North West Airlines World Traveler Magazine*, June 1995, 62.

18. For a further discussion of subpersonalities, see Bryan Robinson, *The Smart Guide to Managing Stress* (New York: Smart Guide, 2012).

Notes to Chapter 8

1. Michael Matthews and Bernadette Halbrook, "Adult Children of Alcoholics: Implications for Career Development," *Journal of Career Development* 16 (1990): 261–68; Janet Woititz, *Home Away from Home* (Deerfield Beach, FL: HCI, 1987).

2. Robert Klaft and Brian Kleiner, "Understanding Workaholics," *Business* 38 (1988): 37–40.

3. Gayle Porter, "Workaholics as High-Performance Employees: The Intersection of Workplace and Family Relationship Problems," in *High-Performing Families: Causes, Consequences, and Clinical Solutions*, ed. Bryan Robinson and Nancy Chase (Washington: American Counseling Association, 2001), 43–69; Gayle Porter, "Work, Work Ethic, Work Excess," *Journal of Organizational Change Management* 17 (2004): 424–39; Gayle Porter, "Profiles of Workaholism among High-Tech Managers," *Career Development-International* 11 (2006): 440–62; Gayle Porter and Nada Kakabadse, "HRM Perspectives on Addiction to Technology and Work," *Journal of Management Development* 25 (2006): 535–60.

4. Gayle Porter, "Organizational Impact of Workaholism: Suggestions for Researching the Negative Outcomes of Excessive Work," *Journal of Occupational Health Psychology* 1 (1996): 82.

5. Ibid., 71.

6. Bill Billeter, "Workaholics Are Hurting the Company and Themselves," *Charlotte Observer*, 16 May 1981.

7. Emilie Filou, "Death in the Office," *World Business*, July–August 2006, 19–22.

8. Lesley Alderman, "How to Tell the Boss You're Getting Worked to Death—Without Killing Your Career," *Money*, May 1995, 41.

9. Christine Rosen, "The Myth of Multitasking," *New Atlantis*, Spring 2008, 105–10.

10. Joshua Rubinstein, David Meyer, and Jeffrey Evans, "Executive Control of Cognitive Processes in Task Switching," *Journal of Experimental Psychology: Human Perception and Performance*, 4 (2001): 763–97.

11. Adam Gorlick, "Media Multitaskers Pay Mental Price, Stanford Study Shows," *Stanford Report*, 24 August 2009, 3–5.

12. Nada Kakabadse, Gayle Porter, and David Vance, "Employer Liability for Addiction to Information and Communication Technology," unpublished paper, 2006.

13. Ellen Gamerman, "The New Power Picnics," *Wall Street Journal*, 12 August 2006.

14. Ibid.

15. Alderman, "How to Tell the Boss You're Getting Worked to Death."

16. Sue Shellenbarger, "To Cut Office Stress, Try Butterflies and Meditation?," *Wall Street Journal*, 9 October 2012.

17. Leslie Wright and Marti Smye, *Corporate Abuse: How "Lean and Mean" Robs People and Profits* (New York: Macmillan, 1996), 82.

18. Anne Wilson Schaef and Diane Fassel, *The Addictive Organization* (San Francisco: Harper, 1988).

19. Diane Fassel and Anne Wilson Schaef, "A Feminist Perspective on Work Addiction," in *Feminist Perspectives on Addictions*, ed. Nan Van Den Bergh (New York: Springer, 1991), 199–211.

20. Klaft and Kleimer, "Understanding Workaholics," 39.
21. Scott Reeves, "Workaholics Anonymous," *Forbes*, 20 April 2006, 1–3.
22. John Sheridan, "Workin' Too Hard," *Industry Week*, 18 January 1988, 31–36.
23. Kaitlin Quistgaard, "Stress Buster," *Yoga Journal*, August 2012, 26.
24. Chade-Meng Tan, *Search inside Yourself: The Unexpected Path to Achieving Success, Happiness (and World Peace)* (New York: HarperOne, 2012).
25. Shellenbarger, "To Cut Office Stress, Try Butterflies and Meditation?"
26. Tony Schwartz, "Relax! You'll Be More Productive," *New York Times*, 9 February 2013; Tony Schwartz, *Be Excellent at Anything* (New York: Free Press, 2010).
27. Alderman, "How to Tell the Boss You're Getting Worked to Death."
28. Michelle Conlin, "Square Feet: Oh, How Square!" *Business Week*, 3 July 2006, 100–101; Bryan Robinson, *The Smart Guide to Managing Stress* (New York: Smart Guide, 2012).
29. Klaft and Kleimer, "Understanding Workaholics."

Notes to Chapter 9

1. Ruth van Holst, William Van den Brink, Dick Veltman, and Anna Goudriaan, "Brain Imaging Studies in Pathological Gambling," *Current Psychiatry Report* 12 (2010): 418–25.
2. For more information on the stress response, see Christy Matta, *The Stress Response* (Oakland, CA: New Harbinger, 2012); Ron Siegel and Michael Yapko, "Has Mindfulness Been Oversold?" *Psychotherapy Networker*, March–April, 2012, 44.
3. Bronwyn Fryer, "Are You Working too Hard?" *Harvard Business Review*, November 2005, 90–96.
4. See, for example, Richard Davidson and Sharon Begley, *The Emotional Life of Your Brain* (New York: Hudson Street, 2012). Daniel Amen, *Change Your Brain, Change Your Body* (New York: Three Rivers, 2010); Norman Doidge, *The Brain That Changes Itself* (New York: Penguin, 2007); Richard Hanson and Richard Mendius, *Buddha's Brain: The Practical Neuroscience of Happiness, Love and Wisdom* (Oakland, CA: New Harbinger, 2009); Martin Rossman, *The Worry Solution: Using Breakthrough Brain Science to Turn Stress and Anxiety into Confidence and Happiness* (New York: Crown, 2010).
5. Davidson and Begley, *The Emotional Life of Your Brain* ; Chade-Meng Tan, *Search inside Yourself: The Unexpected Path to Achieving Success, Happiness (and World Peace)* (New York: HarperOne, 2012).
6. Andrew Newberg and Mark Waldman, *How GOD Changes Your Brain* (New York: Ballantine, 2010).
7. Roy Baumeister and John Tierney, *Willpower: Rediscovering the Greatest Human Strength* (New York: HarperOne, 2011).
8. For step-by-step exercises to activate your parasympathetic nervous system, see Bryan Robinson, *The Smart Guide to Managing Stress* (New York: Smart Guide, 2012).
9. Newberg and Waldman, *How GOD Changes Your Brain.*

10. Robinson, *The Smart Guide to Managing Stress*.

11. Sara Lazar, "Meditation Experience Is Associated with Increased Cortical Thickness," *Neuroreport* 16 (2005): 1893–97.

12. Hanson and Mendius, *Buddha's Brain*.

13. Viktor Frankl, *Man's Search for Meaning* (Boston, MA: Beacon, 2006).

14. Cynthia Adams, "Stressed Out? Think Tennis Shoes, Not Tranquilizers." *University of Georgia Graduate School Magazine*, May 2012, 17–21.

Notes to Chapter 10

1. Matthew Killingsworth and Daniel Gilbert, "A Wandering Mind Is an Unhappy Mind," *Science*, 12 November 2010, 932.

2. See Bryan Robinson, *Work Addiction* (Deerfield Beach, FL: Health Communications, 1989), in which I first described brownouts as more frequent and severe in workaholics than in the average worker and as similar to alcoholic blackouts, which are characterized by memory losses of interactions and events.

3. Chade-Meng Tan, *Search inside Yourself: The Unexpected Path to Achieving Success, Happiness (and World Peace)* (New York: HarperOne, 2012).

4. See, for example, Thomas Bien and Beverly Bien, *Mindful Recovery: A Spiritual Path to Healing from Addiction* (New York: Wiley, 2002); Thomas Bien, *Mindful Therapy: A Guide for Therapists and Helping Professionals* (New York: Wisdom, 2006); Richard Davidson et al., "Alterations in Brain and Immune Function Produced by Mindfulness Meditation," *Psychomatic Medicine* 65 (2003): 564–70; the Dalai Lama and Howard Cutler, *The Art of Happiness at Work: The Conversation Continues about Job, Career, and Calling* (New York: Riverhead, 2003); Jon Kabat-Zinn, *Coming to Our Senses: Healing Ourselves and the World through Mindfulness* (New York: Hyperion, 2005); Daniel Siegel, *The Mindful Therapist: A Clinician's Guide to Mindsight and Neural Integration* (New York: Norton, 2010); Daniel Siegel, *Mindsight: The New Science of Personal Transformation* (New York: Bantam, 2010).

5. Tan, *Search Inside Yourself*.

6. See, for example, Daniel Siegel, *Mindsight: The New Science of Personal Transformation* (New York: Bantam, 2010); Daniel Siegel, *The Mindful Brain: Reflection and Attunement in the Cultivation of Well-Being* (New York: Norton, 2007); Richard Hanson and Richard Mendius, *Buddha's Brain: Practical Neuroscience of Happiness, Love, and Wisdom* (Oakland, CA: New Harbinger, 2009).

7. Bryan Robinson, "Mindful Working," *Wise Brain Bulletin* 4 (2010):1–14.

8. Jon Kabat-Zinn, *Wherever You Go, There You Are: Mindfulness Meditation in Everyday Life* (New York: Hyperion, 1994), 5.

9. See, for example, Hanson and Mendius, *Buddha's Brain* ; Martin Rossman, *The Worry Solution: Breakthrough Science to Turn Stress and Anxiety into Confidence and Happiness* (New York: Crown, 2010); Daniel Siegel, *The Mindful Brain* (New York: Norton, 2007); Ronald Siegel, *The Mindful Solution: Everyday Practices for Everyday Problems* (New York: Guilford, 2010).

10. Jim Loehr and Tony Schwartz, *The Power of Full Engagement: Managing Energy, Not*

Time, Is the Key to High Performance and Personal Renewal (New York: Free Press, 2003).

11. Jan Chozen Bays, *Mindful Eating: A Guide to Rediscovering a Healthy and Joyful Relationship with Food* (Boston: Shambhala, 2009), 5.

12. Thich Nhat Hanh, *Peace in Every Step: The Path of Mindfulness in Everyday Life* (New York: Bantam, 1991).

13. Ron Seigel and Michael Yapko, "Has Mindfulness Been Oversold?" *Psychotherapy Networker*, March–April 2012, 55.

14. See Bryan Robinson, *The Smart Guide to Managing Stress* (New York: Smart Guide, 2012), for details on various strategies for managing stress.

Notes to Chapter 11

1. Barbara Fredrickson, *Positivity* (New York: Three Rivers, 2009).

2. Ibid.

3. Ibid.

4. See, for example, Ron Kaniel, Cade Massey, and David Robinson, "Optimism and Economic Crisis," working paper, 15 July 2010; Susan Segerstrom, *Breaking Murphy's Law: How Optimists Get What They Want from Life—and Pessimists Can Too* (New York: Guilford, 2007); Michael Scheier et al., "Dispositional Optimism and Recovery from Coronary Artery Bypass Surgery: The Beneficial Effects on Physical and Psychological Well-Being," *Journal of Personality and Social Psychology* 57 (1989): 1024–40; Paul Schofield et al., "Optimism and Survival in Lung Carcinoma Patients," *Cancer* 100 (2004): 1276–82.

5. Segerstrom, *Breaking Murphy's Law*.

6. Kaori Kato, Richard Zweig, Nir Barzilai, and Gil Atzmon, "Positive Attitude towards Life and Emotional Expression as Personality Phenotypes for Centenarians," *Aging* 4 (2012): 359–67.

7. See, for example, Sadie Dingfelder, "Our Stories, Ourselves," *APA Monitor on Psychology* 42 (2011): 42; Stephen Joseph, *What Doesn't Kill Us: The New Psychology of Post-Traumatic Growth* (New York: Basic, 2011); Laura King, Christie Scollon, Christine Ramsey, and Teresa Williams, "Stories of Life Transition: Subjective Well-Being and Ego Development in Parents of Children with Down Syndrome," *Journal of Research in Personality* 34 (2000): 509–36; Kathleen McGowan, "The Hidden Side of Happiness," *Psychology Today*, 1 March 2006, 36–37.

8. Kristin Neff, *Self-Compassion* (New York: HarperCollins, 2011); Christopher Germer, *The Mindful Path to Self-Compassion* (New York: Guilford, 2009).

9. Neff, *Self-Compassion*.

10. Kirsten Weir, "Golden Rule Redux," *APA Monitor on Psychology* 42 (2011): 42–45.

11. Neff, *Self-Compassion*.

12. Ibid.

13. Catherine Price and Carmel Wroth, "Compassion Remains a Gift of the Spirit," *Yoga Journal*, August 2012, 78–81, 100.

14. Neff, *Self-Compassion*.

Notes to Chapter 12

1. William Maddux and Adam Galinsky, "Cultural Borders and Mental Barriers: The Relationship between Living Abroad and Creativity," *Journal of Personality and Social Psychology* 96 (2009): 1047–61.
2. Erin Kelly, Phyllis Moen, and Eric Tranby, "Changing Workplaces to Reduce Work-Family Conflict: Schedule Control in a White-Collar Organization," *American Sociological Review* 76 (2011): 265–90.
3. Bryan Robinson, *The Smart Guide to Managing Stress* (New York: Smart Guide, 2012).
4. Gayle Porter, "Workaholic Tendencies and the High Potential for Stress among Coworkers," *International Journal of Stress Management* 8 (2001): 147–64.
5. Marianna Virtanen et al., "Overtime Work and Incident Coronary Heart Disease: The Whitehall II Prospective Cohort Study," *European Heart Journal* 31 (2010): 1737–44.
6. Robinson, The Smart Guide to Managing Stress.
7. Melinda Beck, "Why Relaxing Is Hard Work," *Wall Street Journal*, 15 June 2010; Esther Sternberg, *The Balance Within: The Science Connecting Health and Emotion* (New York: W. H. Freeman, 2001); Stephanie Stephens, "When Relaxing Makes You Sick," *High Energy for Life*, 20 June 2012, 1–2, http://www.bottomlinepublications.com/content/article/travel-a-recreation/when-relaxing-makes-you-sick, accessed 13 June 2013.
8. Information on Workaholics Anonymous in this section (The Steps of Workaholics Anonymous, History of Workaholics Anonymous, Signposts of Workaholics, Tools of Workaholics Anonymous, The Problem, and The Solution) is reprinted by permission of Workaholics Anonymous World Service Organization, © 1991 WA World Services, Inc.
9. See Robinson, *The Smart Guide to Managing Stress*, for more process-oriented activities to dodge stress and burnout and a further discussion of "the sweetness of doing nothing."

Notes to the Appendix

1. Mario del Llorens, Marisa Salanova, and Wilmar Schaufeli, "Validity of a Brief Workaholism Scale," *Psicothema* 22 (2010): 143–50.
2. Bryan Robinson, Phyllis Post, and Judith Khakee, "Test-Retest Reliability of the Work Addiction Risk Test," *Perceptual and Motor Skills* 74 (1992): 926.
3. Bryan Robinson, "The Work Addiction Risk Test: Development of a Self-Report Measure of Workaholism," *Perceptual and Motor Skills* 88 (1999): 199–210.
4. Bryan Robinson and Phyllis Post, "Split-Half Reliability of the Work Addiction Risk Test: Development of a Measure of Workaholism," *Psychological Reports* 76 (1995): 1226.
5. Bryan Robinson and Phyllis Post, "Validity of the Work Addiction Risk Test," *Perceptual and Motor Skills* 78 (1994): 337–38.

6. Bryan Robinson and Bruce Phillips, "Measuring Workaholism: Content Validity of the Work Addiction Risk Test," *Psychological Reports* 77 (1995): 657–58.
7. Bryan Robinson, "Concurrent Validity of the Work Addiction Risk Test as a Measure of Workaholism," *Psychological Reports* 79 (1996): 1313–14.
8. Charles Spielberger, *Self-Evaluation Questionnaire (STAI Form X-2)*, Palo Alto, CA: Consulting Psychologists, 1968.
9. James Blumenthal et al., "Development of a Brief Self-Report Measure of the Type A (Coronary Prone) Behavior Pattern," *Journal of Psychosomatic Research* 29 (1985): 265–74.
10. David Jenkins, Ray Rosenman, and Meyer Friedman, "Development of an Objective Psychological Test for the Determination of the Coronary-Prone Behavior Pattern in Employed Men," *Journal of Chronic Disease* 20 (1967): 371–79.
11. Sandra Swary, "Myers-Briggs Type and Workaholism," honors thesis, Georgia State University, 1996.
12. Del Llorens, Salanova, and Schaufeli, "Validity of a Brief Workaholism Scale."
13. Samantha Rush, "Problematic Use of Smartphones in the Workplace: An Introductory Study," PhD diss., Central Queensland University, 2011.

Index

Culture: technically driven work, 1; work-
 obsessed, 27
"Cultures of sacrifice," 146

Death from overwork (*karoshi*), 19
Decision-fatigued brain, 172
Denial, 225–26
Depression: of children, 63, 123, 124, 125,
 126, 127, 134; of families, 50, 56, 114;
 manic, 121; of workaholics, 2, 4, 17,
 18, 35, 100
Desk potato, 215
*Diagnostic and Statistical Manual of Mental
 Disorders* (DSM-5), 6–7
Diary, for mindful working, 188–89
Disease, workaholism as, 51–53, 62–63, 223
Divorce, 106
Dopamine release, 92
Double bind, of spouses and partners,
 113–14
Downsizing, 146
Driven to Distraction (Hallowell and Ratey),
 46
Driving while working mentally (DWW),
 34–35
Drug addiction program, 30–31
Drug rehab program, 31
DSM-5. See *Diagnostic and Statistical Manual
 of Mental Disorders*
DWW. *See* Driving while working mentally
Dysfunction, of family, 88–89
Dysfunctional childhood: of Art, 195; self-
 regulation and, 90–92

Economic Policy Institute, 5
Einstein, Albert, 213
Emotional bankruptcy, 97
Emotional brain, 168
Empowerment, 26
Enabling, 55–56, 63, 112
Engaged workaholics, 6
Epidemic, of work addiction, 8
Epinephrine, 46
Equanimity, 208–9
Exercises: for mindfulness, 183–85, 190;
 mindful working, 190–91, 193; for
 workaholic mind, 74; written, 80

Exploitation and abuse, in workplace,
 145–46
Externalized thinking, 76, 78

Failure: fear of, 71; of Kathy, 68–69
Families: breakdown of, 52; clinician tips
 for, 60–65; depression of, 50, 56, 114;
 imperfect, 89; perfect, 89; support for,
 64–65; vilification of, 56–57; work addic-
 tion and dysfunction of, 88–89; work
 addiction's impact on, 50–51; workahol-
 ism as disease of, 51–53, 62–63
Families and Work Institute, 4
Family-of-origin work, 100
Family systems addictions model, 51–53
Fear, of failure, 71
Fight-or-flight response, 167, 186
Focused attention mindfulness meditation,
 189
Frankl, Viktor, 176–77

Gastrointestinal problems, stress-related,
 14
George: career of, 164; childhood of,
 163; education of, 163–64;
 recovery of, 165–67; workaholism of,
 164–65
Global High Intensity Activation (GHIA),
 90–92
Goals, 25, 45–47
Gray matters, of brain, 166–67

Habits, of workaholics, 3, 4, 198–99
Hallowell, Edward, 46
Hard work, workaholism and, 16, 20–23
Haste concern, 127
Health: Cooper's crisis of, 179–80, 186;
 optimism's impact on, 204; Roger's
 problems of, 30
Healthy work habits checklist, 198–99
Helpless thinking, 75, 77
High-powered couples, 45
High-stim ADD, 46
Homework, 227–28
"How Stressed Are You?," 169
How to Win Friends and Influence People
 (Carnegie), 130

About the Author

Bryan E. Robinson, PhD, is Professor Emeritus at the University of North Carolina at Charlotte, a Fellow of the American Institute of Stress, and a licensed psychotherapist in private practice in Asheville, NC. He is the author of over thirty-five self-help and academic books, the latest of which is *The Smart Guide to Managing Stress*.

Robinson has published his research in over a hundred scholarly journals. He received the American Counseling Association's Research Award and the University of North Carolina at Charlotte's First Citizen Scholars Medal for his pioneer research on the negative consequences of workaholism. He hosted the PBS documentary *Overdoing It: When Work Becomes Your Life* and has been featured on numerous television programs, including ABC's *20/20*, *Good Morning America*, and *World News Tonight*; the *NBC Nightly News*; and the *CBS Early Show*.

Robinson's debut novel, a murder mystery titled *Limestone Gumption*, was published in 2014. You can visit his website at www.bryanrobinsononline.com or contact him at his e-mail address: bryanrobinson@bryanrobinsononline.com.